BOSTON UNDER MILITARY RULE

1768-1769

A Da Capo Press Reprint Series

THE ERA OF THE AMERICAN REVOLUTION

GENERAL EDITOR: LEONARD W. LEVY

Brandeis University

BOSTON
under MILITARY RULE
❙[1768~1769]❙

as revealed in

A JOURNAL OF THE TIMES

COMPILED BY

OLIVER   MORTON   DICKERSON

DA CAPO PRESS · NEW YORK · 1970

A Da Capo Press Reprint Edition

This Da Capo Press edition of *Boston under Military Rule,*
1768–1769, is an unabridged republication of the first edition
published in Boston in 1936.

Library of Congress Catalog Card Number 70-118029

SBN 306-71943-6

Copyright 1936 by Chapman & Grimes

Published by Da Capo Press
A Division of Plenum Publishing Corporation
227 West 17th Street, New York, N.Y. 10011

BOSTON
under MILITARY RULE
⊫ 1768~1769 ⊨
as revealed in
A JOURNAL OF THE TIMES

B O S T O N
under MILITARY RULE
⊫1768~1769⊪

as revealed in

A JOURNAL OF THE TIMES

COMPILED BY

OLIVER MORTON DICKERSON, PhD.

ARTI ET VERITATI

BOSTON

CHAPMAN & GRIMES

Mount Vernon Press

Printed in the United States of America

Mount Vernon Press, Boston

CONTENTS

JOURNAL OF TRANSACTIONS IN BOSTON

OR

A Journal of the Times

❦ ❦ ❦

EDITORIAL INTRODUCTION

This JOURNAL OF THE TIMES is a unique historical document. In most cases the historian has to reconstruct past events from a series of fragmentary accounts, such as personal letters, diaries, journals, memoranda of commercial transactions, and official documents. Many of these were not prepared for publication, and few of them were intended to give a distant public a continuous picture of events over a considerable period of time.

In a JOURNAL OF THE TIMES, however, we have a day-to-day record of happenings that were politically significant to the whole British empire, prepared consciously for publication by a group of men who intended to supply definite, concrete pictures of conditions in the town where they were living. To add to its uniqueness and its importance as a moulder of public opinion, the English-speaking world had no other common source of information concerning what was happening in Boston; hence it was dependent upon this account to learn the policies of Government and their effects at the most important trouble center of the time in the entire empire.

One must keep in mind the setting that produced this document. In 1768 only five years had elapsed since the close of the greatest world war up to that time. England had become the undisputed mistress of the seas and head of the second greatest colonial empire, with unprecedented taxation and debt problems as a part of the price of glory. Hence, across the difficulties of post-war reconstruction, had come those of colonial relations, imperial taxation, colonial resistance to the processes of collecting new revenues, an application to America of real economic sanctions, and a flood of periodical and pamphlet discussion of the new constitutional questions thus raised. American possibilities and American problems were more prominent in the minds of Englishmen than ever before. Then had come the political revolution at home and the apparently satisfactory compromises under Pitt, only to have the entire question reopened by the unfortunate revenue legislation under Townshend.

Grenville and his followers had severely condemned the Government for quietly submitting to the open defiance of parliamentary laws by unrestrained mob violence in America; and there seems to have been considerable public opinion in England disposed to demand that there must be no repetition of the supine abandonment of the fiscal agents of the Government, as had occurred in 1765.

The flaring up of renewed colonial opposition to the new measures was met with official resistance by the Ministry. From America had come news of concerted measures, similiar to those that had succeeded in forcing a repeal of the Stamp Act: the Massachusetts Circular Letter, resolutions of protest from legislative bodies, a renewal of non-importation agreements, and in Boston and other towns angry mobs attempting to treat the new revenue officials as they did the stamp distributors. Along with these reports had come panicky letters from British officials: Governor Bernard, Charles Paxton, Admiral Hood, and others, which pictured Boston as in a state of revolt and insisted upon adequate military force to support government. The new Commissioners of Customs supported this demand, and transferred their headquarters from Boston to Castle William on the ground that they were not safe elsewhere.

Patriot leaders in Boston believed that they had been the victims of wicked misrepresentation at the hands of designing men, and planned an extraordinary campaign to supply the King, both houses of Parliament, the British public, and people in the other colonies with a truer picture of actual conditions. In this campaign they used personal letters, newspaper articles, resolutions and representations of town meetings and of the House of Representatives, and even the protests of a great convention of delegates from the Massachusetts towns. Colonial agents in London presented petitions, appeared before legislative committees and administrative boards, wrote articles for the newspapers and magazines, and in other ways sought to convince the British public that the Boston people were loyal and law-abiding, and had been grossly maligned by the official reports.

The sending of troops to Boston was a most serious episode in the history of the empire. Nothing similar to it had happened before. Troops had to be gathered from Halifax, from the frontiers in Florida, from the West Indies, and from Ireland. Only real war had ever before led to such formidable military and naval measures. These conditions created a demand for information from the seat of trouble that existing agencies were not prepared to meet. In the days when there were no war correspondents, no feature writers for newspapers, and no associated press dispatches, the means of disseminating information were limited. Libel laws were severe; articles signed by individuals protected publishers, but were discounted by the reading public as indicative of personal bias or some selfish design; and there was a limit to the patience of the public with articles signed with fictitious or pen names. There was real need for an agency that could portray conditions in Boston, and supply a service now rendered by the public press.

It was to give this service, that some inspired individuals conceived the plan of a daily journal of happenings in this beleaguered town, written in simple, direct English and supplied to the newspapers of the empire. The copy was prepared in Boston by men who were in a position to know what was going on and who had a flair for effective newspaper writing. From Boston the material was sent secretly to New York and there first published in Holt's

New York Journal on Thursday, and reprinted in the *Pennsylvania Chronicle* on the following Saturday. It would seem difficult at that time to have transmitted a printed newspaper from New York to Philadelphia, set new type, and printed a second edition between Thursday and Saturday.

It is possible that two sets of manuscript were prepared and dispatched simultaneously, one to New York and the other to Philadelphia. Careful comparison of the two printed copies, however, shows an identity of composition that would have been difficult to secure from separate pen copies.

This material was originally published under varying titles. The first installment of the JOURNAL, covering the dates September 28 to October 3, 1768, was first published in the *New York Journal* on October 13, and subsequent portions appeared regularly with an average lapse of ten days to two weeks between the dates of happenings and the time of publication. The first title of this material was "JOURNAL of Transactions in BOSTON." In the next issue the title was a "JOURNAL of the TIMES." By the fourth issue the heading became a "JOURNAL of OCCURRENCES", with Boston used as a place heading as in all news items. This last title was regularly used by the *New York Journal* until publication ceased. The first title used in the *Boston Evening Post* was "JOURNAL of Transactions in BOSTON," but later portions carry the heading "JOURNAL of the TIMES." Thus of the three headings used for this material only two were used regularly: "JOURNAL of the TIMES" in the Boston papers and those that copied from them; and "JOURNAL of OCCURRENCES" in the New York papers and their followers. It seems clear that the authors in Boston preferred the heading "JOURNAL of the TIMES", and that title will be used in the following discussion.

The first installment of the JOURNAL had a note to other publishers as follows: "*The above Journal you are desired to publish for the general satisfaction, it being strictly fact.*". A similar note at the close of the first installment in the *Pennsylvania Chronicle* is somewhat longer and is signed "Amicus." It would be interesting to know who this particular "Amicus" was. Did he live in New York, in Philadelphia, or in Boston? Was he a patriot intrigued by the style of the first portion of the JOURNAL, or was he some one who knew the full scope of the plans back of the publication? No satisfactory answer can be given, although one suspects that this "Amicus" was one of the authors of the JOURNAL. With this exception, the JOURNAL is entirely anonymous, no other signature of any kind ever appearing in connection with it.

After publication in the New York and the Philadelphia papers, it was printed in the *Boston Evening Post*, and widely copied in other American newspapers and in some publications in England. A considerable portion of it was reprinted in pamphlet form in England for circulation there, probably at the expense of Massachusetts. Apparently no other pre-Revolutionary colonial writing was so widely circulated in the colonies and in England, except Dickinson's *Letters from a Pennsylvania Farmer*. It furnished a common background of information as to what was going on in Boston that was known from one end of the empire to the other.

The authorship of the JOURNAL is shrouded in secrecy. Frothingham says it was mainly the work of William Cooper, the town clerk of Boston, but does not give his source of information. He concedes that other patriots had a hand in it. Governor Bernard ascribed it to Sam Adams and his associates.

Some of the possible authors are: Henry Knox, at that time running a book store in Boston and later prominent in the Revolution; Benjamin Edes, one of the joint publishers of the *Boston Evening Post* and an ardent patriot; William Greenleaf, who was an employee of Edes and Gill in their printing establishment; and possibly Isaiah Thomas, who was acquiring his preliminary experience in the printing business and was soon to found the *Massachusetts Spy*, the most radical of the patriotic papers.

The JOURNAL certainly was not the work of a single individual. There are sections dealing with legal questions that could not have been prepared by a town clerk without material assistance. The nature of the legal information suggests that either John Adams or Josiah Quincy had a hand in its preparation. The discussion of Writs of Assistance on April 28 and April 29, 1769, suggests very strongly John Adams' reputed report of James Otis' speech in 1761. Possibly this was one of the sources he used to refresh his memory, some half century later. There are other sections that suggest the style of "Mucius Scaevola," who is said to have been Joseph Greenleaf.[1] The retained papers of Samuel and John Adams contain no reference whatever to the JOURNAL. Apparently the work was carefully hedged about with secrecy, and all evidence that could be traced to single individuals completely destroyed.

The JOURNAL is singularly unknown to historians. Winsor does not refer to it either in his *Memorial History of Boston* or in his *Narrative and Critical History of America*. Moses Coit Tyler fails to refer to it in his *Literary History of the American Revolution*. Frothingham alone knew of it and used it to some extent in his "Sam Adams' Regiments", although he apparently never discovered the widespread publication of the JOURNAL in American newspapers. His comment upon it is the only material reference by a historian that has come to light. The main portions are quoted below:

"In one way and another the troops became sources of irritation. The Patriots, mainly William Cooper, the town clerk, prepared a chronicle of this perpetual fret, which contains much curious matter obtained through access to authoritative sources of information, private and official. This diary was first printed in New York, and reprinted in the newspapers of Boston and London, under the title of 'Journal of Occurrences.' The numbers continued until after the close of Bernard's administration, usually occupied three columns of the *Boston Evening Post* and constituted a piquant record of the matters connected with the troops and general politics.

"It attracted much attention, and the authors of it formed the subject of a standing toast at the Liberty celebrations. Hutchinson averred that it was composed with great art and little truth. After this weekly

---

[1] Justin Winsor, *Memorial History of Boston* (Boston, 1880–1882), II, 136.

'Journal of the Times' as it was now called, had been published for four months, Governor Bernard devoted to it an entire official letter to Lord Hillsborough. He said that this publication was intended 'to raise a general clamor against His Majesty's government in England and throughout America, as well as in Massachusetts'; and in this way the patriots 'flattered themselves that they should get the navy and army removed, and again have the government and Custom House in their own hands.' The idea of such disloyal purposes excited the governor to the most acrimonious criticism. 'It is composed,' he informed Lord Hillsborough, 'by Adams and his associates, among which there must be some one at least of the Council; as everything that is said or done in Council, which can be made use of, is constantly perverted, misrepresented and falsified in this paper. But if the Devil himself was of the party, as he virtually is, there could not have been got together a greater collection of impudent, virulent, and seditious lies, perversions of the truth, and misrepresentations, than are to be found in this publication. Some are entirely invented, and first heard of from the printed papers; others are founded in fact, but so perverted as to be the direct contrary of the truth; other parts of the whole consists of reflections of the writer, which pretend to no other authority than his own word. To act about answering these falsities would be a work like that of cleaning Augeas's stable, which is to be done only by bringing in a stream strong enough to sweep away the dirt and collectors of it all together.' Doubtless there are exaggerations in the JOURNAL. It would be strange, if there were not.....But in the main the general allegations as to grievances suffered by the people from the troops, are borne out by private letters and official documents, and a plain statement of the cause of Francis Bernard shows that they did not exceed the truth as to him." [1]

The JOURNAL starts with the landing of troops in Boston in September, 1768, and continues until late the next summer, by which time Bernard had been recalled as governor and many of the troops removed from the city. It was obviously written to appeal to three audiences. In the first place, it was to inform the rest of the Americans just what was going on in Boston and give them a concrete picture of what arbitrary government, supported by large numbers of troops, meant from day to day in the largest American city. In the second place, it was written for consumption in England so that the people there, and especially members of Parliament, could know how fundamental principles of British liberty were being daily violated by the military occupation of the city, how the revenues arising under the Townshend measures were squandered and misapplied, how trade was hampered and injured by operations of the Customs Commissioners, and how the effect of the entire policy was to encourage the development of home manufactures here to the injury of British commerce and industry at home. Finally, it was a means of passing on to the people of Massachusetts a considerable mass of information that could not have been made public in any other way.

When one realizes that this material was printed as authentic news items with the specific month and day when the alleged events occurred, that it appeared week after week, and that there was no other source of information whatever and no formal contradiction, the almost diabolical cleverness of the appeals to these specific audiences begins to appear.

The quarrel in 1768 was largely with Boston and New England, but the support of the great southern colonies was necessary if grievances were to be removed. Slavery was common to all of the colonies, but was especially important in the southern and West Indies groups. Items in the JOURNAL which related the attempts of soldiers in Boston to tamper with Negro slaves and to encourage them to attack their masters, followed by specific details of court charges against individual members of the military, must have made interesting reading when circulated as they were in southern newspapers. Here is the beginning of the charge, later included in the Declaration of Independence, that the King "has sought to encourage domestic insurrection."

A similarly clever appeal to the British

audience is in the account of the exposure of the frontier to Indian attacks by the removal of troops for service in Boston, followed by detailed accounts of their not being needed in their new location, of their misconduct, and of the added expense of their transportation and quarters. It was difficult for the ministerial adherents to explain this situation to the British people, who were already heavily taxed to support an increased military establishment allegedly to protect the American frontier from a repetition of such Indian uprisings as Pontiac's Conspiracy. We know that these items struck home by the protests and memorials sent to the home government and by General Gage's enforced explanation of conditions in his letter to Hillsborough of March 4, 1769.[1] Many other illustrations can be cited of similarly successful appeals of portions of the JOURNAL to particular sections of the British public.

There are two main themes that run through the JOURNAL. The first is the evils of military rule in a city like Boston, its inevitably demoralizing effects upon the soldiers, and the constant friction with and mistreatment of the civilian population. Along with this goes a constant stream of evidence that the military rule was illegal, that the local authority was subservient to the military, that soldiers and officers were encouraged to be insolent, abusive, and criminal; and that, so long as they remained in the city, there was no effective remedy at civil law. Instance after instance was presented of the most flagrant offences by the soldiery, followed by specific charges in the local courts, and a few days later evidence printed that crown officers, whose business it was to prosecute such offenders, had dismissed the charges, often after indictments had been formally returned. It was this picture, painted week after week for months, that effectively prepared America and Britain for the outbreak of March 5, 1770, and led them to accept it as a "massacre." No amount of explanation could convince the American or the British public that the fault was not with the soldiers and the policy of an administration that had sent them to Boston.

It was not so much the occurrence itself as the careful preparation for it that had gone on through the JOURNAL OF THE TIMES during 1768 and 1769 that led to the general condemnation of those responsible for the tragedy.

General Gage's papers reveal the attempt to build up in America an office of Governor General through the army. Official reports and correspondence, if studied by themselves, may lead to the conclusion that real union could have been built up in that way, and that even the Americans might have accepted such a system.[2] But against these official letters one must place the story, so effectively retailed through the JOURNAL, of what military rule meant in Boston and what it threatened to all of the rest of America. After that publication had done its work, troops not only had to be removed from Boston, but they could never again be sent into any colony on a similar errand without starting civil war. It was the evidence supplied by the JOURNAL that laid the foundation for the charge in the Declaration of Independence against the King, that "he has affected to render the military independent of, and superior to, the civil power."

The second constant theme is the Customs Commissioners with their bad manners, haughty behavior, false information sent to London, their army of informers, and their personal profits in the enforcement of the revenue laws. This portion of the JOURNAL reads much like the clamor against our coast guard service over the enforcement of the prohibition laws. The effort was to discredit both the law and the enforcement officials. In the case of the colonists, however, there is no boasting about evading the law. Rather, the colonial offenders are held up as honest, seafaring men who are trying to live within the law and are being victimized by a wicked set of thieving revenue officers.

In addition to these two main themes the JOURNAL is a mine of information concerning many other sources of irritation. Outstanding among these is the attempted seizure of Hancock's fortune over the sloop *Liberty* affair. Here is the story of his arrest,

---

[1] Clarence E. Carter, *The Correspondence of General Thomas Gage* (New Haven, 1931), I, 218–220.
[2] See Carter's "Introduction," *ibid.*, xii.

his trial, and the final dismissal of the charges against him, covering the dates of November 3, 7, 28; December 14, 1768; January 2, 5, 7, 28, 30; February 17, 21, 24; March 2, 26, 1769. Along with this is the story of the indictment for perjury of the chief informer against Hancock by a local grand jury, the failure to bring him to trial, and the Customs Commissioners rewarding him with a position on the confiscated *Liberty*. Hancock thus was introduced to the people of America and of England, not as a smuggler, but as the near victim of as unscrupulous a "racket" as had ever been exposed in an age that was notorious for official corruption in England. In the light of material contained in the JOURNAL, biographers of Hancock are likely to revise their estimates of him, and find new reasons why he should have been President of the Continental Congress and the most prominent signer of the Declaration of Independence.

Other points that unquestionably made their impression upon public sentiment were the protests against the impressment of American seamen for service on the ships of the royal navy; the steady subversion of the judiciary to ministerial pressure; and the development of an extensive spoils system in America with which to reward the pimps and parasites that were a part of the irresponsible, arbitrary government in England at that time, and as thoroughly hated there as in America. Evidently one of the objects of the JOURNAL was to expose the system as it had developed under Bernard, to hold him up to contempt and ridicule, and thus effectually to destroy his capacity to do harm. In this the authors of the JOURNAL achieved their end: Bernard was not only recalled, but his name became a symbol for infamy and deceit, and in toasts and resolutions of the patriots was used as an epithet to indicate the extreme limits of condemnation as applied to particular individuals.

The JOURNAL is also interesting as an example of a developing newspaper technique. As a source of current happenings it reflects the first systematic gathering and retailing of news found in American newspapers. The success with which its reproduction was secured in American and British publications further suggests the later news organizations and modern syndicated articles. Prior to the Revolution editorial comment on the news was practically unknown. The newspaper publisher was a craftsman, who printed such items of local and foreign information and advertisements as he could secure and did not consider it his business to mould public opinion by editorial interpretations and comment. The news items in the JOURNAL, however, are edited in a most novel and effective manner. There is first of all the news item, then the editorial comment in italics at the end of the item. As italics were customarily used for emphasis, this made the editorial addition especially prominent and effective, as it was read as a part of the news itself. No other propaganda material of the period had this unique feature.

The JOURNAL was discovered while making an extensive study of contemporary sources of opinion on the eve of the Revolution. Careful examination of its content, and the extent of its publication, led to a decision to gather it together and republish it in book form for use by students of American history. In the opinion of the editor, it is a veritable mine of information for conditions in Boston in 1768-1769, and of the general sources of colonial irritation. Here is material that cannot be found in journals, diaries, private letters, or public documents, because some did not know the facts and others did not dare permit written records of such facts to be found in their possession.

In preparing this material for publication, the form of the original has been retained except in the matter of capitalization. Newspapers were photostated and compared. Spelling and punctuation have been retained exactly as they appeared, even when inconsistent and evidently erroneous. The use of capital letters, however, was found to be a matter of uneven practice in the composition rooms of newspapers, and varied with the whims of the publishers. The *New York Journal* capitalized practically every noun; the *Boston Evening Post* approximated present day usage. As there was no uniformity in this matter, it was decided to reduce capitalization to approximately modern standards, as it was evident that the practice in this particular could not contribute information that might ultimately lead to the identification of the authors.

As the JOURNAL was first printed in the *New York Journal,* and apparently all other forms were copied from that original edition, it has been used as the chief source for this volume. The *Boston Evening Post* has been the other main dependence for copy, because the JOURNAL was prepared in Boston and important changes were made in reprinting it in that paper. So far as could be determined, colonial newspapers copied generally from the *New York Journal* or the *Boston Evening Post.* Wherever the title "JOURNAL OF OCCURRENCES" is used, it indicates that the copy has come directly or indirectly from the *New York Journal.* The form "JOURNAL OF THE TIMES" indicates that the copying has been from the *Boston Evening Post.*

Thanks are especially due to Julius H. Tuttle and the Massachusetts Historical Society for the use of their incomparable files of colonial papers covering this period, and for their courtesies in supplying photostatic copies on an extensive scale. Similar thanks are due to Mr. V. Valta Parma and his associates of the Rare Book Room of the Library of Congress. The writer also desires to acknowledge the assistance of Victor H. Paltsits and the New York Public Library for photostats and incidental research. Finally, the editor's thanks are due to the custodians of the files of other colonial newspapers in Connecticut, Rhode Island, Pennsylvania, Maryland, Virginia, and South Carolina, who have so courteously and faithfully placed their treasured copies at his disposal.

OLIVER MORTON DICKERSON

September, 1936.

The BOSTON  Evening-Poſt.

Containing the freſheſt & moſt important   *Advices, Foreign and Domeſtick.*

September 28, 1768 [1]

ADVICE received that the men of war and transports from Halifax, with about 900 troops, collected from several parts of America, were safe arrived at Nantasket Harbour, having very narrowly escaped shipwreck on the back of Cape Cod, which disaster would have left the extensive sea coast of North America, almost bare of ships of war, and troops, but in no worse state than are the inland fortresses and settlements, from whence the garrisons had been before withdrawn.—Time must account for such extraordinary steps in our Ministry.

September 29

The fleet was brought to anchor near Castle William, that evening there was throwing of sky rockets, and those passing in boats observed great rejoicings, and that the Yankey Doodle song was the capital piece in their band of music. —This day his Majesty's Council received a billet from Governor Bernard, requiring their attendance at Castle William, and informing them that the officers of his Majesty's fleet and army, would be present,—they attended accordingly, and notwithstanding all intimidations, adhered strictly to their votes, published in the last papers; the Governor's arts were ineffectual to induce them to give the least countenance to any troops being brought into Boston, as the barracks at Castle William were sufficient to receive the whole of them arrived from Halifax. —The treatment they received from his Excellency, during their tarry at the Castle, was very uncourtly, and even rude [2]

September 30

Early this morning a number of boats were observed round the town, making soundings, &c. —At 3 o'clock in the afternoon, the Launceston of 40 guns, the Mermaid of 38, Glasgow 20, the Beaver 14, Senegal 14, Bonetta 10, several armed schooners, which together with the Romney of 60 guns,[3] and the other ships of war before in the harbour, all commanded by Capt. Smith, came up to town, bringing with them, the 14th Regiment, Col. Dalrymple, and 29th Regiment, Col. Carr; none having been disembarked at Castle Island,—So that we now behold Boston surrounded at a time of profound peace, with about 14 ships of war, with springs on their cables, and their broadsides to the town! —If the people of England could but look into the town to see the utmost good order and observance of the laws, and that this mighty armament has no other rebellion to subdue than what existed in the brain or letter of the inveterate G——r B——d and the detested Comm—s—rs of the Board of C——s. What advantages the Court of Versailles may take of the present policy of the British Ministry, can be better determined hereafter.

October 1

THIS morning rumours that representations had gone from hence to General Gage at N— York,[4] from our good friend, &c. that we are in a state of rebellion; an express its said has arrived in consequence, with advice that more troops may be expected from N— York. —Sheriff Greenleaf and his deputy pressing carts, &c. for the use of the troops, this

---

[1] All items from September 28 to October 2, inclusive, are from the *New York Journal*, October 13, 1768, p. 2.
[2] The last three words are omitted from the corresponding account in the *Boston Evening Post*, December 12, 1768, p. 1.
[3] The *Boston Evening Post* has "50 guns" and gives the *Mermaid* 28. *Ibid.*
[4] The *Boston Evening Post* has "New York."

and other motions indicate that they medi-
tate a landing this day, to encamp in [1] the
Common, in hopes of intimidating the
magistrates to find them quarters, which
they cannot force until the barracks are
filled without flying in the face of a plain
act of Parliament. At about 1 [2] o'clock, all
the troops landed under cover of the cannon
of the ships of war, and marched into the
Common, with muskets charged, bayonets
fixed, colours flying, drums beating and fifes,
&c. playing, making with the train of artillery
upwards of 700 men. —In the afternoon it
is said an officer from the Col. [3] went to the
Manufactory House, with an order from the
Governor, and requested Mr. Brown and the
other occupiers to remove within two hours,
that the troops might take possession; instead of a compliance the doors were barr'd
and bolted against them. —This evening
the Selectmen were required by the Colonel
to quarter the two regiments in this town,
which they absolutely refused, as his Majesty's Council had done before, knowing
that whoever should conduct in violation of
an act of Parliament must be answerable for
the consequences,—The Colonel as it is said,
waving a demand for quartering, earnestly
entreated that out of compassion to the
troops; one regiment of which were without
their camp equipage, they would allow

Fanueil-Hall, and Chambers, that, and the
following night, as a shelter from the weather.

The next day being the Sabbath, on which
all confusion should be avoided,—at 9
o'clock this night they were permitted to
enter said hall, in which were a large number
of stands of the towns arms: Thus the
humanity of the city magistrates permitted
them a temporary shelter, which no menaces
could have procured.

October 2

Being Lord's day, the town quiet no disorders having risen on any side,—this
evening, by order of Governor Bernard, the
Secretary of the Province opened the Town
House, and even the Representatives Chamber for the reception of the troops. [4]

*The above Journal you are desired to publish
for the general satisfaction, it being strictly fact.*

October 3 [5]

We now behold the Representatives'
Chamber, Court-House, and Faneuil-Hall,
those seats of freedom and justice occupied
with troops, and guards placed at the doors;
the Common covered with tents, and alive
with soldiers; marching and countermarch-
ings to relieve the guards, in short the town
is now a perfect garrison. —This day the
Court of Sessions met at the Court-House,

---

[1] Instead of "in" the Boston account has "on." *Ibid.*

[2] This is written out in full. *Ibid.*

[3] This becomes "Colonel" in the Boston account. *Ibid.*

[4] The portion of the *Journal* covering the dates, September 28 to October 2 was published in the *Pennsylvania Chronicle*, October 17, pp. 2–3. The closing paragraph, however, is longer and was inserted at the beginning just under the title. It is as follows:

"Though you have already published an account of the arrival of the fleet and army at Boston, yet many of your customers would be pleased to see the following Journal, which is strictly fact, in your useful paper—you are therefore desired to give it a place.

Amicus"

The above sections appeared in the *Boston Evening Post*, December 12, 1768, p. 1. The introduction is more elaborate, however, and is reproduced in full below. This appears at the beginning of the *Journal* items instead of at the close of the first installment as in the case of the *New York Journal*.

"*Messrs* FLEETS

Though you have already published an account of the arrival of the fleet and army at Boston, yet a great number of your customers would be glad to find the following Journal of Occurrences *published in your useful and impartial paper, so that they may see in one comprehensive view, the extraordinary transactions of the present day.*

"[In compliance with the above request we shall devote a part of our paper for some time to that purpose; and if any of the facts shall appear to have been misrepresented, a place shall always be open to any gentleman who shall think proper to correct them.]"

The very nature of these headings indicates concerted planning for the publication of this material. The portion of the *Boston Evening Post* regularly devoted to the *Journal* was the entire first page, and sometimes more.

[5] All items from October 3 to October 9, inclusive, are from the *New York Journal*, October 20, 1768, p. 2. Items for October 4 to October 10, inclusive, are omitted from the *Boston Evening Post*, December 12, 1768, p. 1. The item listed October 3 is the same as that of October 10 in the *New York Journal*. All material published in the *New York Journal* under the dates October 3 to October 9 are omitted in the *Boston Evening Post*.

when a motion was made by one of the bench, that the troops be ordered to remove at a distance, he being determined not to assist in administering justice under the points of bayonets. In the afternoon our artillery company appeared in the field and were exercised, their Capt. was informed by the officer of the regulars, that it was not customary to beat drum, or fire after the evening cannon was discharged, the hint was taken. In King-Street, the soldiers being gathered, a proclamation was read offering a reward of 10 guineas to such soldier as should inform of any one who should attempt to seduce him from the service, after which it is said the Col. advised them not to refuse any money offered as a temptation to desert, but to bring the offender to him, when he would take care that it should be the last offer he should make. This day the Council met, when Col. Dalrymple informed them he had procured quarters, and demanded billeting for the troops.

October 4

Report, that James Murray, Esq; from Scotland, since 1745, had let his dwelling house and sugar houses, for the quartering of troops, at £15 sterling per month, and that Mr. Forrest from Ireland had let them a house lately purchased for about £50 sterling, at the rate of £60 sterling per annum.——

Captain James Scott, master, of the brig Lydia, owned by John Hancock, Esq; having his clearance and pass, and being ready for sailing, informs, that a boat from Commodore Smith's ship came along side, and acquainted him that it was Capt. Smith's orders, that he should not leave this harbour without his permission.

October 5

The Council now met, and were obliged to pass the guards placed in the passage way, entering their chamber. Col. Dalrymple again informed them that he had provided quarters for his troops in this town, and again required of them, that they might now be billetted, and this notwithstanding the barracks built at the charge of this government for the reception of the King's troops were standing empty. It is said that after

consultation had thereon, the C-n-l advised the Governor to appoint a person to make provision accordingly, *provided* said person would be willing to *risque* his being repaid therefor by the next General Court—thus we see the provision made by act of Parliament for the ease and safety of the subject and the convenience and benefit of the troops, may be set aside and rendered useless by any commanding officer, who will take upon himself to hire quarters amongst the inhabitants at any rate, in expectation that such expence will be finally thrown upon the people.

October 6

In the morning nine or ten soldiers of Col. Carr's regiment, for sundry misdemeanors were severely whipt on the Common;—to behold Britons scourg'd by Negro drummers, was a new and very disagreeable spectacle. We are told that Capt. Allen of the Gaspee, goes passenger in the Lydia, Captain Scott, for London, with dispatches from the commander of the troops, on the New England expedition. No doubt with the glorious news, that he had effected a landing in the heart of the country, without the least loss or opposition to his Majesty's troops. This day, by order of Governor Bernard, the south battery was delivered up to Col. Dalrymple. If this people had not more patience and loyalty, than some others have tenderness and sound policy; what a scene would soon open! From Cambridge we learn, that last evening, the picture of —— ——,[1] hanging in the college-hall, had a piece cut out of the breast exactly describing a heart, and a note, —that it was a most charitable attempt to deprive him of that part, which a retrospect upon his administration must have rendered exquisitely painful.

October 7

Men of war pressing our inward bound seamen, as they have done for some time past, to the great damage of the merchant.—The transactions of the Council relative to billeting the troops, &c. greatly misrepresented in the Thursday's paper by G—— B——, and the S—— abuses of this sort have of late years been many and numerous,

---

[1] Obviously Governor Bernard.

to the infinite prejudice of Britain and the colonies.

October 8

This day we have the mortification to hear from one of our carpenters, that a barrack-master was contracting with him for the erecting a large building as a guard-house on the town's land, at the only entry way into this city by land, encouraged thereto by G——B——'s declaration that said ground, and also the Common, was the King's: Those lands have been taken possession of by the troops without any application to the proper owners. The store-house on the south battery repairing by the barrack-master, and the stores belonging to the town, have been turned out upon the wharf.

October 9

This being the Sabbath, Mr. Kneeland, the chaplain of one of the regiments, preached to the soldiers on the Common, and in the afternoon read prayers; no disturbances throughout the day. This night the frame of a guard-house, designed to be erected on the town land at the entrance of the town, was cut and otherwise destroyed by persons unknown.

The Governor has by proclamation offered a reward of £20 for the discovery of any of the persons concerned.

October 10[1]

Two circular letters of Lord Hillsborough's this day seen in print, whereby it appears that the Commissioners of the Board of Customs had repeatedly complained of being obstructed in the execution of their office. The proceedings of Council on the 27th and 29th of July last, which G——r B——d hitherto prevented being made public, declares to the world, that no insult had been offered to the Commissioners; That, "what happened on the 10th of June, seems to have sprung wholly from those who complain of it, and that it seems probable, an uproar was hoped for and intended to be seconded by the manner of proceeding, in making the seizure of the sloop Liberty; that their quitting the town was a voluntary act, without any sufficient ground for the same,

and that when at the Castle, there was no occasion for men of war to protect them." "That it is their unanimous opinion, the civil power does not need the support of troops; that it is not for his Majesty's service, nor the peace of this province, that any troops be required, or that any came into the province; and that they deem any persons who may have made application for troops to be sent hither, in the highest degree unfriendly to the peace and good order of this government, as well as to his Majesty's service and the British interest in America."

How detested and abhorred by the people must that G——r and those men then be, who, not content with having by their misrepresentations introduced troops into this province, are now leaving no stone unturn'd in order to procure quarters for them in this metropolis, to the great vexation and distress of the inhabitants, as also in violation of law and justice, which must be the case, while they are quartered in the town, to disturb and annoy the inhabitants, and while the barracks provided by the province, at a very considerable expence, remain empty!—

The prints of this day contain a very extraordinary advertisement, published by order of the commissioners of Customs, whereby it appears that the inhabitants of Nantucket, who are mostly of the persuasion called Quakers, have not accommodated Mr. Samuel Procter, an officer of the customs lately sent among them, with an office, and that therefore orders are issued to their several officers in America, to make seizure of all vessels, and their cargoes, that shall arrive from that island, without proper documents, signed by the Collector and D. Comptroller of the port of Boston. —*If quarters are to be provided by the people for Custom-House officers, who are daily increasing upon us, as well as for his Majesty's troops, we shall quickly perceive that we are without quarters ourselves.*

October 11

We have certain information, that at a full meeting of the inhabitants of Lebanon, a large town in Connecticut, convened the 26th of September last, in consequence of intelligence that troops were soon expected in

---

[1] "Items from October 10 to October 16, 1768, inclusive, are from the *New York Journal*, October 27, 1768, pp. 2–3. The item for October 10, is the same as that given under the date of October 3 in the *Boston Evening Post*.

Boston, to be quartered upon the town; said inhabitants unanimously expressed their sentiments and resolutions as follows, "That a union of measures is absolutely necessary, at this important crisis, in order to maintain our liberties and immunities, and that they fully agreed with their brethren of Boston, in the resolves they passed in a late town meeting; and that considering themselves connected by the strongest ties to their fellow subjects, in this and the neighbouring colonies, they should look upon an attack upon them, as though they themselves were the immediate sufferers, and that with a determinate, unalterable resolution and firmness, they would assert and support their American brethren, at the expence of their lives and fortunes; should their welfare, which is so intimately blended with their own, demand the sacrifice." *As it is thought the above shows the disposition, not only of the other towns in that colony, but of the rest of the provinces; how must the friends of Britain applaud the prudence and wisdom of the late Committee of Convention in Boston, who in tenderness to the mother country, and loyalty to their sovereign, under all their grievances, while they adhered strictly to their rights, yet strongly recommended peace and quietness to the people, until the effect of their last representation, and petitions could be known.*

October 12

Advice received that the merchants in Connecticut, have agreed as those in Massachusetts, and New York, &c. had done before them, not to import any goods from Great Britain, till the late revenue acts, &c. are repealed. —*A measure that must have the greatest tendency to awaken the attention of the mercantile and manufactoral part of Britain to their own immediate interest, which they lately seem to have quite lost sight of.* The rumor of Castle William being delivered up by the G——r to the King's troops, arose from his having permitted a number of mariners from the ships of war, to land at Castle Island, six of whom it is said went off in a boat the last night.

Reports of great desertions and a general disposition to desert from the regiments here, which it is said left Halifax under great dejection of spirits; about 21 of the soldiers absconded the last night, and parties from the troops with other clothing, instead of their regimentals, are sent after them. —*Some of the consequences of bringing the troops into this town, in direct violation of the act of Parliament, and disregard to the advice of his Majesty's Council, instead of quartering them in the barracks on Castle Island, are like to be the scattering proper tutors through the country, to instruct the inhabitants in the modern way of handling the firelock and exercising the men, and also in the various manufactures which the ingenuity and industry of the people of Great Britain have hitherto furnished us with.* —This night a surgeon of one of the ships of war being guilty of very disorderly behaviour, was committed to gaol by Mr. Justice Quincy, as was also a person not belonging to this province, by Mr. Justice Hutchinson, on complaint of a soldier, that he had been enticing him to desert; said stranger was first taken and confined by Captain Willson, in the Town House for some time, without warrant or authority from any magistrate— *If the oaths of soldiers who are promised 10 guineas for such discoveries, are to be taken as sufficient proof, we know not what proscriptions may take place.*

October 13

A private letter from Halifax contains some particulars relative to the Boston expedition, not known before, viz. "That in consequence of orders received Sept. 11th, from this place, all the workmen in the King's yard, necessary to equip the ships, were set to work on Sunday; a strict embargo laid, and guard vessels sent to the mouth of the harbour to prevent intelligence being sent, and more caution used than when fixing out for the Louisbourgh expedition; the embargo so strict, that an open shallop going a mackerel catching, was stopt and sent back to town; and that the troops embarked in as great hurry as was ever known in time of war. —*What a tragi-commick scene is here presented! and how must it be viewed by European politicians?*—

Another letter mentions, that as Halifax must sink without the support of troops and ships of war, some of their patriots were about erecting a liberty pole, and employing some boys to sing the Liberty Song through the streets, in hopes it may procure the return of those ships and forces or a larger number from Britain, in order to quell such disturbances. Accounts received from various parts of this province and the neighbouring colonies, that the tea table furniture and other foreign superfluities, have given place to spinning wheels, looms, and other utensils of industry; and that the aversion to British manufactures increases in proportion to the measures taken to impoverish and enslave us. It is said the officer who gave out the orders last evening, observed to the soldiery, that the practices of the inhabitants to entice them away from the service, was not out of affection to them, but from disaffection to the Government. —*Such insinuations are a little ungenerous, as the town is under the greatest uneasiness that the troops are not placed in the government's barracks, which being on Castle Island, would have prevented any desertion, and many other evils and disorders, which are daily taking place.*

His Majesty's C——l met this day, when we are told the G——r was informed that it was the opinion of the B——d, that they were not held by their oaths as C——l——rs to keep such matters and things as he has or may commit to them, as a secret, unless the B——d shall judge it for his Majesty's interest so to do.[1]

October 14

The troops still keep possession of Faneuil Hall, the Court House, Representatives Chambers, &c, guards placed at the passage way into the town, near the Neck. Patrolling companies near the ferry ways, and parties sent into the country to prevent desertions: In the forenoon one Rogers, a New-England man, sentenced to receive 1000 stripes, and a number of other soldiers, were scourged in the Common by the black drummers, in a manner, which however necessary, was shocking to humanity; some gentlemen who had held commissions in the army, observing, that only 40 of the 170 lashes received by Rogers, at this time, was equal in punishment to 500, they had seen given in other regiments.

October 15

A deserter from the 14th Regiment was brought in the last evening by one of the decoy parties, sent into the country, also a labouring man from Roxbury, with a soldier's regimentals on his back, he was confined for some time in a tent, without lawful warrant, and afterwards committed to prison by Mr. Justice Hutchinson. —This afternoon the troops were drawn up, on the Common, on the appearance of General Gage; at sunset there was 17 discharges from the field cannon; he passed the front of the battalion in his charriot, preceded by a number of aid de camps on horseback. — *The arrival of this gentleman from N. York' at this time, is a very agreeable circumstance, to the friends of their country; as his mild and judicious behaviour in that province, has been justly applauded; and he comes here determined to see and judge for himself.*

October 16

This day Capt. Jenkins arrived from London, who brought a print of August 13th, in which there is the following article,— "There are 4000 troops ordered for Boston, which it is thought will sufficiently intimidate those people to comply with the laws enacted in England; especially as the other colonies seem to have deserted them."—The design of sending troops among us, was before fully comprehended; all the colonies that have been permitted to meet, have united with us in humble petitions and remonstrances, and it is hoped that the merchants of Philadelphia have, or will soon co-operate in a measure our friends at home represent as the most likely to procure a redress of grievances.

October 17 [2]

We have received certain accounts that at a town-meeting held at Norwich, a large and populous town in Connecticut the 4th instant, they voted, that their representatives be instructed— "That the several Colonels within the colony be obliged upon sufficient penalty, to have a general muster or review of their respective regiments, in order that the militia be at all times properly furnished —That proper encouragement be made for necessary manufactures in the colony—and that the most effectual measures be taken to keep up a union with all the neighbouring

---

[1]" The *Boston Evening Post* omitted the last part of the above item, beginning with "such insinuations."
[2]Items from October 17 to October 23, 1768, inclusive, are from the *New York Journal*, November 3, 1768, p. 2.

colonies," they also unanimously voted, "That they fully approve of and justify the votes and resolves of the town of Boston in their late meeting, of the 12th of September last, and the spirited conduct of the Committee of Convention, declaring their allegiance to his Majesty, George the Third, as well as their resolving in the most spirited manner to maintain all their undoubted rights and privileges sacred and inviolable; that they consider the noble cause we are engaged in, as the common cause of their country; and that they will unite both heart and hand in support thereof, against all its enemies whatsoever."—

A captain of the Regulars having a night before greatly insulted some young gentlemen in the coffee-house, calling them Liberty Boys, rebels, &c. who he was come to take care of, ordering them to disperse, and throwing out very indelicate threatenings, being apprehensive of receiving a caning from one of them, had the precaution to come into King-Street with S. G.[1] who brought the Riot Act in his pocket, and its said, threatened to read the same unless the gentlemen dispersed, which he has since declared was by order of G—— B——. *A greater indignity than which could not have been offered, and would have shown to what an odious use, that act may be applied by the tools of power.* The gentleman who had called said officer to account, took him into a private room in the coffee-house, after which he publickly asked pardon of him, and the rest of the company he had in his cups affronted. *It is to be hoped that this specimen of the spirit of the inhabitants upon a justifiable occasion, may prevent a repetition of such gross insults.*

October 18

Council summoned in the morning of yesterday, which broke up in the evening, after coming into a vote of the following import—"His Excellency Gen. Gage, having acquainted the Board that he was in daily expectation of the arrival of two regiments from Ireland to Boston: And this Board being desirous to do all in their power to accommodate the King's troops, agreeable to the act of Parliament in that case made and provided, do advise, that his Excellency the Governor, give immediate orders for the clearing the Manufactory-House in Boston, being the property of this province, of those persons who are in the present possession of the same, to receive those of said regiments who cannot be accommodated in the barracks at Castle William, or otherways agreeable to said act. —*Notwithstanding the restrictions of the above vote, it proves very disagreeable to the people, who are not a little apprehensive that the G——r who it was thought, in a manner dragooned them into the same, will not fail to improve it to their disadvantage.*

At the above Council a worthy member in rep'y to what the G——r had observed to Gen. Gage, respecting the vote of the 5th inst. for billetting the troops, told the General, that the proviso in that vote, viz. "That the person nominated to provide billetting must risque his being repaid therefor by the next General Court," was made with great deliberation and with express design to prevent such person from being deceived by that vote into an apprehension, that it was in their power to procure a reimbursement for such advancements, but that it must be wholly left to the next General Assembly to do thereon as they might think proper. —*If the troops quartered themselves upon us, directly contrary to an act of Parliament, can it be thought then, that any G——l Assembly will ever defray the charge of billetting such troops.*

October 19

The people dwelling in the Manufactory House, again secured themselves with bolts and bars. His honour the Lieut. Governor, condescended to come with Sheriff Greenleaf, and to use many arguments and devices in order to effect their removal; but he was plainly told, that it was their opinion and that of others, that they could not be *legally* turned out of doors in consequence of the vote of Council, which was not an act of the General Court, and that it surely could not be intended that they should be ousted in any other way; to which his honour replied, that the remaining part of Government had given the order. Several persons have been taken up within these few days by the soldiery, and confined without war-

[1] Evidently Sheriff Greenleaf.

rant for their so doing; some of our first merchants greatly affronted by a sea captain or two, who have been, or probably will be called to account therefor. —Gentlemen and ladies coming into town in their carriages, threatened by the guards to have their brains blown out unless they stopped. Parties of soldiers going about the country in disguise and pretending to be deserters, are guilty of great impositions, and may occasion much mischief if not checked in time.

October 20

This morning the justices of the town were called upon to meet the Governor, General Gage, and King's-Attorney, at the Council Chamber; when met the Governor required of them to provide quarters for the troops in this town, but received for answer, that they apprehended that this application did not then come properly before them. About noon the inhabitants were greatly alarmed with the news that Mr. Sheriff Greenleaf, accompanied by the soldiery, had forced an entry sword in hand, into one of the cellars in the Manufactory-House; Mr. Brown one of the inhabitants, in attempting to disarm him, received several thrusts in his cloaths, the sheriff's deputy entered with him; he then gave possession of the cellar to some of the troops: A large number of soldiers immediately entered the yard, and were placed as centinels and guards at all the doors of the house, and all persons were forbid from going in and out of the same, or even coming into the yard. The plan of operation being as it is said to terrify or starve the occupants out of their dwellings. —Great numbers of the inhabitants assembled to be eye witnesses of this attack of the sheriff, upon the rights of citizens, but notwithstanding they were so highly irritated at his conduct, there was no outrageous attempts made upon him or his abettor, the people having had it hinted to them, that our enemies in advising to this step, had flattered themselves with the hopes that some tumults and disorder would arise, which might be improved to our further prejudice.[1] The sheriff refused giving Mr. Brown a copy of his warrant or orders for this doing, and only referred him to the

minutes of Council for his justification, a copy of which was also refused him. *We now see that the apprehensions of the people respecting an ill improvement of the late vote of Council was not without just grounds.* This night the sheriff procured guards of soldiers to be placed at his house for his protection, *a measure that must render him still more ridiculous in the eyes of the people.*

October 21

The siege of the Manufactory House still continues, and notwithstanding one of their bastions has been carried by assault; the besieged yet shew a firmness peculiar to British Americans: The children at the windows crying for bread this morning, when the baker was prevented supplying them by the guards, was an affecting sight. Some provision and succours were however afterwards thrown into the Castle with the loss of blood, but no lives. The Council met in the forenoon at the G——rs, those of them who were in the late vote greatly disturbed, that such an illegal method should be taken by the G——r to carry it into execution, they were still more disturbed at the treatment received. Council met in the afternoon at their own chamber, and are to meet again on the morrow. *The C——l have been really in a most uncomfortable situation for some time past, tho' very frequently called together by the G——r, it is rather to give a colour and countenance to what he had done or is projecting, than to receive their information and advice.* Col. Dalrymple was required by the Selectmen to remove from Faneuil-Hall this day or on the morrow, agreeable to his word of honour, the troops which have occupied it for too long a time already. —The Common this day presented more scenes of distress. *Dissertions, drunkenness and innumerable disorders, which give uneasiness to the citizens and procure punishment for the soldiers, are to be imputed to their being placed in this town rather than on Castle Island, and is what General Amherst and other commanders in the late war publickly declared would be the case, if troops should be ever quartered in this town, and this opinion induced the government to be at the expence of providing suitable barracks at said island.* In the evening terms of accomodation were pro-

---

[1] The item for this date in the *Boston Evening Post* stops at this point.

posed to Mr. Brown of the Manufactory, but rejected with disdain.

October 22

This morning we are told that the sheriff, whom to carry on the allusion we will call the General, has raised the siege of the Manufactory, with the trifling loss of all his honour and reputation—the troops were withdrawn under cover of the night, and it is hoped as the season is now advanced, that they will be soon ordered into winter quarters at Castle Island; sufficient supplies have however been sent into the Manufactory to serve in case the attack should be renewed. The G——r not liking the late determination of the justices who refused the demand for quartering, their attendance on the G——r yesterday was required, and they are to meet again this forenoon. Reports that Commodore Hood has been sent for, and his arrival from Halifax soon expected. A Court Martial, of which, by commission from the General, Colonel Dalrymple is president, held this day for the trial of a soldier of his regiment for dissertion, who had been brought in by one of their decoy parties. Plenty of rum has procured many whippings on the Common this evening, the man cannot be restrained from it in town.

The justices adhere to their vote respecting the G——rs demand for quartering the troops.

October 23

Advice is received, that six more regiments may be soon expected from Ireland, and another from Halifax. *If pensions of £10,000 sterl. per annum had been settled upon G——r B——d and his partisans during life, rather than making so unnecessary a military parade, it would have been a vast saving to the nation.* We have accounts from Louisbourg, that several of the settlers upon that island have been lately killed by the savages. *This is what has been expected from the late withdraw of troops from that place, and it is to be feared our inland settlements will suffer from the like cause.*

October 24[1]

Large quantities of tea have been sent from hence by the merchants to the other colonies, they not being able to make sale of it to here. *It will give pleasure to many among us to hear that the owners thereof not finding a vent for so superfluous and baneful an herb in any other part of the continent, have been obliged to reship the same for a European market.*[2]

This day the brig Tryton, owned by Mr. D——s, a merchant in this town, was seized by order of the Board of Customs, on supposition it is said, that she had some time ago been employed in an illicit trade; and that they may oblige the owner to prove where and how she has been employed. —*This seizure exhibits another instance of the generosity of the Commissioners, and their friendly disposition towards trade, in as much as it is said, that they have not now any more cause of suspicion than they had four months past; during which time she has remained in port undisturbed till the owner had spent £100 sterling in repairs, and had taken a freight for Hull, the insurance of which has been some time past wrote for by the several freighters.*[3]

The following complaint was this day regularly made, viz.

Suffolk, SS.) To the worshipful Richard Dana, John Ruddock, and Joseph Williams, Esqrs. justices of the peace in and for the said county of Suffolk.

HUMBLY SHEWS,

JOHN BROWN of Boston, in said county, weaver, that Stephen Greenleaf of Boston aforesaid, Esq; and Joseph Otis of said Boston, gentleman, together with divers other malefactors and disturbers of the peace of our said Lord the King, (whose names to the said complainant are yet unknown, on the 20th day of October instant, with force and arms, and with strong hand, at Boston aforesaid, unlawfully and injuriously did break and enter into the dwelling house of the said John Brown, then and there being in the possession of the said John Brown; and that the said Stephen Greenleaf, and Joseph Otis, together with the said other malefactors,

---

[1] Items covering the dates, October 24 to October 30, 1768, inclusive, are from the *New York Journal*, November 10, 1768, pp. 1–3.

[2] The above paragraph is omitted from the *Boston Evening Post.*

[3] The italicised portions directly above are omitted from the *Boston Evening Post.*

then and there with force and arms and with strong hand, unlawfully and injuriously did expel, amove and put the said John Brown from the possession of the said dwelling-house, and the said John Brown, so as aforesaid expelled, amoved, and put out from the possession of the said dwelling-house, then and there with force and arms, and with strong hand, unlawfully and injuriously did keep out, and still do keep out, to the great damage of him the said John Brown, and against the peace of our said Lord the King, his crown and dignity, and the laws of this province in that case made and provided. Dated at Boston, this 24th day of October, in the eighth year of his Majesty's reign, Annoque Domini, 1768. The complainant aforesaid, prays relief, and that he may be restored to the possession of the premises.

JOHN BROWN.

Advices from N. York, are, that the inhabitants of that city highly approve of our conduct, and seem resolved to risque their lives & fortunes in the common cause if the infatuation of an ab——d M——y, or wicked G——r, should reduce them to that necessity: And that letters from London mention, that they know of no people since the ruin of the Roman commonwealth, that entertain more just ideas of liberty than the brave sons of North-America do; that the petitions of their merchants, the remonstrances and resolves of their assemblies, and all their public transactions, display a manly resolution and quick discernment, that is not to be equalled by any body of people in the world: And that if things are not accommodated soon, the late measures will be attended with almost a general bankruptcy on that side the water. *It cannot but be very flattering and encouraging to Americans to have their conduct and exertions in support of their just rights and liberties thus applauded by the more sensible and discerning part of the nation, may success attend their and our efforts to ward off the ruin impending over both countries—.*[1]

We are told that Mr. Fisher, late Collector of the port of Salem, and a brother-in-law of Governor Wentworth, of New Hampshire, has been displaced by the Commissioners,

and another appointed in his room, notwithstanding Mr. Fisher's books were well approved of by the Inspector General and others in office; and that the principal ground of complaint, excepting his standing fair with the merchants, is his not having obliged the poor fishermen to contribute to the support of Greenwich-Hospital, which they have not done from the first settlement of the country to this day, and with good reason, as no one of them ever has or can expect an admission into that hospital. —*Perhaps Administration may think a demand of this sort the more necessary at this time, as a gentleman it is said has been lately appointed to receive the hospital money, collected from the seamen employed in a foreign trade, from our collector, who used to remit the same clear of charge; for which important service this new officer is to be allowed two hundred pounds sterling per annum.*

A vessel at Marblehead with molasses, has been seized and libelled in the Court of Admiralty, on presumption that the whole quantity she bro't had not been reported. Two vessels from Newbury-Port with molasses, which had been entered and gauged, and the duty paid thereon, has had officers put on board in order to regauge said molasses. All our shipping employed in the coasting business from one part of the province to another, are now obliged to enter and clear under all the restrictions of those which are engaged in foreign voyages. —*The late extension of those acts of Parliament to the colonies made at first to prevent the running of wool to France, and such like destructive commerce; the vast multiplication of custom-house, revenue and other cown officers, and the extravagant fees demanded on pretences before unheard and unthought of. The many injudicious and perplexing restrictions laid upon our foreign trade, on pretext of preventing the contraband, nine-tenths of which is more profitable to the mother country than to the colonies; and the unbounded power given to the Commissioners to embarrass and distress, rather than relieve and assist the merchant, has opperated so effectually to the destruction of our trade: that necessity is now obliging us fast to lay aside the use and consumption of foreign superfluities, and to fly to the ground and manufactures for a support and maintenance.*

---

[1] All of the above paragraph was omitted from the *Boston Evening Post.*

October 25

It being the King's accession-day, there was a general appearance of the troops in the Common, who went through their firings, evolutions, &c. in a manner pleasing to the general. A divine of the punny order, being in the field, was pleased to observe, that we might now behold American grievances *red-dressed:* The glitter of the arms and bayo-nets, and this hostile appearance of troops in a time of profound peace, made most of the spectators very serious, and reminded me of what a late traveller relates in his account of Turkey, "That being present on a day when the Grand Signior was passing from his palace to his mosque, and observing that the Janissaries stood without their arms, and with their hands across, only bowed as the Sultan passed; he was led thereby to ask a captain of those guards why they had no arms? Arms said he thou infidel, they are for our ENEMIES; we govern our subjects with the LAW. *There was also a time when Britain was well governed without the aid of a standing army, and when she would have thought that a colony held by the sword was not worth the keeping.*

It is said the officers intended a grand assembly this evening, but the ladies of the town could not be persuaded into the propriety of indulging themselves in musick and dancing with those gentlemen who have been sent hither in order to dragoon us into measures, which appear calculated to enslave and ruin us.

For this, when beauty's blooming charms
   are past,
Your praise, fair nymphs, to latest times
   shall last.[1]

The justices of the town met twice yesterday to consider of the Governor's reiterated demand to provide quarters, &c. for the troops; when Mr. Justice Hutchinson, informed them, that his Excellency required their answer not in the usual way, but in writing, and under their hands; which intimation was so far from intimidating them into a compliance, that they this day waited upon the[2] Governor with the following reply:

May it Please Your Excellency,

YOUR Excellency having been pleased to demand of us to quarter and billet a number of officers and soldiers in the publick-houses in this town: we would beg leave to observe that in the act of Parliament, a number[3] of officers are mentioned for that purpose, namely constables, tytheing-men, magistrates, and other civil officers of the town, which upon enquiring we cannot find have been applied to; and also that by the same act of Parliament the justices are not empowered to quarter and billet the said officers and soldiers, but in default or absence of the aforementioned officers; your Excellency will therefore excuse our doing anything in this affair till it is properly within our province.

William Stoddard,	:	*John Hill,*
Richard Dana,	:	*Edmund Quincy,*
John Ruddock,	:	*John Avery,*
Nathaniel Balston,	:	*John Tudor.*

The ware-houses on Wheelwright's-wharf, exclusive of the use of wharves and cellars, have been this day taken up by the barrack-masters for the purpose of quartering troops, at the rate of £ 300 sterling per annum.

October 26

A general Council met this day upon summons; the Governor proposed in the forenoon their submitting the dispute relative to quartering troops in this town, to the opinion of the judges of the Superior Court; which extraordinary motion was with great propriety rejected. He also recommended their appointing one or more persons, to join with General Gage, in hiring barracks for the troops in this town; the G——r apprehending it best that those who it is likely will finally be saddled with the expence, should be assisting or at least advising in this matter.[4] The Council were utterly against this proposal, as the barracks at Castle-Island still remained empty, and it would have countenanced the quartering of troops in this town; and as the barrack-masters had

---

[1] The italicised poetry and the paragraph directly above are omitted by the *Boston Evening Post.*

[2] In the *New York Journal,* 1349, p. 1, it is "they," an obvious misprint.

[3] In the *New York Journal,* 1349, p. 1, this is "numbers," another obvious printer's error.

[4] The portion back to the last semicolon is omitted from the *Boston Evening Post,* but was included by the *Pennsylvania Chronicle.*

before taken upon themselves to hire barracks at their own direction and risque. —*Is it possible to conceive that any Minister will hereafter have the modesty to make a requisition on the town or government for a reimbursement of the charge of quarters, &c. when taxes are laid and monies daily collecting from this people, one design of which as is declared in the act of Parliament imposing those duties, being for the defraying the charge of a military establishment for securing and defending his Majesty's American dominions?—*

In the afternoon the Governor laid before the Council a letter he had received from the Commissioners, intimating that they now tho't they might come up to town with safety to their persons, provided the magistrates were disposed to do their duty; and requesting the opinion of the Board on this matter: Whereupon one of those honourable gentlemen was pleased to say, that he believed if they should come up from the Castle disposed to behave themselves as they ought to do, which must be very differently from what they had done before, they might then remain among us with safety; another of those gentlemen declared his mind, that all his Majesty's good subjects would be safe in this town, that the Council had already published to the world that their withdraw to Castle William was an unnecessary tho' voluntary act of their own, designed to answer certain purposes which it has appeared the Council were fully aware of: However the Governor pressing for an answer, a sort of a vote with the help of the S——y, was drawn up relative to this important matter, wherein the Council give it as their opinion, that the Commissioners might come up to town with safety.

The Governor also laid before the Council extracts from a letter of Lord Hillsborough's which clearly discovers how much this government as well as individuals are still misrepresented and injured by G——r B——d and others among us; and also affords the most striking specimens of that lord's abilities as a M——r, his thorough

knowledge of, and regard to the British constitution; and that his kind endeavours to promote the peace and welfare of poor America, has been scarce exceeded by a Grenville.

We hear the G——r was so courtly as to tell his C——l, that he required their answers and advice on such matters and things as he might lay before them, before they left the Chamber, and that he should not permit them to meet together to consult and agree upon any votes or answers without his being present with them at those debates. —*Poor gentlemen he cannot forgive them in as much as by some late votes and publications they had preferred the honour and good of the province, to the credit and private views and interests of a G——r.*[1]

October 27

The people were this morning filled with astonishment on hearing that the G——r had nominated and appointed the J——s M——y[2] already noticed in this Journal, as one of his Majesty's justices of the peace for the county of Suffolk; no appointment of this sort could have been more unpopular, or have raised a more general indignation. The inhabitants being fully persuaded that by means of the steady conduct of our bench of justices in refusing to quarter and billet troops in this town contrary as they apprehend to an act of Parliament, this gentleman was added to their number, and that the G——r will not now want a Justice Gillam, or a more fit instrument to carry his purposes into the utmost execution. It is given out that when this nomination was made, there was silence for a space of time, and such signs of disgust as raised the passions and voice of this G——r, who afterwards condescended to use arguments and intreaties with his C——l in favour of his said friend, which finally prevailed to obtain the consent of a majority of two only.

This day Fanueil-Hall was cleared of the troops and delivered up to the Selectmen by Col. Dalrymple.[3]

---

[1] All of the above paragraph was omitted from the *Journal* by the *Boston Evening Post*, also all of the items for October 27.

[2] James Murray.

[3] The above item appears in the *Boston Evening Post* at the close of the *Journal* for October 26. As this correction was made in the *Journal* as printed later in Boston it is obviously a correction to make the *Journal* agree with the facts. An error of one day in the removal of troops would not have been noticed outside of Boston.

October 28

In the morning it was known that the troops which lately occupied Fanveil-Hall, had been placed, or had quartered themselves in the buildings, which had been hired of James Murray, Esq; but owned by James Smith, Esq; of Brush-Hill, such a procedure in the face of an act of Parliament, may well surprise the inhabitants, and lead them to think that some gentlemen of the civil or military order have concluded that they have a right for *certain purposes*, of dispensing with those acts at their pleasure: However this may be, it is hoped that the people will soon have the satisfaction of knowing whether such steps can be taken by any with impunity; or whether every order and person among us is not equally held to the due observance of law.

The prints and letters brought by Capt. White, who arrived here yesterday from London, leads us to hope that American affairs will quickly take a new turn, as some late publications, had served to awaken the attention of the people to their own interest, which they now find has been ill consulted by those in power, who either by giving credit to the accounts received from hence, thro' interested and false mediums, or in order to answer purposes merely ministerial, had gone into such measures as have thrown the nation into the utmost confusion and distress, and if not changed must end in its total destruction.—A gentleman of this town now in London, writes that at an interview with L——d H——lls——gh, he was told that it was determined right or wrong to inforce an obedience to the late regulations. Several ministerial pieces justify G——l Amherst being displaced, and Lord Botte̅tourts being appointed in his room upon this principle, that every one who held any post from the Crown, ought to be ordered to their several stations in the colonies, in order to exert their whole influence to carry down the late regulations. *In pursuance of this ministerial plan of policy, we now behold a standing army and swarms of crown officers, placemen, pensioners and expectants, co-operating in order to subdue Americans to the yoke. Our hopes are that the people of Britain do now, or*

will soon fully perceive that they cannot have our monies in the way of a revenue, and trade both; that what the merchants and manufacturers receive, serves to increase the wealth and oppulence of the naition, while the other only tends to destroy trade and increase ministerial dependence.

This day the following address was prsented to General GAGE by several gentlemen of the Council in behalf of themselves and the other members who subscribed it, being all that were present.[1]

To his Excellency General GAGE, *Commander in Chief of his Majesty's forces in* America.

The ADDRESS of the subscribers, members of his Majesty's Council of the Province of *Massachusetts Bay:*
SIR,
A general Council being held yesterday gives the distant members of it, together with the members in the town and neighbourhood, the pleasure of addressing you. — We take the first opportunity of doing it; and at the same time to pay our compliments to your Excellency.

In this time of public distress, when the General Court of the province is in a state of dissolution; when the metropolis is possessed by troops, and surrounded by ships of war; and when more troops are daily expected, it affords a general satisfaction that your Excellency has visited the province, and has now an opportunity of knowing the state of it by your own observation and enquiry.

Your own observation will give you the fullest evidence that the town and province, are in a peaceful state—Your own enquiry will satisfy you, that tho' there have been disorders in the town of Boston, some of them did not merit notice; and that such as did, have been magnified beyond the truth.

Those of the 18th of March and 10th of June are said to have occasioned the above-mentioned armament to be ordered hither. —The first was trivial, and could not have been noticed to the disadvantage of the town, but by persons inimical to it; especially as it happened in the evening of a day of recreation. The other was criminal, and

---

[1] The above paragraph and all of the address of the Council and General Gage's reply are omitted by the *Boston Evening Post.*

the actors in it were guilty of a riot; but we are obliged to say it had its rise from those persons who were loudest in their complaints about it, and who by their over-charged representations of it have been the occasion of so great an armament being ordered hither. We cannot persuade ourselves to believe they have sufficient evidence to support such representations; which have most unjustly brought into question the loyalty of as loyal a people as any in his Majesty's dominions.

This misfortune has arisen from the accusation of interested men, whose avarice having smothered in their breasts every sentiment of humanity towards this province, has impelled them to oppress it to the utmost of their power: and by the consequences of that oppression essentially to injure Great-Britain.

From the candour of your Excellency's sentiments, we assure ourselves you will not entertain any apprehension, that we mean to justify the disorders and riotous proceedings that have taken place in the town of Boston. We detest them, and have repeatedly and publickly expressed that detestation; and in Council have advised Governor Bernard to order the Attorney General to prosecute the perpetrators of them: but at the same time we are obliged to declare in justice to the town, that tne disorders of the 10th of June last, occasioned by a seizure made by the officers of the customs, appear to have originated with those who ordered the seizure to be made. The hour of making the seizure (at or near sunset) the threats and armed force used in it, the forcibly carrying the vessel away, and all in a manner unprecedented, and calculated to irritate, justify the apprehension that the seizure was accompanied with these extraordinary circumstances in order to excite a riot, and furnish a plausible pretence for requesting troops. —A day or two after the riot, and as if in prosecution of the last mentioned purpose, notwithstanding there was not the least insult offered to the Commissioners of the Customs, either in their persons or property, they thought fit to retire, on the pretence of security to themselves, on board the Romney man of war, and afterwards to Castle William; and when there, to keep up the idea of their being still in great hazard,

procured the Romney and several other vessels of war to be stationed as to prevent an attack upon the Castle: which they affected to be afraid of.

These proceedings have doubtless taken place to induce a belief among the officers of the navy and army, as they occasionally came hither, that the Commissioners were in danger of being attacked, and to procure from those officers representations coincident with their own, that they really were so. But their frequent landing on the main, and making excursions into the country, where it would have been easy to have seized, if any injury had been intended them, demonstrates the insincerity of their declarations, that they immured themselves at the Castle for safety. This is rather to be accounted for, as being an essential part of the concerted plan for procuring troops to be quartered here: in which they and their coadjutors have succeeded to their wish: but unhappily to the mutual detriment and uneasiness of both countries.

We thought it absolutely necessary, and our duty to the town and province required us, to give your Excellency this detail, that you might know the sentiments of this people, and that they think themselves injured, and injured by men to whom they have done no injury. —From the justice of your Excellency, we assure ourselves your mind will not admit of impressions to their disadvantage from persons who have done the injury.

Your Excellency in your letter to Governor Bernard, of the 12th of September, gave notice that one of the regiments from Halifax was ordered for the present to Castle William, and the other to the town: but you was pleased afterwards to order both of them into the town.

If your Excellency when you know the true state of the town, which we can assure you are quite peaceable shall think his Majesty's service does not require those regiments to continue in the town, it will be a great ease and satisfaction to the inhabitants, if you will please to order them to Castle William, where commodious barracks are provided for their reception; or to Point Shirley, in the neighbourhood of it: in either of which or in both they can be well accommodated.

As to the two regiments expected here from Ireland, it appears by Lord Hillsborough's letter of the 30th of July they were intended for a different part of North-America.

If your Excellency shall think it not inconsistent with his Majesty's service that they should be sent to the place of their first destination, it would contribute to the ease and happiness of the town and province, if they might be ordered hither.

As we are true and faithful subjects of his Majesty, have an affectionate regard for the mother country, and a tender feeling for our own, our duty to each of them makes us wish, and we earnestly beg your Excellency to make a full enquiry into the disorders above mentioned, into the causes of them and the representations that have been made about them; in doing which your Excellency will easily discover who are the persons that from lucrative views have combined against the peace of this town and province: Some of whom it is probable have discovered themselves already by their own letters to your Excellency.

In making the enquiry, tho' many imprudencies and some criminal proceedings may be found to have taken place, we are persuaded from the candour, generosity and justice that distinguish your character, your Excellency will not charge the doings of a few individuals, and those of an inferior sort, upon the town and province. And with regard to those individuals, if any circumstances shall appear justly to extenuate the criminality of their proceedings, your Excellency will let them have their effect—On the same candour, generosity and justice we can rely, that your Excellency's representations of this affair to his Majesty's ministers will be such as even the criminals themselves shall allow to be just.

Harrison Gray,	Sam. Danforth,
James Russel,	John Hill,
John Bradbury,	Isaac Royall,
Royal Tyler,	John Erving,
Samuel White,	James Bowdoin,
James Pitts,	Gam. Bradford,
Samuel Dexter,	Tho. Hubbard,
Na. Sparhawk	

Boston, October 27, 1768.

To the foregoing address the General gave the following answer.

To the honourable Messieurs Danforth, Hill, Royall, Erving, Bowdoin, Bradford, Hubbard, Sparhawk, Gray, Russell, Bradbury, Tyler, White, Pitts, *and* Dexter, *members of his Majesty's Council of the Province of Massachusetts-Bay.*

GENTLEMEN,

I *return you thanks for the honour you do me in this address, and am greatly obliged to you, for the good opinion you are pleased to conceive of me.*

Whatever may have been the particular causes of the disturbances, and riots, which have happened in the town of Boston, those riots, and the resolves which were published, have induced his Majesty to order four regiments to this town, to protect his loyal subjects, in their persons and properties, and to assist the civil magistrates in the execution of the laws.

The discipline and order which will be preserved amongst the troops, I trust, will render their stay, in no shape distressful to his Majesty's dutiful subjects, in this town; and that the future behaviour of the people, will justify the best construction of their past actions, which I flatter myself will be such, as to afford me a sufficient foundation, to represent to his Majesty the propriety of withdrawing the most part of the troops.

Boston, Octo. 28, 1768.   THOMAS GAGE.

October 29

The inhabitants of this town have been of late greatly insulted and abused by some of the officers and soldiers, several have been assaulted on frivolous pretences, and put under guard without any lawful warrant for so doing. A physician of the town walking the streets the other evening, was jostled by an officer, when a scuffle ensued, he was afterwards met by the same officer in company with another, both as yet unknown, who repeated his blows, and as is supposed gave him a stroke with a pistol, which so wounded him as to endanger his life. A tradesman of this town on going under the rails of the Common in his way home, had a thrust in the breast with a bayonet from a soldier; another person passing the street was struck with a musket, and the last evening a merchant of the town was struck down by an officer who went into the coffee-house, several gentlemen following him in, and expostulating with the officers, were treated in the most ungenteel manner; but the most atrocious offence and alarming behaviour was that of a captain, the last evening, who in company with two other officers, endeavoured to persuade some Negro servants to ill-treat and abuse their masters, assuring them that the soldiers were come to procure their freedoms, and that with their help and assistance they should be able to drive all the Liberty Boys to the devil; with discourse of the like import, tending to excite an insurrection. Depositions are now taking before the magistrates, and prosecutions at common law are intended, the inhabitants being determined to oppose by the law such proceedings, apprehending it the most honourable as well as the most safe and effectual method of obtaining satisfaction and redress; at the same time they have a right to expect that General Gage will not remain an unconcerned spectator of such a conduct in any under his command. —*Here Americans you may behold some of the first fruits springing up from that root of bitterness a standing army. Troops are quartered upon us in a time of peace, on pretence of preserving order in a town that was as orderly before their arrival as any one large town in the whole extent of his Majesty's dominions; and a little time will discover whether we are to be governed by the martial or the common law of the land.*

October 30

Last evening the encampment on the Common broke up, and the soldiery retired into winter quarters in this town, but by whom they have been quartered remains yet to be enquired. —To the further astonishment of the inhabitants of this town, we are told that libels were registered the last evening by order of the Commissioners, against twenty-one merchants and others of this town, for upwards of the sum of £100,000 sterl. on pretence of their having broke some of the late revenue acts. —*What an enemy has our trade been to the mother country, that it is thus dealt with!*

October 31[1]

In consequence of the late practices upon the Negroes of this town, we are told that orders have been given by the Selectmen to the town watch, to take up and secure all such Negro servants as shall be absent from their master's houses, at an unseasonable time of night.

The following complaint was regularly made this day, viz to the worshipful Richard Dana and John Ruddock, Esqrs. two of his Majesty's justice of the peace for the county of Suffolk, and of the quorum.

The subscribers Selectmen of the town of Boston, complain of John Willson, Esq; a captain in his Majesty's 59th Regiment of foot, a detachment whereof is now quartered in the said town of Boston, under his command, that the said John, with others unknown, on the evening of the 28th day of October current, did, in the sight and hearing of divers persons, utter many abusive and threatening expressions, of, and against the inhabitants of said town, and in a dangerous and conspirative manner, did entice and endeavour to spirit up, by a promise of the reward of freedom, certain Negro slaves in Boston aforesaid, the property of several of the town inhabitants, to cut their master's throats, and to beat, insult, and otherwise ill treat their said masters, asserting that now the soldiers are come, the Negroes shall be free, and the Liberty Boys slaves—to the great terror and danger of the peaceable inhabitants of said town, liege subjects of his Majesty, our Lord the King, and the great disturbance of the peace and safety of said town.

Wherefore your complainants, solicitous for the peace and wellfare of the said town, as well as their own, as individuals, humbly requests your worship's consideration of the premises, and that process may issue against the said John, that he may be dealt with herein according to law.

Joshua Henshaw, : *John Rowe,*
Joseph Jackson, : *Sam. Pemberton,*
John Hancock, : *Henderson Inches.*

What must the good people of England think of our new conservators of the peace,

---

[1] Items from October 31 to November 6, inclusive, are from the *New York Journal*, November 17, 1768, pp. 2–3.

or rather what would the present Ministry have thought and done, had the inhabitants of this town stood chargeable upon the oaths of creditable witnesses, with the crime of having solicited the soldiers now quartered upon us, and as is apprehended contrary to an act of Parliament and the Bill of Rights, to cut their officers throats and desert the service with promises of rewards for so doing?

All the troops in town marched into the Common this morning, drumming the dead beat; at 8 o'clock, Richard Arnes, a private of the 14th Regiment, dressed in white, having just before had the sacrament administered to him by the Revd. Mr. Palms, chaplain of the regiment, who also accompanied him, was pursuant to the sentence of a General Court Martial, shot for desertion: The regiment then marched round the corpes as it lay on the ground, when it was put into the coffin, which was carried by his side into the Common, and buried in a grave near where he was shot, and the church service read over him. This was the first execution of the kind ever seen in this town, tho' during the late war a much larger body of troops, had been encamped here: Some of the first ladies among us presented a petition for his pardon the evening before, and we flattered ourselves (as it was his first desertion, and in a time of peace, and which could not have happened had he been quartered agreeable to act of Parliament on Castle-Island) it would have met with success; but the numerous desertions from so important a service as the troops are now engaged in, it seems prevented this act of grace.

for this behaviour, for which boldness he was knocked down with a musket and much wounded, they went off undiscovered; another had a thrust with a bayonet near his eye, and a gentlemen of this town informs, that a day or two before the physician already mentioned met with his abuse, he overheard several officers discoursing, when one of them said, if he could meet that doctor he would do for him.

The troops still occupy the Town-House, and the main guard is fixed in a house on the south-side of the same, and two pieces of mounted cannon planted before the door.

In pursuance of a complaint made to Mr. Justice Dana, and Ruddock, relative to Capt. Willson and others, a warrant was issued by those justices for taking up said Willson and bringing him before them, which was delivered to Benjamin Cudworth, a deputy sheriff of the county, who being opposed in the execution of it, applied to the high sheriff, who with divers constables went to apprehand him; at first he also met with opposition from one of the officers, but the said Willson soon after surrendered himself to the sheriff, who brought him before the justices at Faneuil-Hall, which was crowded with people; and after the examination of divers witnesses upon oath, the complaint was so well supported, that the justices ordered him to become bound with sufficient sureties for his appearance at the Superior Court in March next, to what shall then be alledged against him, touching the matters complained of, as also for his good behaviour in the mean time.

November 1

THE last night a soldier passed the guards, at the south part of the town, and was haled, but not answering, they followed and fired at him several times, and being impeded in running by the sea-weed on the beach, he was taken and brought back to the guards: This man was present at the execution in the morning, but nothing is like to prevent desertion while the troops remain in this place.

An householder at the west part of the town, hearing the cries of two women in the night, who were rudely treated by some soldiers, ventured to expostulate with them

November 2

Two men and a lad coming over the Neck into the town, were haled by one guard and passed them: soon after they were challenged by another, they replied they had just answered one, but they hoped they were all friends; upon which a soldier made a pass or two with his bayonet at one of them, who parried the bayonet at first, but was afterward badly cut on the head and grievously wounded in divers parts of his body. One passing the south town watch was challenged but not stopped, he drew his sword and flourished it at the watch, using very insulting language; he was then discovered to be an officer a little disguised, another soon joined him, full as abusive, both declared that if they had been challenged in the street and no orders shewn, they would have deprived the watchman of his life. A country man also coming into town, was thought to have approached nearer the guards than he should have done, for which offence he was knocked off his horse with a musket. The other evening three officers unknown being together at the south part of the town, were heard to say, by a person of credit, "that if the Negroes could be made freemen, they should be sufficient to subdue these damn'd rascals," *perhaps these doings and others of a like nature, are exhibited as specimens of the lenient and persuasive methods, which Lord H——ls——gh intimates are to be taken to bring back his Majesty's misled subjects to a sense of their duty; be this as it may, the sufferers and the abused, are seeking satisfaction in a legal manner.*

Capt. Howard arrived from Corke, which he left the 7th September, in company with the man of war and 11 cats, having on board as was reported 2000 troops for Boston. But know it Britons! 50,000 will not give you so good a hold, as you once had, in the *affections* of this people.

This night orders were it is said read to the officers to hold the troops in readiness against the morrow, as a large mob was then expected.

November 3

We can now account for the orders of the last night. This morning Mr. Arodi Thayer, marshal of the Court of Admiralty for three provinces, with a hanger at his side, came to the house of John Hancock, Esq; to serve him with a precept for £9000 sterling, and having arrested his person, demanded bail for £3000 sterling. Mr. Hancock offered him divers estates to the value thereof, which were absolutely refused; he then made him an offer of £3000 in money, and afterwards of £9000, which were also refused; Mr. Thayer alledging that such were his directions. Mr. Hancock however having heard of the orders and expectations of last evening, prudently determined to give bail, as did five other gentlemen arrested for the same sum, and on the same account from the

like prudent motives. Thus the Commissioners of the Customs not satisfied with the seizing and forfeiture of the sloop Liberty, for a non-entry of a part of her cargo of Madeiria wines, which before the American Revenue Acts were duty free, have gone beyond every thing of the kind before heard of in America, in prosecuting the supposed owner and each person they imagined concerned in unloading the wines, for the value of the whole cargo and treble damages. — *The public will now impartially judge whether this conduct does not bear much the same complexion which his Majesty's Council expressly declared of the seizure of said sloop, namely to occasion a tumult, and thereby give the same colouring for a necessity of quartering the troops contrary to act of Parliament in the body of the town, instead of the barracks at Castle-Island, that was originally given for their being ordered here.*

This day at a general Council, the G——r as we are told, reminded them of an important article of Lord Hillsborough's letter, viz. where he "strongly recommends a reform of the magistrates of the town, since they have some of them been heretofore deficient in the execution of their trust, and hopes that such gentlemen will be found to fill up those important places, who will be zealous to support the law and the constitutional authority of Parliament." As to the first part the G——r was pleased to say, that he should not at present enter upon it, but as to the latter he had and should be casting about in his mind, who were the proper persons to be appointed; he then was pleased to nominate the new appointed Justice Murray, as a justice of the quorum, but the Board are to have it under consideration till the next general Council.[1]—It appears Lord Hillsborough has been greatly abused in the accounts sent him from hence: We know of no magistrate who has been deficient in the execution of his trust, but this we know, that no one of them had the presence of the G——r to countenance them, nor did the sheriff whose duty on all such occasions is to be present and active, even make his appearance, but the inhabitants were left to exert themselves, and finally by their own virtue surpressed the tumults and restored

---

[1] From this point on the rest of the item for **November 3** is omitted from the *Boston Evening Post.*

order to the town. —The nomination for the quorum may shew the people how much the G——r despises the murmurs or sentiments relating to any part of his conduct.

November 4

The following letter taken from a gazetteer of August 26, has been shown in the last Thursday's paper, viz. Whereas it has been publickly reported, that the Earl of Hillsborough has neglected to deliver a petition from the Assembly of the Massachusetts Bay, to his Majesty at a time when his lordship had not even seen the said petition. I think it my duty to inform the public that such insinuations are entirely groundless. My reasons for any delay and proceedings therewith, I have duly given the Assembly in my letters to them of the 12th and 18th of March, and 27th of June.

DENNYS DE BERDT.

By this letter it appears that a young secretary has been able to make a screen of an old agent: The truth is, that our Assembly were informed, that when this letter first got to hand, the great were still engaged in electioneering, which prevented its being handed to Lord Hillsborough; but we were soon led to understand that a petition offered by Mr. De Berdt, could not be presented to his Majesty, he being an agent for the House only; a block thrown in the way by our good G——r, who had the last winter endeavoured that the Assembly might join the Council in choice of an agent, who if not chosen through his influence, would yet have been subjected to his negative; and be it known, that in all provincial letters and instructions to their agent, the concurrence of the several branches of government has not been thought necessary; in which case our representatives could never in a regular way have conveyed to Administration, or the people of England, the pure unadulterated sentiments and views of their constituents, as has been done by them for some time past; tho' our enemies have falsely asserted, that they were only the sentiments of a faction.

November 5

Last evening the guards were withdrawn from the cellar of the Manufactory House, and Mr. Brown and the other manufacturers are again permitted to pursue their several businesses; they have still a right of action for damages against the sheriff and other trespassers; and it may be remarked, that he is the first civil officer of the province, who ever applied for the aid of the King's troops, and this before he had taken the previous steps which the law required. —This day the Pope and other effigies were carried through the town, as on these anniversaries is customary, with great decency and decorum, agreeable to their resolution of 1765, which has been practiced ever since.

November 6

This being Lord's day, the minds of serious people at public worship were greatly disturbed with drums beating and fifes playing, unheard of before in this land — *What an unhappy influence must this have upon the minds of children and others, in eradicating the sentiments of morality and religion, which a due regard to that day has a natural tendency to cultivate and keep alive.*

November 7[1]

John Fenton, Esq; allied by marriage to the late Surveyor General; has been removed from his place of Deputy Receiver of the new duty, and Nath. Coffin, Esq; appointed in his room. The Receiver General resides in this town.

A Court of Admiralty this day, when the libels entered against John Hancock, Esq; and others were read and the court adjourned to the 28th inst.

Letters from Jamaica acquaint us, that the General Assembly there was dissolved on the 22d of September last, by the Lieut. Governor of that island for their not complying with his Majesty's express command, for payment of the monies issued by the treasury of Great Britain, for the island subsistance of the troop stationed there during the discontinuance of their Assembly. —*A dispute may also arise with us relative to the barracks and billeting of troops here, during the discontinuance of our General Assembly: The G——r as also Col. D——lple, declared before the Council that they made no demand for the hiring of barracks, but only for the*

---

[1] Items for November 7 to November 13, inclusive, are from the *New York Journal*, November 24, 1768, p. 2.

utensils and billeting, they being at liberty to hire barracks on the King's account; this was perhaps to draw the C——l into a vote for providing barracks, utensils, and billeting, which was then represented as the utmost that would be desired on account of the troops; but it is now intimated by the G——r that the charge of barracks must be finally defrayed by the province.——

We have also advice from South-Carolina, that their new Assembly was to meet on the 25th ultimo: As it was imagin'd they would not recede from the resolutions of the Massachusetts ninety two,[1] which are highly applauded in the province, a dissolution of that Assembly was expected soon after. *—The British ministry seems to have adopted French maxims and customs with respect to their treatment of American parliaments, which must not only be well relished by a free people, but be soon productive of very salutary effects.*

November 8

The Commissioners of the American Board of Customs, have this day thought proper to leave Castle William, the seat of their chosen residence for some months past, and to make their re-entry into this metropolis. *—We wish we had full evidence, that during this recess, they had not been fully employed in transmitting such accounts, and projecting those measures, that have had too direct a tendency to enflame and further embroil the mother country and the colonies; and this at a time when a return of mutual affection and confidence is so necessary for the preservation and happiness of both.——*

A letter makes its appearance in the Court Gazette, exactly in the stile of the *true patriot*, the writer asserts, "That Mr. HOLLOWELL, by his temperate caution and care not to aggravate any thing in his accounts, has given general satisfaction," he condoles us as "fatally misled by evil-minded men of malicious dispositions, into measures which tend to public ruin," and declares "that the nonsense of Wilkes and Liberty is now at an end; that no one ever made a question about the propriety and necessity of shooting forty men among the rioters at Huxam, in 1757, but when *ill humours are*

set afloat, (a phrase borrowed from a governors speech) the clearest point will be disputed; that the King's servants seem determined to maintain the supreme legislative authority of Great Britain, and if our people flatter themselves with indulgence in their frowardness, they will be deceived; as in short all men of understanding, except *a few interested merchants* who are afraid of their American debts, are calling out for a much greater exertion of authority."

Whether the above is London or Boston manufacture, the public may judge, be this as it may, it certainly carries *the plain mark of the beast in its forehead;* the writer, who is probably the one that has been soliciting for a thousand a year out of the American revenue in addition to his present salary, seems to make quite light of the interest of the British merchants; The revenue, the revenue, is all and in all with him; to secure which he calls out for still greater exertions of power, and what cares he, tho' these merchants should loose the several millions due to them from America, in so ridiculous a scuffle: *But know it B——d,[1] so soon as the people of Britain shall put the whole produce of American revenue into one scale, and the profits and advantages of their colony trade in the other, they will perceive the former at once to kick the beam;—then, and not till then may we expect to see some men, who from selfish views have projected and recommended schemes destructive to the commerce of Britain and the welfare of the colonies, reap the fruits of their doings, and those who have generously prefered the interest of the nation to their own, the honours and applause they are justly entitled to.*

November 9

Yesterday the Superior Court met by adjournment at the Court House. In the afternoon a motion was made by J——s O——s, Esq;[2] one of the bar, that the court would adjourn to Faneuil-Hall, not only as the stench occasioned by the troops in the Representatives Chamber, may prove infectious, but as it was derogatory to the honour of the court to administer justice at the mouths of cannon and the points of bayonets.—This day the troops were re-

---

[1] This refers to the number of the members of the Assembly who refused to rescind the Massachusetts Circular Letter on the demand of Lord Hillsborough.
[2] Bernard, Governor of Massachusetts.

moved from that Chamber, much to the satisfaction of the people who have looked upon their being placed there at first by the G——r as an insult upon the whole province.

The Town-House watch being on the return at 2 o'clock in the morning, heard a great noise and uproar in the streets, they soon found it was made by a number of officers, and presuming to speak to them, tho' with great mildness, they were threatened with being seized and put in irons, and otherways insulted in a gross manner. — Several soldiers, late at night, entered the house of Mr. Justice W——ls, and in humble imitation of some of their superiors, were very free with the blacks, to whom they declared a liking, and that their assistance was wanted; the justice being confined by sickness, was obliged to call in the assistance of some neighbours, who coming armed soon forced those intruders to decamp. —A married woman living in Long Lane, returning home in the night, was seized by the neck and almost strangled, she was then thrown upon the ground, and treated with great indecencies: Another woman at New Boston was rudely handled. Mr. N——w——l of Needham, passing near the town gates, was struck with a musket and without the least provocation, received another stroke from a drunken guard, which stunned him. —*The mention of such abuses as these is by no means intended to insinuate a want of care in the commanding officers, but to show the great impropriety and grievance of quartering troops in the town, in as much as even under the eye of the General, the inhabitants are exposed to such great insults and injuries.*

A large guard house for the soldiery is erected on the town land, near the Neck, and almost finished, notwithstanding Mr. Pierpont, who had hired it of the Selectmen for about 4 years past, did, by their order, and before witnesses, forbid their erecting the same. —*These are times in which no inhabitant knows what ground he stands upon, or can call his own.*

A general Council this day, at which we hear the G——r proposed his publishing a proclamation relative to the justices of the town, founded on what Lord Hillsborough has written, concerning their conduct in the late times; *the Council did not approve of this proposal, being aware it would have led some*

to conclude that they were not of the mind that said Lord had been imposed upon in the accounts transmitted from hence, respecting the behaviour of those magistrates.

November 10

This day the G——r required the attendance of his Majesty's justices of the peace, at the Council Chamber; they attended accordingly, James Murray, Esq; the first made justice on the *reforming plan* being among them; when to keep up the appearance of their having been negligent in their duty, Lord Hillsborough's letter was read to them, after which they were exhorted by the G——r to a faithful and diligent discharge of the duties of their office;—*we do not hear that it was recommended to them to proceed according to law, with those who have quartered the troops upon us, or against such officers and soldiers as have insulted the public, injured and abused the subject, and thus broken the King's peace.*

Several large transports just arrived from Cork, having on board part of the 64th and 65th Regiments, the remainder with the Hussar frigate were parted with in a storm ten days ago. —*It is to be hoped that the arrival of these troops will lead some officers to conclude that the aid and countenance of our Negro gentry may now be dispensed with.*

November 11

What an appearance does Boston now make! One of the first commercial towns in America, has now several regiments of soldiers quartered in the midst of it, and even the Merchants Exchange is picquetted, and made the spot where the main guard is placed and paraded, and their cannon mounted; so that instead of our merchants and trading people transacting their business, we see it filled with red coats, and have our ears dinn'd with the music of the drum and fife. —*How would the merchants of London be startled if they should behold their exchange thus metamorphosed.*

November 12

Reports that the small-pox is on board some of the Irish transports; we have certain information that several had that distemper on board one of them since she left Cork; notwithstanding which, said ship has been suffered, contrary to the law for preventing the spread of infectious disorders to come up into the town, and numbers of the passengers have been seen walking the streets. —*The bringing the small-pox among us at this time would open a new scene of distress, as we have a great addition to our numbers, and the risque of taking the infection would deter our coasters and country people from coming in this winter, with the necessary supplies of provision and fuel.*

November 13
The parade of the guards on week days, grander than in time of war, and nothing lessened or omitted this Sabbath; Commodore Hood, and several men of war arrived from Halifax. ——

November 14[1]
The Commissioners of the Customs again hold a board in this town; as the day of their appointment is noted in their callender as a holy day, on which no business is to be done in the several offices, we may probably hear that the day of their restoration is alike distinguished; *however it is to be hoped that the restoration of sound British policy may soon make a reform in their callender, and obliterate such public marks of vanity and folly.*

The inhabitants of Windham, a considerable town in Connecticut, have lately instructed their representatives to "encourage a spirit of industry and frugality, and the woolen, linen, glass, and paper manufactures," *rightly judging that under the difficulties brought upon them by the late Revenue Acts, no step can have a greater tendency to procure them relief.* —They also instruct their representatives "to come into effectual measures to cement and confirm the union between that and the other governments in America; and that they endeavour to bring about a general congress,"—*all founded upon the sound maxim, respecting the colonies, divided they fall, united we stand.*

November 15
We are informed the Assembly of the lower counties of Philadelphia, have appointed Dennis De Berdt, Esq; their agent

in England, and have petitioned the King, Lords and Commons for redress of the grievous burdens laid on America. —*No one Assembly upon the continent have, that we hear of, receded from the resolutions of the Massachusetts ninety two, and every of them excepting Halifax and Pensacola, whose existence depends on the smiles of a court, have harmonized with this province in their resolves and petitions respecting the new regulations; measures which must in the end prove more detrimental and ruinous to Britain than the colonies.*

Letters from South-Carolina inform, that all the King's troops were withdrawn from the out posts and ordered for Boston, and that the companies stationed at Bermuda and New Providence, were also withdrawn from those islands.—And we have accounts from West Florida, that the settlers there were in great fear and distress at the removal of the fifteen companies from that province, as they lay surrounded by savages, from whom they have no defence; that one of their planters had lost 30 head of cattle, supposed to be carried off by the Indians, and that they could not account for so singular a measure, as the taking off troops from a frontier province to place them in an interior country.—*The conduct of our present Ministry may convince the nation that there are mysteries in politicks as well as religion.*

The inhabitants of town and country, greatly disturbed, that numbers of the passengers of those ships which have had the small-pox on board, have been permitted to land in this town; and we hear that the Selectmen waited upon General Gage, and acquainted him with the laws of this province for preventing infectious sickness in the town; and proper measures are taking for the prevention of those ill effects which are apprehended.

It is confidently reported that the principal design of Lord George Campbell, the Governor of Halifax, who came passenger in the Romney man of war, Commodore Hood, is to make a representation to General Gage, of the present deplorable state of that colony, occasioned by the withdraw of the King's troops and ships of war; Halifax it is

---

[1] Items from November 14 to November 20, inclusive, are from the *New York Journal*, December 1, 1768, pp. 1–2.

said is like to be deserted on this occasion, the tradesmen and many others being obliged to follow the fleet and army, upon which in that new settlement they depended for a subsistance. —*Thus thro' the misrepresentation of interested and designing men, and under the pretence of aiding the civil government in the old colonies, where such aid is not only entirely needless, but highly affrontive and grievous; the new colonies, both north and south which have been thought by former Administration to be of so much consequence, and upon which such large sums have been expended by the crown, are now not only exposed to a foreign enemy and the savages, but deprived in a great part, of the very means of subsistance.*

November 17

Capt. Watts arrived from London, which he left about the 25th of Sept. in coming into the harbour, he received a shot from an armed schooner, which carried away one of his yards. Her boat then boarded him and took away sixteen of his seamen:—*the importance of the service in which the fleet is now engaged may perhaps apologize for their thus distressing our merchants.*—

It has transpired, that our G——r and those of the other colonies have orders from the American S——y, not to lay before their several Assemblies any of his letters, or even extracts from them for the future, without special directions for so doing. —*The freedom with which even the people of Britain have treated his circular letters may account for this prohibition, but however prudent it may be with respect to himself. Judging by the specimens before given us, it cannot be very agreeable to the public to have the matter of such letters partially dealt out to them, and interlarded with the comments and glosses of a G——r, or the creatures of a G——r in whom there is no ground for placing the least of our confidence.*

We are told that Robert Auchmuty, Esq; Judge of Admiralty for this province, &c. has a yearly salary of £600 sterling allowed him out of the American revenue; and that three other Judges of Admiralty for North-America will be appointed with the like salaries. —*The only recompence former Judges of Admiralty have received for their services was an allowance of 5 per ct. out of the pro-*ceeds of all condemnations; and a fixed allowance of £100 sterling per annum, would have satisfied the first lawyers among us for capacity and character; and will administration ever be able to persuade Americans that the intention of this revenue is to lessen the national debt, when they behold it so lavishly bestowed one way and another upon the tools of power; or rather must it not serve fully to convince them, that the fruits of our toil and labour torn from us by that project, is to be held out as bates and lures to such base Americans as can sacrifice their country in order to realize them.*

The little new settlement on the island of St. John has been so noticed by Administration, that Isaac Deschamps, Esq; is appointed Chief Justice there with a salary of £300 sterling per annum, which is above double what any first justice ever received in this province,—*what pretty Ministerial pickings does the American revenue already afford!*

November 18

The following ships of war now ride at anchor in this harbour and more expected. Romney, Mermaid, Glasgow, Beaver, Viper, Senegall, Bonetta, Magdalene, Hope, Little Romney, and Sultana, besides the ships which brought the troops from Ireland. The 64th Regiment of those troops Col. Pomroy, are landed and quartered in town, the 65th Regiment Col. Mackey, at Castle Island; they consist of 500 men each.—The battalion-men of the detachment of the 59th are to return to Halifax. —*What an amazing expence must be occasioned by the movements of the troops and ships of war throughout the whole extent of this continent: Modern statesmen are extremely dexterous in figuring in and out, it is to be wished for the good of the nation, that they were as expert in figuring up.*

November 19

Before the dissolution of our Assembly in June last, the Council thought it their duty to petition his Majesty and both houses of Parliament on the American revenue; a draft of a petition to the King was reported and the C——l entreated that the Assembly might continue till this and their other addresses were completed, which would not have taken them a day; the Court[1] was

---

[1] General Court, i.e. the combined legislative body of Massachusetts.

prorogued notwithstanding. The Council were still for proceeding in their petitions; but the G——r insisted upon it that the C——l were annihilated in their legislative capacity; that they existed only as a privy C——l and in this latter capacity could not act without his presence and permission, which he should not afford them in the business they were upon. The C——l complained of this *novel injurious treatment,* and were it not for the critical situation of our affairs, would probably have remonstrated to Administration; after much altercation they were *allowed* to petition the King, but astonishing as it is, were *prohibited* addressing *either houses of Parliament.* The first petition was completed, going rather on the inexpediency of the late acts, than considering the matters of right, and was committed to the G——r, at his own desire, to be transmitted to Lord Hillsborough, and by him presented to his Majesty.—The Court Gazette now informs us that "the petition of his Majesty's Council of this province, has been graciously received by his Majesty; and that the petition with his Excellency the Governors *reasonings in support of it,* would have a due consideration before the meeting of Parliament!"

The mention made in the Gazette of the *reasonings* of Mr. B——d in support of said petition has greatly alarmed the C——l, who it is said, are very suspicious that the G——r has been capable of a piece of chicanery below the character of the meanest member of community; it has some how got abroad that the B——d in their petition humbly intreat that his Majesty would be graciously pleased to interpose with his Parliament for the prevention of any monies *being drawn* from his Majesty's American subjects by way of revenue, and that the G——r's glosses upon this and other paragraphs, are calculated to mislead Administration into an apprehension that they are not so desirous of a *repeal of those acts,* but that the monies arising therefrom might not be *drawn* out of the country, but *expended among us,* whereby the *great objection* to those acts would be removed out of the way: It is said the C——l have had several meetings on this occasion, and diverse committees have waited upon the G——r for a sight of *his letters and reasonings* without obtaining that

satisfaction, and are therefore, as it is said, taking measures to detect his management with Lord H——sb——h. —*We have here a striking specimen of the arts that have been made use of by some men, to beget, increase, and continue the misunderstanding between Great-Britain and her colonies, that threatens the ruin of both;—how infatuated must that man be, who from the success of former tricks and subterfuges, at length becomes bold enough upon affairs of the greatest importance, and at the most critical season, to hold out false lights to Administration, and through them to a British Parliament, and even Majesty itself? To such a degree does ambition and avarice sometimes blind the human mind.*

The G——r we are informed not long since expressed himself to a gentleman of character in something of the following manner, I believe the petition of the C——l will be granted, for I have endeavoured to shew Administration the reasonableness of the petition, and that the whole revenue should be *expended in America;* and as my own support is not adequate to my station, *I expect a good share of it myself.*

This exactly agrees with what the public papers have years ago declared to be the views of that gentleman from a *civil* and *military* establishment in America. —The *revenue,* the *American revenue,* too trifling indeed to be the object of a *national* concern, has been held up to Administration by *designing* and *interested men* on this side the water, with a view to *enrich themselves;* and some *late appointments* in America, plainly shew what bates have been held out to engage a number of warm coadjutors in this dishonourable cause. Hence Administration has been abused by being told that only *a very few* in America were *dissatisfied* with the late acts of Parliament, and hence disturbances have been *created* and greatly *exaggerated* in order to form a pretence for the *dissolution* of the government of this province, and the *introduction* of a military force to *stifle* the complaints of this loyal and suffering people.

November 20

It is to be wished that some part of the parade of relieving the guards, &c. might be dispensed with upon the Sabbath; whereby the inhabitants would be less disturbed, and the soldiery have more time to attend the more important duties of this holy day.

November 21[1]

An order of G——r B——d's for a Thanksgiving was yesterday read in the several churches[2]; in which we are called upon to give thanks, among other public blessings, "for the opening of new sources of wealth to the nation." If the *American* revenue is hereby intended, we believe it will scarcely serve to slack the thirst of those M——s and G——s[3] who have opened it. This we know, that it has entirely choaked up or diverted another way, a trade, which tho' unhappily for Great-Britain, she has made contraband, was in truth a grand source of national wealth. Before the project of an American revenue, our adventurers in that trade had nothing to encounter more formidable than the Spanish and French *guarda costa's;* duties were indeed then laid upon foreign sugars, molasses, and a few other articles, but Administration, not intending a *revenue,* they were wisely winkt out of sight: Then it was, that the silver and gold, together with the various products of the French and Spanish West-Indies, the Spanish Main, and the Mediterranean, were drawn from these places, in exchange for the produce of the continent, and British manufactures; this trade increased our shipping and seamen, and by yielding the best of remittances, enabled us greatly to enlarge the import and consumption of British made goods; and scarce an article of *foreign ware*, interfering with those of our mother country *introduced into the plantations thro' this channel;* tho' from *selfish* motives it has been otherwise reported to Administration: But now, unhappily for the nation, in order to secure the duties from which the American revenue was expected; custom-house officers, &c. have been multiplied, and they enabled by new acts of Parliament, and the extention of former acts to the colonies, to harrass and ruin the adventurer: and what is still more surprising, modern ministers, by adopting the Spanish policy, have converted the ships of war into mere *guarda costa's,* which instead of aiding and assisting the merchant in the prosecution of this trade, have been wholly employed in seeking its destruction: The Dutch and other European nations have availed themselves of our infatuation, and are now enriching their several countries by a trade, which has been thus torn from the colonies, and lost to the nation, notwithstanding we have such peculiar advantages for the carrying of it on.

November 22

Lord Botetourt of Virginia, in the room of the much respected General Amherst, lately displaced, we find is arrived at his capital, and agreeable to prediction has begun his administration with an action of eclat, having not only dissolved the patriotic Assembly of that province, but been able to do it with the advice of Council. *The dissolving and suspending American parliaments, a fashion introduced by Lord H——s——gh, instead of warding off and preventing, will rather serve to hasten and accomplish the great event.*[4]*

*[It may be doubted whether the Assembly was dissolved for the reason this gentleman supposes, since it does not appear that the Governor gave the least hint of any such reason; or if he had, that the Council would on that account have advised him to a dissolution—for the Council perfectly concurred with the Assembly in asserting their rights—in the petition to his Majesty, the memorial to the Lords and the remonstrance to the Parliament; the Council therefore with respect to these proceedings, were equally obnoxious to the Ministry as the House of Representatives; and could never have advised the Governor to a dissolution of that house for a conduct which they could not censure without condemning themselves. Besides the least hint from the Governor, or even suspicion, that the Assembly was dissolved for such a cause, would have been a sure means of the re-election of every man of them that concurred in the measures, and of the rejection of every one who did not; which would entirely have defeated the

---

[1] Items from November 21 to November 27, inclusive, are from the *New York Journal*, December 8, 1768, pp. 1–2.
[2] In the *Boston Evening Post* this begins "A proclamation for a thanksgiving was yesterday read in the churches."
[3] Evidently ministers and governors.
[4] This long paragraph in brackets is in small type.

supposed design of the dissolution, by producing an Assembly much more unanimous and firm than the last, in opposition to the ministerial scheme of enslaving the colonies.]

November 23

This day C——m——r P——n exhibited himself upon change for a few minutes; *and appeared a striking instance* of the *contempt* and *hatred* which those men draw upon themselves from their fellow citizens, who have dared to misrepresent and injure their country in order to gratify their avaricious cravings.

General Gage this day set out on his return to New-York (without doubt fully) convinced, that it is owing to the basest misrepresentation, that this loyal and orderly people have been treated with so great *insult* and *indignity*, as to have an army and fleet sent among them, as it is expressed by the M——r, to preserve order and assist the civil magistrate in the due execution of the laws.

November 24

It is confidently reported that Commodore Hood has requested the B——d of C——s ——s to let him know in writing, what ships of war they apprehend may be necessary to winter in this port, for the better protection of their persons from insult, and the better to enable them to secure and collect the American revenue; that he may then dispatch the remaining ships to their several stations, before the winter sets in. —*Can we wonder that C——m——rs, P. H. B. and R. have been so intoxicated with the ideas of their own importance, when a British M——r seems to have thought them capable of directing the movements of so considerable a part of the fleet and army?*

We hear that a petty officer of the Mermaid man of war, having left his station and deserted, has been sentenced by a courtmartial held for his trial, to be hanged on a yard-arm of said ship. —*It is to be feared the N. E. expedition will occasion a greater loss of men than we at first apprehended.*

November 25

The town watch has been lately greatly abused and interrupted in their duty by some officers, two of them came to the Town-House watch with swords under their arms, calling them damned scoundrels, forbidding them to challenge officers as they passed, or to give the time of night in their rounds as also from keeping in the watch house, threatening that in such case they would have them in irons, and bring four regiments to blow them all to hell; also telling the watchmen they were the King's soldiers and gentlemen, who had orders from his Majesty, and they were above the Selectmen who gave them their orders: Upon another night, other officers came to the dock-watch, one of them with a drawn hanger or bayonet, striking it against the door and asking, whether they thought the times were now as they had been, and that they could stand four regiments; also damning them, and threatening to burn all of us to ashes, and to send us all to hell in one month's time:—At another time the south watch was also assaulted, one of the men struck at, and much abused with profane and threatening language. The last evening a gentleman of distinction, seeing an officer of a man of war in the coffee-house, who had two evenings before called out to him in a rude manner, thought proper to ask him why he was thus accosted; upon which the officer desired him to go into a room, for he wanted the pleasure of taking his life; that as he did not suppose him acquainted with the sword, pistols would do; he then called out to the gentleman will you not fight me? upon which the gentleman desired, and the officer agreed to meet him at his house in the morning, to determine what was to be done; the officer not coming, we hear the gentleman having learned that he was a Lieut. of marines, intended a prosecution, but was prevented by his confining himself to his ship. Captain W——n, of the regulars, tho' bound to his good behaviour for the Negro business, has notwithstanding repeated his offences, by drawing his sword upon some persons the last evening and otherwise abusing them, and we hear complaint has been made to one of our magistrates respecting this affair. —*If such proceedings in our new conservators of the peace were not so common, these doings would appear strange, but that they are so common,—this is stranger still.*

We have advice from New-York, that on the 14th inst. there was exposed and burnt in that city, the effigies of G. B. and S. G.[1] in resentment at the parts they acted in endeavouring to get the troops quartered in the town; contrary to the letter and spirit of the act of Parliament relative to billetting troops in America, as also to the advice of his Majesty's Council. —It is said the former has given out, that the mistakes of the billetting act will be corrected this session of Parliament,[2] and from the success he has hitherto met with in imposing upon a M——r, he is now vain enough to insinuate, that he shall be able to influence even a British Parliament to give him power to trespass upon the citizens.

November 26

By the ships just arrived from London and Bristol, we have the agreeable advice, that the political tide was turning fast; the merchants and manufacturers are looking more about them, and Ad——m——n are confounded to find that instead of a little faction in one province only, as G. B. represented it; the whole continent are united in opposition to measures, which they apprehend to be not only anti commercial, but quite incompatible with their rights as men and as British subjects: That all parties among them disavow the late revenue acts, and as its great fautor is among the dead, those acts being now destitute of all support, will be repealed, and some men among us whose importance grew out of them, be returned to their primitive insignificancy, if not called to a severe account. American publications are now read with eagerness; the principles upon which they turn, and the spirit and energy appearing in many of them are highly applauded: Our cause is at length brought where we have long wished it to be, before the public; it can be no longer injured by false glosses, and the basest arts: A vast majority is already in our favour; and shall we now renounce the principles, in defence of which we have already gained such merit and applause from our brethren in Britain, many of whom, had at first apprehensions on the contested points, different from our own? Some tools of power would persuade

us to this, they even beseech us not to mention our rights; but this would be to relinquish the best of causes when we have the fairest prospects of success. The enemies to our rights and liberties have done their worst, their machinations and gross misrepresentations have procured a standing army for this town; the inflamed accounts, great movements, and vast expence, by which this has been effected, serve to fix the attention of the parent country, upon the American dispute; the side that is supported by truth and equity and constitutional principles, needs only attention, in such a nation as Britain in order to prevail; instead of being discouraged we are invited by many on the other side of the water, of the first character for political wisdom, and of no small influence in government, to keep our foot upon that constitutional ground, where from the beginning we have placed it; they have assured us that this ground will support us, and we trust in God we shall never be driven from it. The Ministry as well as the nation will find reason to rejoice at the prudent manner in which we received the troops, and in that loyalty to our sovereign, and affection to the parent country, which in this people has prevailed over all resentment. While the nation are anxious till they hear the event, none we know are more distressed than those who influenced or gave the order for so rash and impolitic a step:— The apprehension of destroying by its own military force, the channels of its commerce and the fountain of its wealth, or of losing in the affections of America, a resource which nothing else can supply, has at length thoroughly alarmed the nation: Who would have thought that any M——r would have driven so near a precipice! We are now told that a retreat is wished for, in consistence with the honour of Government; this is what we sincerely wish. Selfish and wicked servants, with a tolerable share of art may hold out false lights, especially, when the scene of action is distant, by which wise and great men may be misled; but is it not true honour to rectify mistakes upon the avowed principles of truth and equity? however this

---

[1] Governor Bernard and Sheriff Greenleaf.
[2] The *Boston Evening Post* omits the rest of the item for this day. Possibly the direct reference to the governor may have given ground for a prosecution for libel if printed in a Massachusetts paper.

may be, we hope America will never renounce the rights of British subjects to form
a screen for any Minister.

November 27

It seems not improper for the day, to
reflect with concern on the drunkenness,
debaucheries, and other extravagancies which
prevail by means of the troops being quartered in the midst of a town, where distilled
spirits are so cheap and plenty; as also on
the many severe whippings which have been
occasioned thereby the last week; and we
cannot but express our fears, that Boston
will before the spring, produce as great a
change upon a parcel of the best soldiers of
Britain, as the city of Capua did in a shorter
space of time upon Hannibal's brave army
impolitickly quartered therein.

November 28[1]

A countryman named Geary, who was
taken up and bound over by the Chief
Justice to answer at the Superior Court, to
the complaint of his having endeavoured to
entice some soldiers to desert from one of
the regiments quartered in this town, had
his trial last Thursday; and was acquitted
by the jury. *It was a trial of some expectation,
being the first of the kind since the troops arrived: If it had turned out otherwise, it might
have induced the artful and designing of the
soldiery to have practiced upon the simple and
unwary among us, if not to have complained
of them, in order to obtain the rewards they
have been encouraged to expect for services of
this nature.*

The Court of Admiralty for the trial of
the libels entered against Mr. Hancock and
others, which was to have met this day, is
further continued until Tuesday the 6th of
December next, and it is as true as it is
grievous, that none of the interrogatories on
behalf of the informers have been as yet
lodged in the registers-office. *The severe
treatment given these gentlemen, cannot be well
relished by their townsmen, who heartily wish
that the Co——s——rs may still toil in their
infamous fishery, without catching any evidence that may operate to their prejudice.*

November 29

Letters from England, not only confirm
Robert Auchmuty, Esquire, being appointed
Judge of Admiralty for this province, but
acquaint us that Jonathan Sewall, Esq; of
this town, is appointed for Nova-Scotia,
Jared Ingersol, Esq; for New-York, and
Augustus Johnson, Esq; for South-Carolina,
each as it is said with salaries of £600 sterl.
per annum, but the fund from which these
are to come is not yet ascertained. —From
these extraordinary appointments, and more
extraordinary allowances, some are apt to
think that G. B.'s[2] reasoning, especially in
support of the part of the Council's petition
to his Majesty, that no monies may be
drawn from America; has had such effect,
that we shall soon hear of the doubling of
some salary, and of a considerable increase
of colony placemen, in order to prevent our
monies being *drawn from us* by the American
revenue; with which application of said
revenue the M——y have been led to
imagine that the people of the colonies will
not only be satisfied, but that government
and its officers may be supported therefrom
in the most honourable and firm manner;
but some advices lead us to suppose, that
the American revenue will be given up, and
another fund appropriated for the service of
the M——y.

November 30

An honourable gentleman of his Majesty's
Council, lately riding over Boston Neck in
his coach, was stopped by some soldiers on
guard, one of which had the assurance to
open the door, and put in his head; upon
being asked what had occasioned such freedom, he had the insolence to reply, that he
was only examining whether any deserter
was concealed there.

A number of gentlemen passing in the
night by the Town-House, were hailed by
the guards three several times, without answering; whereupon they were stopped and
confined in the guard-house for a considerable time: A young gentleman in another
part of the town, having a lanthorn with
him, was challenged by some soldiers, but

---

[1] Items from November 28 to December 4, inclusive, are from the *New York Journal*, December 15, 1768,
pp. 1–2.

[2] Governor Bernard's.

not answering so readily as was expected, he was threatened with having his brains immediately blown out unless he stopped: A merchant of the town passing the grand guard this night about ten o'clock, was several times challenged by the soldiers, and upon telling them, that as an inhabitant he was not obliged to answer, nor had they any business with him; they replied that this was a garrison town, and accordingly they presented their bayonets to his breast, took and detained him a prisoner for above half an hour, when he was set free; having procured the names of those who had thus used him, he is prosecuting them for the same; and we may expect soon to have it determined, whether we are or are not a proper garrison town. *Perhaps by treating the most respectable of our inhabitants in this sort, it is intended to impress our minds with formidable ideas of a military government, that we may be induced the sooner to give up such trifling things as rights and privileges, in support of which we are now suffering such great insults and injuries.*

December 1

A GENTLEMAN of great distinction in the province of Nova-Scotia, in his letter of October last, writes, "I want to hear the consequences of the troops arrival in Boston; it seems extremely singular that they should be drawn off from a frontier province, when there are so many garrisons left standing, well supplied with artillery and ammunition, and no one to prevent a small body of enemies from taking possession of them, and sent to such a place as Boston, where they cannot be wanted or desired; unless your constitution of government is to be altered, and the great men at home are apprehensive it may occasion some opposition, I see not why they are sent there; and if there should be an opposition, what can *one thousand* do towards *enforcing* those measures?"—*It must certainly be an ease to the writer of this letter and other well wishers to the safety and prosperity of Nova-Scotia, to find that Lord George Campbell, has so far succeeded in his applications and negotiations this way, as to be able to return to his government with one man of war and a draft of not less than twenty-five battalion men from the 59th Regiment, which has been spared from the Boston service for the protection of Halifax this winter.*

December 2

We have advice that the people of the back settlements in South-Carolina, who have lately made movements very alarming, and dangerous to the peace of that colony, are now quiet, and waiting for a redress of their grievances in a constitutional way. From that province the regular troops had been withdrawn, in order as it was said to *assist* the civil magistrates of Boston in the *execution* of their duty; however, it seems the *prudence* and *moderation* of their *governor* and *lieutenant governor*, has done more to restore order, and give *efficacy* to the laws, than would have been effected with all the military force now in America.

The accounts from North-Carolina are, that a great number of men who call themselves Regulators, had mustered in the back part of that province for a redress of grievances; against this body the Governor marched 1500 of the militia, and when within about 12 miles of each other, they came to a parly; and upon assurances given the Regulators by the Governor, that methods should be taken for their relief, they separated, and returned to their settlements. We do not learn that *Governor Tryon*, notwithstanding this grand and alarming confederacy, has made any application for *regular troops to quell and disperse it*, when he might reasonably have expected to have received at least as many regiments as has been sent, as it is said to assist our G——r and the C——m——rs in *quelling disturbances in Boston;* but on the contrary, like a *wise* and *brave* governor, he adventured with the *militia* of the province to perform that service, whereby the people have been less *irritated*, and a *vast expence saved to the nation*, for which he will be more entitled than some other governors, to a *national allowance.*

A fire broke out the last night in the barracks, called Murray's, which had it not been discovered just as it was, must not only have proved fatal to many of the soldiers, and the women and children quartered therein, but might have occasioned the destruction of a considerable part of the town; those buildings having been judiciously pitched upon for barracks, tho' standing in the very centre of the town, and within a few feet of the largest pile of wooden buildings in the province.

This night about ten o'clock, as some principal gentlemen of the town with their ladies were returning home, having lanthorns with them, they were hailed by a military guard placed at West-Boston, and refusing to declare themselves friends, tho' they informed them they were inhabitants, who thought themselves, not under a military, but a civil government; and therefore not liable to be thus called upon, they were stopped and detained so long in the street, in a very cold season, that one of the married ladies, through the cold and surprise, is now much indisposed. —*The practice of challenging the inhabitants, for a short time was laid aside; we cannot say to what influence it is owing, that it is re-assumed by all the guards scattered thro' the town, tho' it is thought we are obliged for it to those persons whose misrepresentations have procured troops to be quartered among us, and who have been all along endeavouring to create plausible pretences for their continuance in this town.*

The man who was the last week condemned to be hanged, by a Court-Martial held on board his Majesty's ship Mermaid, was this day brought on deck for execution; no formalities used on such solemn occasions were omitted, and when the condemned person, the people in the ships of war and on the wharfs, were expecting his being turned off, a pardon was brought to him. —*Commodore Hood, in this act of humanity and mercy, has given no unfavourable idea of his prudence and capacity as an officer.*

December 3
Arrived his Majesty's ship Rose, of 20 guns, from England, last from New-Providence, where she landed his Excellency Thomas Shirley, Esq; lately appointed governor of the Bahama-Islands, in the room of his father Major General William Shirley, who was governor of this province when the famous expedition to Louisbourg was projected, and that fortress and island reduced by a body of New-England forces, in 1745. This army was wholly raised, equipped and supplied in less than six weeks time, without *the knowledge* of, or any *assistance from* the

British administration; the arrival of Admiral Warren, with some ships of war being *purely accidental.* This was an acquisition *so important,* that Mr. Pelham, the then Prime Minister, declared in the House of Commons, that for the restoration thereof, France had *relinquished* all the fruits of several successful campaigns, and *given peace to Europe;* but notwithstanding this essential service rendered the mother country during that war, as also in twice preserving Nova-Scotia to the Crown with the militia sent from hence which repelled the French invaders, and the vast aid in men and money cheerfully afforded the Crown in the late war on the requisition of that great minister Mr. Pitt, which involved us in a debt we are still staggering under; Besides what the colonies yielded to Britain by way of trade, which the great Commoner declared in Parliament, amounted to two millions, and was what *chiefly contributed* to the astonishing success of the war. We say notwithstanding all this, the colonies in general, and this province in particular, seem to be considered by some of the successors of the great Commoner, to be of little or *no consequence* to the nation, but rather *a burden upon them;*—hence it is that the support of a number of before unheard of officers has been thought of so much importance, that the *trade, security, peace and happiness* of all North-America, have been in effect sacrificed to those *voracious* state collectors; and the colonies, and this province in particular, by the *suspension* of its legislation, and the quartering a *standing army* upon them in a time of peace; has been treated with a *severity* and *indignity,* that can never *be forgot,* unless this people are under the powerful actings of those principles of Christianity, which some modern bishops have represented to the nation, and the world, that Americans, *have wholly* lost since their emigration from their native country.

The Rose man of war is remembered by New-England men as the ship that carried off their famous G——r Sir Edmond Andross; but whether she is now to carry off the more—famous G——r B——d, as was reported, cannot as yet be ascertained. A *Shirley* and a *Pownal,* recommended themselves to Administration, the *first* by the influence he had in his Assembly to engage them in the Louisburgh expedition and other expensive and successful services for the Crown; the *latter* in that he was able to obtain a vote and carry it into effect for the raising 7000 men in his province, to join the army under General Amherst, in the reduction of Canada; notwithstanding the aid he had given in the former campaigns of that war, and that about 3000 of our men were then engaged in other services, for the common cause. G. B. has hardly been able for years past to carry *one single point* with the Court;[1] he has made *the best connections* in the province his *personal* enemies, and incurred the *hatred* and *aversion* of at least *ninety nine* in a hundred of the people of his government; as well as exposed himself to the *contempt* and *resentment* of the other colonies; but if we may form any conjecture from the plan of politicks which our late statesmen seem to have adopted; which is to *irritate*, *inflame*, and *drive* rather than *consiliate* and *draw;* we cannot but say that the *chance of a continuance* is in favour of this said G——r, however 'tis thought a little time will determine not only the fate of *such politicians*, but what must essentially affect the whole *British Empire.*

December 4

It is observed with pleasure that the guards are now relieved on Lord's day morning one hour sooner than on other days, which allows the soldiery to attend public worship in season; that there is now much less martial music on the Sabbath then has been heard since the first arrival of the troops.

December 5[2]

The Court of Admiralty for the trial of the libels entered against John Hancock, Esq; and others, is further continued:— The most exorbitant and unheard of demand of about £50,000 sterling, to compensate for a small cargo of wine, would have been shocking to persons of common humanity, had the whole of it been smuggled, which the custom-house book will evince was not

the case, how much is such grievance heightened by frequent continuations, whereby the subject may be kept in suspense, contrary to the principles of equity, and the declaration of Magna Charta. —"*A delay of justice is a denial of it.*"

The chief civil magistrate in the province has, it seems, received, if not asked, the aid of the military; for we now behold centry boxes fixed at the gates of the province house, and guards placed there for his better protection. —*A king of England being once ask'd by a foreign prince, "Where are your guards sire?" immediately replied, "The affections of my people;"—A security, honour, and happiness which all the military force of Great Britain can never restore to our present G——r.*

On Tuesday evening last, between 6 and 7 o'clock, a householder in this town was met by three soldiers; who at first passed by him, the space of a few rods, but soon return'd, damning him, and asking why he did not answer when hail'd; immediately upon which, one of them without any provocation gave him a blow, which was seconded by another, whereby he was brought to the ground; they then stamped upon him, using means to prevent his calling out; when they robbed him of all the money in his pocket, which happened to be but three pistareens.— *Those soldiers doubtless expected a much larger booty: May our great plunderers experience a like disappointment.*

We are assured that the members of his Majesty's C—l of this province have taken effectual measures to clear their late humble petition to his Majesty for the redress of our public grievances, from the misrepresentations and false glosses, which there is too much reason to suspect has been put upon it, by what Lord H—ls—gh stiles the *reasonings* of G. B.[3]—*It has been long a misfortune to this province and the colonies in general, that so much credit has been given by Administration to the* NARRATIONS, GLOSSES *and* COMMENTS *of their enemies here, that the ill effects of them have been often experienced by us, before it was even suspected that such representations had been made.*

---

[1] General Court.

[2] Items from December 5 to December 11, inclusive, are from the *New York Journal*, December 22, 1768, pp. 1–2.

[3] Governor Bernard.

December 6

This day two of the soldiers concerned in stopping an inhabitant of this town the other evening, for refusing to answer when hail'd by the guards, were by warrant brought before Mr. Justice Dana; who considering the nature of the offence, bound them over to answer, to the court of general sessions of the peace for this county, to be held in January next. —*It is our happiness and security, that we have recourse to the common law; and that the times are not so corrupt, but we have magistrates who have spirit enough to exert themselves in support of our common rights; should the time ever come when the law of the land shall be made to yield and truckle to military power,—what a scene of confusion would then open upon a people so jealous of their liberty?*

December 7

A general Council this day, in the minutes thereof we suppose it will be recorded, *James Murray, Esq; nominated and appointed a justice of the quorum;* tho' but TWO of the members, as it is said, *gave their voice* for the same.—While such *wise methods* are pursued for *bracing* up government by putting persons of *family* and *influence* in the province into the magistracy, our enemies may flatter themselves that they shall not for the future hear of any difficulties thrown in the way of *quartering troops upon us;* or of the inhabitants *daring* to express *any sort of dislike* at the behaviour of men in power.

The G—r was pleased to say, that he should not in time to come nominate any more *honorary justices;* but only such as would engage to be acting ones in that office,—whereupon a worthy gentleman whose name had been mentioned at the Board had the go-by; and Mr. William Coffin, jun. was nominated, and appointed a justice of the peace for this town and county, being the *second* made magistrate on the *reforming plan* proposed by Lord Hillsborough.—One of the members of the Council had at the late Board, made a representation and complaint of the great insult which had been offered him by the soldiery, when passing over the Neck in his charriot, but instead of its being properly, if at all noticed by the G——r, he was this day pleased to acquaint the Council, that he understood from Col. Pomeroy, that there was *a combi-*nation *of the inhabitants of the town,* not to answer to the challenges of the guards, which he observed was a breaking in upon the *rules* and *orders* of the *military,* might occasion *disturbances,* and be attended with *ill consequences.* It is said one of the members observed upon it, that he believed there was a *combination,* but that it was a combination of some gentlemen of influence, designed to oppose, in the steps of the law, and prevent the further repetition of violence and disorder, which have been too frequently committed since the arrival of the troops in this town.

December 8

Several pieces of intelligence have been cook'd up in the Court Gazette, with design to prevent the successful operation of the patriotick resolutions of the merchants, respecting a non-importation of goods. In order to disabuse our brethren in the neighbouring governments, they are informed the importation the last summer and this fall, has fallen *much short* of former years, and that some vessels whose arrivals are expected before the first of January next, when the agreement of the merchants takes place, are ordered to return *only ballasted* with hemp and coal; It may also be affirmed with truth, that the sale of goods in the summer and fall, has been *much less* that in former seasons, from whence it may be concluded that the people are grown *much more frugal;* To instance only in *Bohea tea,* several great retailers of that article have declared that they do not now sell *one fifth part* of what they did lately,—People of the best fashion in town, have with one heart and mind, and almost instantaneously banished it their tables; but a number of towns in the country, to stop the consumption have lately signed the following agreement, viz. "Whereas the prodigious consumption of foreign teas used amongst us, is not only very impoverishing to our country, but is also prejudicial to the health of the inhabitants:

We the subscribers being animated with a zeal to promote the good of our country, (in breaking off bad customs) declare for ourselves, respectively, that neither we, nor any for or under us, will entertain any friend or visitor whatsoever, with any tea imported from India or elsewhere, or drink any ourselves, or suffer any to be drank in our houses, until the late revenue acts for imposing taxes on America be repealed."—Perhaps our neighbours may suspect that such agreements, have little or no effect, I will adduce the town of *Sudbury* as an instance to the contrary, by giving a little anecdote.—A young man of that town who had lately married, and was removing to a new settlement where he had purchased a piece of land, on which he had expended his all, was recommended to the parish by the Selectmen for a contribution; the minister had given notice of the Sabbath on which it was to be made; this design'd object of their charity was pleased the Saturday before, to take in a shop about a pound of Bohea tea, promising to pay for the same out of the money to be collected the next day; This soon flew through the town, and was so resented that great numbers of the parish applied to the minister the next morning, for a re-consideration of their vote, which was accordingly re-considered, and the imprudent man thereby deprived of the benefit of the intended contribution.—*If Americans in general, pursue such methods as the foregoing for obtaining relief and a redress of grievances, we may laugh at all the troops sent among us, or rather at those M———rs, who should have procured an act of Parliament depriving Americans of that understanding and good sense, with which nature and providence has endow'd them, before they had attempted with any hopes of success, to dragoon us out of those rights and privileges, which the inhabitants of these colonies inherit and know they are entitled to as men and as subjects.—*

December 9

Orders have been received from Georgia and another province for some articles of American manufacture, which could not be procured in this place,—From hence it may be concluded by some, that New-England manufactures exist only in our news papers; but such a conclusion would be *very erroneous:* We have not it is true any quantities of home made cotton, linen, and woolen goods which can yet be spared for *exports,* but it may be depended upon that those manufactures have *greatly increased* since the Stamp-Act: Almost every house in the country is now a manufactory; some towns

have more *looms* therein than *houses:* The encouragement and countenance given by the *clergy,* our *patriots* and the *college,* by appearing clothed in our own woolens, &c. has raised a spirit in the country, that can hardly be abated; our farmers now look upon it as a *disgrace,* if they and their family, are not clad with the fleece of their flock, and by their own industry: Companies are forming in several parts of the country, for the carrying on several branches of business, with the help of our *new imported artizans,* which must so increase and *improve* New-England manufactures; that if the present restrictions on foreign trade are continued, and the revenue drain for our cash is kept open, we may soon have an *overplus* to spare to those of our southern brethren, who are disposed to favour us with their custom. It is a fact, that our country people are already able to furnish themselves with by far the greatest part of their necessary clothing; The *resentment* of Americans may soon be *strong enough* to banish every *foreign* superfluity; then Britons will be convinc'd by sad experience of the truth of an old English proverb, viz, *Honesty is the best policy.*

December 10

While the friends of their country are recommending and countenancing by their example, the strictest economy, C———m ———r P———x———n and Company are endeavouring to establish a weekly and brilliant assembly at Concert Hall; where their Board is again held in the day time, and a centinel placed for their guard: One of their livery boatmen has waited upon the gentlemen and ladies of the town with the proposals and a subscription paper; which to use a *courtly phrase* has been almost universally treated *with the contempt it deserves,*—C———m—r R———n, in order to throw a splendor upon office, and so to *dazzle* with its brightness, *the eyes of Americans,* that they might not perceive the *incomparable insignificancy* of his person, nor how ridiculously the fruits of their industry are bestowed; intends soon to make his appearance in a suit of crimson velvet, which will cost him *a sum* that would have been a *full support* to some one of the families, that are almost reduced to poverty themselves; who are yet obliged, not indeed by the laws of Christianity, but by the

Revenue Act, to feed the hungry and cloth the naked C——m——rs, not barely with what is *convenient* and *necessary*, but with all the *luxury* and *extravagance* of *high life*.

December 11

We have the melancholy account that a schooner coming from St. John's in Nova Scotia, with a considerable number of passengers, being such as had left their settlements in that colony in order to reside in this province, has been lately cast away on the salvages, near Cape Ann, and not one of the people saved.—*It is to be feared we may hear of more loses of this kind, as necessity has put numbers upon launching from that country in the most dangerous and perilous season of the year: We wish we may not also before long receive some disagreeable tidings from the two Floridas, and other of our new settlements, from whence the troops have been withdrawn, for the Boston expedition.*

December 12[1]

A married lady of this town was the other evening, when passing from one house to another, taken hold of by a soldier; who otherways behaved to her with great rudeness; a woman near Long Lane was stopped by several soldiers, one of whom cried out seize her and carry her off; she was much surprised, but luckily got shelter in a house near by; Another woman was pursued by a soldier into a house near the north end, who dared to enter the same, and behave with great insolence: Several inhabitants while quietly passing the streets in the evening, have been knocked down by soldiers; One of the principal physicians of the town, was the last Friday, about 12 o'clock at night, hailed by an officer, who was passing the street, but not of a patroling party; the doctor refused to answer, and resented this treatment; whereupon the officer seized him by the collar, asserting that he was on the King's duty, and swearing that he would have an answer; this so provoked the doctor that he gave him a blow, which brought the officer to the ground; he then seized him, but a soldier or two coming up at that instant, he thought proper to let him go.

These are some further specimens of what we are to expect from our new conservators of the peace; The inhabitants however still preserve their temper and a proper decorum; in this they have doubtless disappointed and vexed their enemies: Under all the insults and injuries received from a G——r, C——m——rs, and the M——l——y, we are patiently waiting the result of our petitions and remonstrances, for a redress of grievances, and an alteration of measures: We cannot but flatter ourselves that Administration must soon be convinced of the propriety and necessity of putting affairs upon the old footing, which experience now demonstrates to be the best for both countries.

December 13

We are told that Col. Pomeroy upon whom the chief command of the troops quartered in this city now devolves, has given orders to his officers, to suspend challenging the townsmen, as had been practiced for some time.—The inhabitants have steadily persevered in refusing to answer to those challenges of the military guards in the night; choosing rather to be stopped or confined, than by a different conduct to countenance so affrontive an attack upon the rights of citizens; The town watch is appointed for our security in the night; to them and not to the military are the inhabitants legally obliged to give answer, when properly hailed: Several of the soldiers have been prosecuted in the law by those who they have presumed to detain for not answering to their challenges; the insolence of power will forever be despised by a people who retain a just sense of liberty; and while they pursue constitutional methods for the redress of any grievance, they may rationally hope for success.

December 14

The Court of Admiralty for the trial of the libels relative to the sloop Liberty, &c. met yesterday, and again adjourned to the 3d of January next: the interrogatories have been lodged. The Commissioners expected they would have been able this evening with the countenance of the military gentlemen, to have opened an assembly at Concert Hall, for the winter season; but the virtue and

---

[1] Items from December 12 to December 18, inclusive, are from the *New York Journal*, December 29, 1768, pp. 1–2.

discreetness of the young ladies of the town, occasioned a disappointment; It is probable they may have one the next week, with a small number of matrons of their own core: It must ill become American ladies to dance in their fetters.

December 15

There have been many severe scourgings, lately given the soldiery, particularly on Tuesday last, almost wholly occasioned by a too free use of distilled spirits. It is said one of them has died of his wounds, the truth of which we do not avouch, but it is expected that inquiry will be made by the grand jury of the county: The inhabitants are the more affected with these punishments, imagining they might have been prevented, had the troops been quartered at Castle Island, or on a pretty village on a neck of land over against it, called Point Shirley, where they might have been well accommodated, and supplied, and would have received the full protection of the ships of war. Distressing sympathies will force themselves on those who have the greatest humanity; who are the most worthy part of the species: Some such persons among us have expressed their dislike to those whippings, and at the shooting a man for his first desertion in the time of peace.—A pamphlet has made its appearance, said to be written by a clergyman in this town: The author shews that giving more than forty stripes, allowed Deutronomy 25, verse 3d, is breaking a moral law of God; that the Jews were prohibited by that law giving about forty stripes, lest their brother should seem vile unto them, even as if he was a dog, (but the military allows to lay them on by hundreds,) That God intended the forty stripes should be a terror to the Jews; but not like the terrors of death; whereas military delinquents who have been sentenced to receive 1000 or 1500 lashes sometimes choose death rather than life, and beg they may be shot to escape a whipping, that such indignities are a disgrace to the human nature. *Homo sum humanum nihil a me alienum puto;* That when such punishments are decreed as threaten life, the sixth Commandment is broken, and all concerned are guilty of killing the victim, tho' he should not die under the operation; That it is strange that tho' the law of our God, with regard to whipping,

is so religiously observed by the *civil authority*, it should be set at naught by *the men of the sword;* that the weight of military cruelties is rested on the *necessity* of them; a support which must fail,—it being always necessary to keep God's laws; but can never be necessary to break them. The author then introduces this account from Winchester, "That a sergeant belonging to the 14th Regiment, then lying in the city, was found drunk upon guard; and by a Court Martial was reduced to a private man, and sentenced to receive two hundred lashes; next field day; amongst other unusual aggravations of the punishment, the drummers were ordered to strip, to stay a minute between every stroke, and instead of 25, to give only ten lashes. When 190 cuts had been administered in this manner, the surgeon who stood by, declared, that if the man received the remainder, it would be impossible for him to survive the punishment; accordingly he was unloosed from the halberts, and carried back to the guard house; where having languished a few days, his back began to mortify, and the mortification soon reaching his kidneys, he died delirious. The coroners of the city of Winchester interposing on this occasion, *an inquest was taken upon the body of the deceased,* when the jury brought in their verdict *wilful murder against the captain,* who commanded at the punishment, &c. This narration is closed with the following reflection.—Wherever troops are quartered, the civil authority should have a strict eye over them: and as often as death appears to be the effect of a whipping, should imitate the worthies of Winchester; otherwise *blood guiltless* will be brought on the place.—

The case of one Blakeny, as related by Dr. Lucas, the Patriot of Ireland, in his Mirror for Court Martials is also mentioned. He was ordered to receive 500 lashes at the head of the garrison in Dublin; his body was mangled most horribly, and he would doubtless have met his death, had not the Lord Lieutenant remitted 300 of the 500 lashes— and the author further adds, is there not reason to fear, that if some worthy gentleman in Boston had not prevailed for the remitting 300 of the 500 lashes decreed for a criminal (among the troops here) he must have perished, especially as 190 cruel cuts had dispatched the sergeant at Winchester. The author then refers to the memorable Petition of Rights, wherein it appears to be an article of complaint "That certain persons exercised a power to proceed within the land according to the justice of martial law, even against soldiers, by such summary course and order as is agreeable to martial law, and as is used in armies in time of war, as was looked on to be against the form of the Great Charter and law of the land; that any man within the land, tho' a soldier and mariner, should be judged and executed by martial law, lest by colour there—of any of his Majesty's subjects may be destroyed or put to death, contrary to the law and franchise of the land." In consequence of which petition, the King revoked his commission.—The author concludes with expressing his hopes, that tho' in these perilous times, some friends of power tells us, we must not say a word about *rights* (than which nothing could be said more *satirical against the Ministry*) The time will come when our rights shall be restored to us as at *the first*, and our privileges as at the *beginning:* When the *civil* authority shall have its free course and his Majesty's subjects be no longer *disparaged* and *distressed* with court martials *in time of peace.*

December 16

The people of Salem, Marblehead, and other towns from whence our fisheries are carried on, complain greatly of the new act of severity in demanding from the poor fishermen pay for Greenwich Hospital. In 1732, this point was settled, and orders transmitted from home to desist from demanding that duty from the fishermen; but now a gentleman concerned in that revenue having as it is said 12s 2d per cent on all the money raised this way for doing nothing, demands and insist upon the payment of said duty: Thus, for the providing for one creature of a M——r; (for the revenue will not be *benefitted*, as the pay of this officer will be equal *to this new duty*) a method is pursued which must greatly affect the interest *of the nation*, as well as of *the province*, it having a direct tendency to *lessen* if not *destroy* so valuable a branch of trade as the fishery.

The prodigious multiplicity of crown and revenue officers, since the project of an American revenue was formed, grows daily more and more alarming, the names of the new-created officers, and the business said to be allotted to them, would make a small revenue dictionary. It is now the general opinion, that large as the sums are that have been drawn from America by this duty, and with them the life-blood of its trade, it will when the officers on the establishment, and incidental lists are paid up, without mentioning the charge of transporting the C——m——rs to America, and the expence accrued by their campaign to the Castle, &c. yield *little* or *nothing* to the revenue: The *revenue* about which so much noise has been made, tho' it may be dear to interested men or *women* on this or the other side of the water, (for Americans now begin fully to comprehend the modern doctrine of quarterings) is quite inconsiderable *to the nation*, and will certainly prove insufficient to defray *a tenth part* of the military force that it has occasioned to be quartered in this single town: What a *sorry pittance* then is this revenue to be the *ground* of so much contention, and the *occasion* of removing *ancient foundations*, upon which the *commerce of Britain* has so greatly *flourished*, and the *colonies* have thought themselves *happy* in their *connection* with her.

One F——s a master of a vessel, who having disposed of a considerable part of his cargo, not quite to the satisfaction of his owner, and being reprimanded therefor, made information, &c. by way of resentment, whereby an addition was made to the loss and damage of his unfortunate owner, by a seizure of said vessel: It is said this fellow has been since so noticed by the Commissioners as to have a small post in the customs given him.—*This is mentioned only to shew that such infamous persons after having betrayed a total want of confidence, even to perfidy, in these times knew where to find their* REFUGE and SUPPORT; This same person was the other day taken with a single writ for a debt due to a trader in this town; when he produced to the sheriff a protection from the Court of Admiralty, that he might be enabled thereby to file his interrogatory, relative to the above seizure.—This day a brigantine from London, where she is owned, last from Nantucket, was seized by order of the C——m——rs, it seems she had landed the chief part of her cargo at Nantucket, and reported to, or entered with the naval officer, as was formerly practised; the particular cause of this seizure is not as yet ascertained.

This evening several soldiers of the guard near the Neck, were detected in stealing leather out of a shop at the south part of the town; they were pursued by the owner, and one of them was overtaken, who defended himself with his bayonet and gave the pursuer a thrust, which struck against his collar bone; he was however mastered, and is now secured in gaol till he can take his trial at the next court of assize.

December 18

There has of late been several smart re-counters between the soldiers quartered in this town and the seamen belonging to the men of war now in harbour, they discover a very particular dislike or rather enmity to each other.—This evening a number of soldiers and sailors happened to meet, when a bloody affray ensued;—in which it is said the seamen were victors: Several of the parties have lost thumbs and fingers and are otherways badly wounded; one of the soldiers dangerously; Care is taken of them at the hospital provided for the use of the troops.—*It is to be feared the indiscretion and animosity of these people may in the course of the winter be productive of other disagreeable consequences; and further evince that the peace and good order of the town is not like to be preserved or promoted by our military inmates.*[1]

December 19[2]

Last evening after church service, there was a considerable gathering of children and servants, near the Town House, drawn by the music of the fife, &c. which is again heard on the Sabbath, to the great concern of the sober and thoughtful inhabitants; some of those youth's having behaved so as to displease the officer, orders were given the guard to clear the parade; they marched up with bayonets presented,—one of the lads was pursued by a soldier to some distance, who made a thrust with his bayonet, which passed thro' his coat, and had he not thrown himself on the ground that instant, its

thought he would be run thro' the body: He has entered a complaint against said soldier, with one of the magistrates of the town; *an application to the military on any such occasions would be resented by the inhabitants, who would by no means countenance the exercise of law-martial in the body of the county, and in a time of peace.*

December 20

Capt. Sweeney, arrived from Halifax with the remains of the 14th, 29th, and part of the 59th Regiments, quartered here, and a number of women belonging to the said regiments. He informs that the schooner Providence, Capt. Campbell, with military stores, was cast away the 19th ultimo, on Betty's Island, in Prospect Harbour, and one man drowned. We also learn from Augustine, that Capt. Chambers was arrived there with the troops with-drawn from Pensacola; on his passage, he met with a violent gale, in which he lost his mast, and had four feet water in his hold, where some of the sick soldiers were drowned. A large ship, one of the Cork fleet, with Col. Mackay, most of the officers of his regiment, and a number of soldiers on board, is still a missing vessel.—*Some important acquisitions were made in the late war from our enemies, with much less expence and loss to the nation, than will be occasioned by the late extensive movements, and very extraordinary American proceedings.*

By letters from Sandusky-Bay, we learn that some gentlemen on their way from Detroit, were robbed of many things of value by some Indians; that the sloop Charlotte, was cast away on Lake Erie; and the schooner Boston burnt in Cat Fish Creek, on the same lake, supposed by the Indians: *Accounts of damages done by the Indians since the withdraw of troops from the out settlements, may be expected to multiply upon us.*

December 21

This day there was a meeting of his Majesty's Council, when the Governor informed them, that an action of trespass, had been brought against Stephen Greenleaf, Esq; sheriff of the county of Suffolk, by Mr.

---

[1] The portion in italics is omitted from the *Boston Evening Post.*
[2] Items from December 19 to December 25, inclusive, are from the *New York Journal, Supplement,* January 12, 1769, p. 2.

John Brown of the Manufactory, for breaking, entering in, and keeping possession of
an appartment in said house. The G——r expressed his hopes and expectations, that the
C——l would *support* the sheriff, who he
said had acted in that business by their
authority, and therefore ought to be *saved
harmless by them.* This motion of the G——r's
having been supported, one or more of the
Council observed to this purpose, that the
vote for clearing the Manufactory House,
was at first obtained by a majority of one
only, or six out of eleven, present,—that it
was intended by the Council to be done in
a legal manner, and that when the affair was
in agitation, they thought it necessary to
wait upon his Excellency and did accordingly wait upon him, and that even the
gentlemen themselves, who voted for the
clearing the house, declared to his Excellency that the *manner* of proceeding, was in
their opinion *illegal,* and *different* from what
they expected, when they voted for it. Upon
which the G——r was pleased to say, that as
the sheriff had acted in this affair, in consequence of the vote of the C——l, it must appear very unaccountable in them not to
support him; that it would have an ill
appearance on the *other side of the water,*
where it would certainly be known, and in
order to intimidate the C——l into his measures, he very delicately intimated that it
would be a subject of *representation:* When
undoubtedly such kind of glosses would be
put upon it, as had before been put upon
their humble petitions, and other parts of
their proceedings. The Council did not
think it adviseable to determine on a matter
as *new* and *unprecedented* as it was *important,*
and therefore referred it for further consideration, to a full board; where its to be
hoped a greater concern will appear to *secure*
the substantial rights of every honest householder, than to *provide a screen* for any
creature of a G——r whatsoever.

But tho' the G——r has upon more occasions than one expressed his concern to save
the credit of his t——ls, —— is it not worthy
of remark, that so little regard was discovered for the honour and dignity of his
Majesty's C——l, as that when one of those
honourable gentlemen complained in C——l

of the treatment he had received in having
his chariot stopt and searched for deserters,
this G——r should treat the complaint with
neglect; and rather defend, than censure the
conduct of the soldiery in stopping the inhabitants; and what is still more astonishing:
At a C——l convened upon the arrival of
the troops to consider of C——l D——s[1]
demand for quarters; an Hon. gentleman
who had long had a seat at the B——d, and
who had freely spoke to this point, as he
thought the good of the province, and the
service of his sovereign required, was modestly told by this gentleman of the sword,
that if he had meant any insult upon him in
his speech, he should have taken his own
satisfaction, as soon as they were off that
floor; and this in the very presence of the
G——r, without his taking the slightest
notice of so gross an affront offered to the
whole B——d.

December 22

A common soldier of one of the regiments
arrived from Ireland, having the last evening made too free a use of spirituous liquors,
was this morning found dead in his barracks:
It is said that the captain he was under, has
ordered all the men belonging to his company to view the corps of the deceased, that
by his unhappy fate they might be deterred
from such intemperance as has brought this
person and many before him to an untimely
end; Its to be hoped a suitable number of
officers will be *pickt out* of the military core,
to lead and accompany the soldiers on this
melancholy service.

December 23

It may now be said that the G——r and
C——m——rs have the last night had a sort
of an assembly at Concert Hall; Never were
the gentlemen concern'd more liberal in
their invitations, even those ladies who
declin'd subscribing, had their cards; the
neighbouring towns were reconnoitred for
females, and the good natured S——r of the
B——d of C——m——rs was so complaisant
as to offer to go as far as Salem to bring two
damsels from thence; their efforts were
finally so successful, as to procure from
among themselves and their connections,
about ten or twelve unmarried ladies, whose

---

[1] Colonel Dalrymple's.

quality and merits have been since related with the spritely humour of a military gallant.—The ball was opened by Capt. W——n, —a gentleman who has been already taken notice of in this Journal; There was indeed a numerous and blazing appearance of men, but the ladies of all ages and conditions so few, that the most precise Puritan could not find it in his heart to charge said assembly with being guilty of the crime of mixt dancing.—

December 24

We are informed by the Boston Chronicle, but know not the grounds the publishers have for such information,—that a packet is soon expected from London, with orders for calling a new Assembly of this province, which is much to be desired. As the Governor expressly declared in his message to the late House of Representatives, that he had laid before them the full of the orders he had then received; it is difficult to account for his not having called one before, or why he should wait for any orders, relating to it; for it did not appear that he was under any prohibition. The ill consequences therefore that have or may arise from the want of an Assembly at this critical time, must be accounted for by the G——r and not by the M——r. But if he has since received such prohibitory orders, is it not an infringement of the honour of the G——r, as well as the rights of the people granted in the charter of the province? In that charter the King has been pleased to devolve the power of calling, adjourning, proroguing or dissolving the Assembly upon the Governor: And he being present and knowing to every emergency that takes place, it must be an advantage to the people to have this matter left to his prudence; But if the being of an Assembly is for the future to be left to the will or humour of a Minister, and he at the distance of a thousand leagues, unconnected with, and independent upon the people for his support, the time may come when we may be in a worse situation than the nation was in, in the reign of Charles the First, when there may be not only a vacation of the General Assembly for twelve years, but *no Assemblies at all:* Or if we should happen to have a Governor *of integrity* and steadiness to assert his own *honour* and the people's *rights,* he would in all likelihood be soon recalled for disobeying the command of the Minister, who would *rescind* them; But the rights of American charters, seem at present to be of very little importance in the opinion of our American G——r, or the M——r in the American Department.

December 25

One great objection to the quartering of troops in the body of a town, is the danger the inhabitants will be in of having their morals debauched; The ear being accustomed to oaths and imprecations, will be the less shockt at the profanity, and the frequent spectacles of drunkenness, exhibited in our streets, greatly countenances this shameful and ruinous vice. The officers of the army are not backward in resenting the smallest disrespect offered themselves by a soldier, and such offences are severely punished, but it seems the name of God may be dishonoured with horrid oaths and blasphemies, in their presence without their looking upon themselves as obliged to punish, or even reprove them for the same; perhaps they take this to be the duty of the civil magistrate, and indeed it appears highly reasonable, that the magistrates of the town should notice those offences, and exert themselves in all legal ways, to restrain the soldiery from such enormities, and check the progress of so terrible a contagion among the inhabitants.—Those who look upon the awful denunciations of God's word against sinners, not merely as bugbears to afrighten, but what will really be inflicted on all impenitents, cannot but compassionately wish that more pains were taken and better means used to reform the army. This set of men are generally made up of the most thoughtless and unprincipled of our youth; The common soldiers are in general destitute of Bibles and proper books of devotion; their pay so small as not to enable their procuring them, or else we might suppose stoppages for them as well as other articles; What a pity is it that the Society for Propagating the Gospel, do not spare a part of their charity for this purpose; and if together with this, due care was taken in the appointment of chaplains, and strict orders given them, diligently to pursue the duties of their office, by rebuking, exhorting, instructing, and daily praying with their regiments, might we not hope for such success, as that the reproach which has been too justly cast upon us by foreigners, "That our army has less appearance of religion among them than there is among any other in Europe," may be soon wiped away?

December 26[1]

This morning a vessel from Salem or Marblehead, having a cask of sugar on board, which it was supposed had not been properly cleared out, was seized by one of the custom-house officers, who brought a number of SOLDIERS! to assist and keep possession of said vessel, but upon discovery that the sugar had been reported at the Custom-House, she was soon released. It is very extraordinary that soldiers should be called in upon such occasions: It seems calculated to lead Administration to conceive that the quartering of troops in this town is necessary to enable the custom-house officers to discharge their duty; but this is so far from being the case, that no one article of goods which has been seized in the port of Boston since the new regulations, and perhaps before, has been rescued from the officers; it is indeed true that soon after the Commissioners retired to the Castle, a poor simple Irishman indeavouring to save the duty upon a few hogsheads of molasses, had the same seized and thereby lost the fruits of several years industry: The petty officer who had the charge of the vessel for some time, was one evening locked up in the cabbin, and a few hogsheads of molasses were carried off; as soon as it was known to the inhabitants, they expressed their resentment at this procedure in such a manner, that the hogsheads of molasses very soon found the way back again to the vessel in full tale and quantity.

December 27

A report is current, that Mr. Alderman T–k[2], has procured a copy of the will or instruments whereby C—m—r P—, gave to the late C. T—d, the reversion of an estate represented to him as worth £50,000—

which he intends to produce in the House of C—m—s next s—s—n, in order to shew what secret influence had been exerted for the procurement of an American B——d of C—s—ms. It might also be of special service to present that H—e with the picture of a certain lady of pleasure, whose influence was powerful enough to procure £500 a year for a B. that those guardians of the people might see how the monies taken from Americans is charmed away and applied not for the lessening of the national debt but for the support of M—l w—h—s and p—si—s[3].

December 28

A further number of libels against the concerned in landing some molasses out of the vessel beforementioned, which was not reported to the custom-house, has been lately entered in the registers-office of the Court of Admiralty. This trade which was formerly considered even by the B—d of T—e as advantageous to the nation, is now treated with great severity; a duty of one penny per gallon on molasses, and five shillings per hundred on F. sugars is not laid for the regulation of the West-India trade, but for the express purpose of a revenue. Ad—st—n has not even endeavoured to save appearances; the molasses produced and imported from our own islands, is burdened with the same duty, and all English sugars shipt from hence to our own markets by an act of Parliament passed in 1765, shall be deemed and taken to be foreign and liable to the same duties and restrictions. The impolitick severity made use of to secure this revenue, if what never reaches the exchequer may be properly term'd *revenue*, has nearly destroyed our trade with the foreign West India Islands, before the late regulations notwithstanding the diligence of French and Spanish guarda-costas, vast quantities of sugar, coffee, indigo, &c. were brought from those islands chiefly in exchange for our fish, the growth of the continent, and British imports; these were again exported to the Mediterranean and other foreign markets, and the greatest part of the neat proceeds thereof remitted

---

[1] Items from December 26, 1768, to January 1, 1769, inclusive, are from the *New York Journal*, January 19, 1769, pp. 1–2.

[2] Alderman Trecothic, a popular member of Parliament and a consistent friend to the colonies.

[3] Ministerial whores and pensioners—a not uncommon appellation at this time.

in bills and cash to the British merchants in pay for the goods we received from thence: But now the North-American merchants are deprived of those advantageous remittances, and instead of having sugars for export, that article has so arisen in price, that what was lately sold at this market for about 17s, will now command upwards of 42s. sterling per hundred: *The monies wrested from Americans by the injudicious project of a revenue, may indeed enable a M—r to create a number of new offices, multiply place men, and increase salaries, but can never countervail the national damage, by the lessening of its navigation and the loss of so profitable a circular trade.*

The C—l met this day, and the G—r renewed his request, that they would agreeable to the petition of Sheriff Greenleaf, indemnify said sheriff as to his conduct at the Manufactory-House, in the action brought against him by Mr. William Brown, and in order to shew the reasonableness of this requirement, he was pleased to tell the C—l, that in this business Mr. Greenleaf pursued *their vote* and did not act as *sheriff* but as their *bailiff*, he having commissioned him so to do. The Council were the more surprised at this *demand*, and G—rs *assertion* to support it, as he could not but remember, that when they first heard of the sheriff's extraordinary procedure respecting the Manufactory-House; they were so alarmed as to have a meeting among themselves on the 22d of October last, when seven of the eleven of the Council, (six of whom, by continual application were drawn into the unhappy vote,) which were all whose presence could then be procured, waited upon the G—r and acquainted him that it was their unanimous opinion, that the whole procedure of the sheriff was expressly contrary to their intention in said vote, which was only general for the clearing the Manufactory-House for the reception of the troops after the barracks at the Castle should be full; and that they never had an idea of the sheriff's making a forceable entry contrary to law; and that notwithstanding this application, the siege of the Manufactory was continued for about twelve days after: One of the C—l then asked the G—r whether the sheriff acted as bailiff when he sent for a number of the regulars to assist him when

he forceably entered the said house, as part of the posse-comitatus, or whether a bailiff could legally do it; and it was then observed that this could not be done; the presumption, was that Mr. Greenleaf had acted only as sheriff in that business: All that was offered by the C—l did not discourage the G—r from exerting his influence in support of this officer, he insisted upon the question being put, and it was according put in words of the following import, viz. Whether the C—l would take upon themselves the defence of said action on the part of the sheriff, or indemnify said sheriff.—To which question the C—l replied in a manner that has brought as much credit upon themselves as it has cast reproach upon the G—r.

That they *would not* at present determine that question, the C—l being of opinion that for them to do any thing that might *give a bias*, either to *court* or *jury*, would be *extremely wrong:* That for the C—l *now to determine*, whether they would indemnify Sheriff Greenleaf, or would not *indemnify* him might *give such a bias*, and therefore they desire to be excused from giving any answer *till the cause shall be determined* in a court of justice. It is said that the G—r was greatly mortified by the foregoing vote of C—l, and could not forbear expressing his resentment, by telling them that if he was in their place he should be *ashamed* of looking the sheriff in the face, and that their conduct would make an ill appearance on the other side the water, where they might depend it would be properly represented, and where he apprehended measures might be taken to procure justice to that officer.

It may throw some further light upon this procedure of the sheriff respecting the Manufactory-House, to observe, that this house is the property of the province, which Mr. Brown has been permitted to improve for about twelve years past, and that altho' it should be supposed, that the G—r and C—l have a right to dispose of the property of the province, upon a dissolution of the General Assembly, or that Mr. Brown was an intruder in this house, points which are by no means granted; yet it does not follow that he could be dispossessed in any other way than by ejectment in a due course of law. The conduct of the sheriff cannot therefore be excused in his forceable entry, or in that aggravating circumstance of it, his calling the soldiery to his assistance, when some respectable inhabitants declared to him they stood ready to aid him in all legal steps upon this occasion, and that he could not but know that this was the disposition of the inhabitants.

The above is another specimen of the conduct of G. B. and the spirit with which he is actuated, this we are persuaded is now so well understood that not a single colony on the continent envies the Massachusetts, such an administration any more than the residence of the Commissioners.

December 29

A number of robberies have been lately committed by the soldiers, for which some of them have been apprehended and committed to gaol. The other evening as a journeyman to a silver-smith, was going through an alley leading into Ann-Street he met a soldier, who took hold of him and ordered him to deliver up his money; a scuffle ensued, when the smith was thrown by the soldier, who clapt his knee upon his breast and a hand upon his mouth, to prevent an alarm, and with the other hand robbed him of the few pence he had in his pocket; a whistling was then made, supposed by some of his comrades, when the soldier ran and made his escape, leaving the journeyman much wounded. This is not the only instance of a street robbery, since the arrival of the troops, which before was a crime unknown in this town, and serves more and more to convince us, how much beholden we are to some persons among us, not only for the introduction of such a set of men into the province, but for influencing to their being quartered in the midst of us, which gives them a still greater opportunity to injure and distress the inhabitants. It cannot but raise our indignation to perceive that altho' G—r B—d, and the Co—m—rs were so ready in *reporting* and *exaggerating* every little trifling *disturbance* that took place *before* the arrival of the troops, they can now behold with *perfect indifference*, if not *satisfaction*, all the riots, outrages, robberies, &c. that are daily perpetrated among us.

December 30

It is said that the animosities which have appeared between the King's soldiers and seamen, which were neither at first fomented, nor have since been encouraged by the inhabitants, has occasioned several serious consultations between their respective officers, as to the best method of checking and removing them; and we hear that General Pomeroy, observing that the severest whippings are ineffectual to restrain the men from a too free use of spirituous liquors, is about substituting some other punishment in the room thereof; a large log, to which a delinquent is to be chained, for a longer or shorter time is talked of, and the experiment trying; but some think that if a drunkard was confined in a dark room, for one or more days, and only fed with bread and water, it would not only serve his health after a debauch, but have the most likely tendency to restrain him from hard drinking for the future.

December 31

Yesterday the Selectmen, waited upon General Pomeroy, to acquaint him that the music of the fife, &c. on the Sabbath, was very disagreeable to the inhabitants, and might have an ill effect upon the younger and more thoughtless part of the community, with respect to the observance of that day; and as they apprehended it contrary to law, they expressed their hopes and desires that it might be omitted for the future, as they had taken notice it had sometimes been in stormy weather; they also took the liberty to observe, that the challinging the inhabitants when passing the streets, was looked upon as a great grievance, and would therefore not be submitted to by the people, who did not look upon themselves in a garrison state, and were therefore determined to seek redress in a legal way, if it was still continued; that they thought it but prudent to mention this to him, that he might by suppressing what was complained of, do justice to the inhabitants, to prevent those disagreeable consequences, which might otherwise follow.

The last evening, we are sorry to say it, as three young gentlemen, were passing the house where General Pomeroy resides, having a large glass lanthorn with them, they were challenged by one of the centinels placed at the gates, and declining giving any other answer to the same, than that they were those who should do them no hurt; they were so ill treated by a centinel, as that one of the young fellows received several blows from him, and another of them a push from the muzzle of the musket in his face, which much wounded him; the General upon application gave the names of the two centinels, who were ordered under guard; the abused, applied to a magistrate, and information will be given in, to the grand jury of the county, that they may be proceeded with, according to the merits of their offence.

January 1

THE soldiery are obliged, the Lord's day not excepted, to attend twice or thrice a day at the calling of the rolls. There being now four regiments and part of another among us, who have much leisure on their hands, what pity is it that they are not ordered to attend prayers in the churches nearest to them, once a day at least; and if their chaplains would give a few words of exhortation at those seasons, and employ but one hour in a week, in catechising or instructing the soldiers in the fundamental principles of Christianity, many of whom appear to be as ignorant thereof, as those who are inlisted under the banners of Mahomet.—Might it not be hoped and expected, that their morals would be reformed, whereby they would become better soldiers, and render their residence in any town less intolerable to the sober inhabitants.—

The noise of the fife was this day more general and offensive than it has been upon any Sabbath, since the troops came among us.

January 2[1]

This day the Court of Admiralty for the trial of the libels against Mr. Hancock and others, on presumption that a few pipes of Madeira wine had been landed, more than was entered, again sat, and a number of witnesses were examined by the court, in a most extraordinary and curious manner; Mr. Hancock's nearest relations, and even his tradesmen were summoned as evidences; but nothing turning up, that could support

the libel against him, the court was again adjourned to the 4th instant, for a further examination.

A vessel, which was loaded and just upon sailing for the West-Indies, has been lately seized, by order, as it is said, of the C—m—rs, to the great damage of the concern'd in the present adventure, only on supposition that a voyage or two before, some wines brought from the Western Islands, had been landed out of her, without an entry, and paying the duties; which Americans look upon as illegal and unconstitutional, being laid not for the regulations of trade, but for the *express purpose of a revenue.* The duty upon wines from the Western and Portugal islands, is seven pounds sterling per ton; half the value of some of those wines; while the duty in England on the best Portugal wines is not half that sum; this is at once destroying our trade with those islands, which took off great quantities of our lumber and fish, and often enabled us to make remittances to Great-Britain, in wines, direct, or in a circular way of trade, which the heavy duty now prevents; there being no draw-back allowed on exportation: Those *restrictions* and *incumbrances* must prove as baneful to the *mother country as to the colonies:* the depriving us of *any article* of remittances, must *lessen* the importation of British manufactures in the same proportion.

January 3

A letter signed by upwards of two hundred of the merchants and traders of Philadelphia, has been transmitted to the merchants and manufacturers of Great Britain, acquainting them that they look upon the late statutes, imposing duties on paper, glass, &c. as *unconstitutional* and destructive of their rights, as their brethren and British subjects; which the Assembly of their province have, with decency and firmness remonstrated against, to the British legislature; they also represent in a clear and striking manner the impolicy of those acts, and the other *burdens* and *restrictions* upon trade; that unless they are speedily relieved from those *unnatural* and *useless* fetters, it is their

---

[1] Items from January 2 to January 5, 1769, inclusive, are taken from the *Boston Evening Post*, February 20, 1769, pp. 1–2.

serious and candid opinion the commerce between Great Britain and her colonies, must of necessary consequence *greatly diminish*, and as they add, the general importation of goods suddenly cease.—*It is our hearty wish that the mild and cautious efforts of the Philadelphia merchants, may be equally effectual with the more spirited and disinterested measures of their brethren in the neighbouring colonies, to obtain immediate relief; or in case of a contrary effect, serve to convince them of the justice, as well as necessity of carrying their significant intimation into speedy execution.* The instructions of the freeholders of the city and county of New-York, and of Queen's county, to their representatives in the General Assembly, now sitting, being replete with patriotic sentiments, and discovering their disposition to confirm the present happy union subsisting between the colonies; have been read with pleasure, and as they convey the political sentiments of so great a part of that respectable province; we flatter ourselves, that their Assembly, before their present session is ended, will fully harmonize with their constituents therein, which they have till now been prevented from doing, by frequent prorogations.

We have the pleasure to find that the General Assembly of South-Carolina, with respect to the Massachusetts Circular Letter, have acted with their usual spirit, and in a manner becoming the dignity of the representatives of a free people; their whole proceedings relative thereto, have been transmitted to the Hon. Thomas Cushing, Esq; Speaker of the late House of Assembly of this province, with a letter from the Hon. speaker of that house—the greatest part of which is as follows,—

SIR,

It is with a satisfaction equal to the importance of the subject, that I obey the order of the house, in informing you of their unanimous resolutions upon the subject matter of your letter; in acquainting you of their entire approbation, of the measures taken by the late House of Representatives of the province of Massachusetts-Bay, to obtain a redress of our grievances; and in thanking the members of that house, in their name, for communicating to their fellow subjects and sufferers, in this, and the other provinces, their proceedings upon that trying occasion. I inclose you the journals of the proceedings of our House of Assembly, during the short, but interesting period of their existence, as printed by their order: Which must convince the impartial world, that they have acted with duty and affection to his Majesty, at the same time, that they have supported with firmness, the rights they hold under the constitution.— The House was dissolved by proclamation in the evening of the day, that they entered into their resolutions—This method of proceeding, may for a time involve the province in some difficulties; but I trust that nothing which the Ministry can invent, will ever prevail upon a Commons House of Assembly of South-Carolina, tamely to surrender the liberties and privileges of the people, to any power upon earth. I am, Sir, with great respect, your obliged and obedient servant,

P. MANIGAULT.

Those who have distinguished themselves in our Assembly, by their zeal for the rights of their constituents, and of America in general, cannot but receive a very sensible pleasure from such weighty and honourable testimonies, to the justice of their sentiments, and the importance of the cause in which they have shewn such firmness; while they have been represented to Administration, by some among ourselves, as the dregs of a faction, confined even to a single town in this province. It is universally acknowledged, that Lord Hillsborough's letter was a most impolitick measure, and that it has had an effect directly contrary to his Lordship's intention: Nor is it to be supposed that this and similar measures would have been taken, had those upon whose representation his Lordship formed his idea of American affairs, transmitted him a just and candid account of them; those persons ought therefore to be answerable for the *dishonour* and *embarrassments*, which their own representations have occasioned.

January 5
The Court of Admiralty on Mr. Hancock's libels, sat yesterday, and again this day, by adjournments; the examination of witnesses still continues; It is said they have been summoned by orders given immediately by

the Commissioners, and by the warrants which the Commissioners had taken out blank, and filled up with such names as had been kept secret, even from the register, and their own advocate;—adjourned to Saturday.

A vessel with molasses, owned by a merchant in this town, which had been obliged to put into Salem, by stress of weather, reported her cargo there; as she was proceeding for this port, where the same was to be legally entered, at the Custom-House, she was taken by one of our little guarda coastas, the captain of which it is said gave £100 sterl. for his commission, and is detained on the frivolous pretence, that in searching her, they found three or four casks of molasses more than was reported at Salem, tho' the entry was to be made in this port.

A coasting sloop owned in George Town, at the eastward, when proceeding to that place, was stopt and searched by one of our guarda coastas, having some goods on board which were not specified in her clearance, she has been seized and now detained, its to be feared, to the distress of many inhabitants there, who being remote from supplies, depended on receiving by her the chief part of their winter provisions and stores: Formerly our coasting vessels going from one part of the province to another, did not clear out; lately it has been practiced to clear them out with ballast and stores, as the poor people who send up their memorandums by those vessels for supplies, must put the master to great difficulty in obtaining a clearance or cocket, as well as themselves to a charge; this vessel was thus cleared out, as was another which sailed in company, having much the same articles on board, which was also stopt, but immediately suffered to proceed: Such advantage taken of one and not of another, now puts the shippers to the great trouble and charge of clearing out even a jarr of olives, or the smallest article of English goods, going from one part of the colony to another.—It is said the merchants of So. Carolina disputed clearing out enumerated goods, going from one part of the province to another some of which were seized and libelled in a court of admiralty, but the decree went in favor of the merchants,—a like dispute happened at New-York.

Another vessel bound from hence to Portsmouth, in Piscataqua, has been taken into possession by one of our guarda coastas; this cruising captain, having found by searching, there was a barrel of Madeira wine on board, which had been shipt unknown to the coaster, as a barrel of vinegar; it seems those English guarda coastas, are more haughty & severe then are the French and Spanish; for they bore and tap casks and practice every art to discover a mistake, which they may take advantage of; in short a simple coaster must now be fully acquainted with the whole *science* of trade, or expose himself, owners and freighters, to great loss, if not ruin.

It is said one of our English guarda coastas pursued a vessel to sea, which had sailed on a foreign voyage, and actually took out a seaman, which they *suspected* might make a good witness against a Cape Ann sloop, lately seized for having landed more molasses than was entered.—As the vessel thus deprived of a seaman, may be lost by this management, its supposed a good action for damages lies against the captain of the guarda coasta.

Several other vessels, besides those already mentioned have been stopp'd by our guarda coastas, from proceeding to their ports, on one pretence or another, and if brought upon trial, and acquitted, the misfortune of Americans is, that a judge of admiralty, by declaring it as his opinion, that there was *probable cause of action*, it shall bar the claimant from recovering damages, or even charges: But what is a still greater misfortune, those American judges have now as it is said, a salary fixt of £600 sterling per annum, whose commissions run during good behaviour, and their continuance in office must depend on pleasing a minister, or those interested men in all seizures on this side of the water, whose approbations or complaints, unhappily for us, have lately had too much credit and regard paid to them by Administration.

January 6[1]

The winter does not prevent the people of

---

[1] Items from January 6 to January 8, 1769, inclusive, are from the *New York Journal*, February 2, 1769, p. 1.

Halifax from flocking over to us; a number of vessels have lately arrived from thence, with passengers; one schooner has brought not less than a hundred, chiefly women; the dregs and refuse of all nations, which the army and navy had collected together in that place; those miserables are daily applying to the Selectmen, and overseeers of the poor, for relief: The inhabitants of this town have been justly applauded, for their compassion, not only to their own poor, but unto strangers; our loss of trade, upon which we chiefly depend for a support, which is wholly owing to the late injudicious restrictions, and the imprudent severities of a G—r, C—m—rs, and custom-house officers, has brought us into great distresses; our alms house and work house, tho' large and commodious, are now fill'd; a great proportion of those objects, are strangers and not inhabitants of any town in this province; many of our own poor are thro' necessity supported out of the alms house; and their numbers daily increasing; what must then become of those who are posting to us from all quarters! Charity, however extensive has its bounds.

A vessel is just arrived from New-York, the master of which it is said, gives out, that he has brought from thence for the C—m—rs 10,000 ounces of silver, which had been collected in that port, from the new duties; about 700 ounces of which is in *wrought plate*, which some of the principal merchants in that city had been obliged to part with from their side boards; by reason of the scarcity of coin'd silver and bullion; we also learn that other merchants have been necessitated to deliver up sugars and other articles to the custom-house officers, which have been housed in the King's warehouses, for want of cash to discharge the duties. The same has been done by our merchants on the like occasion. *What can more clearly point out, the impolicy, not to say cruelty of the projects for an American revenue? our laws restrain the most hard hearted sheriff from levying their executions on a tradesman's tools, which are considered as the life of his family; the wisdom of late politicians, have permitted the most cruel and voracious of all men; C—m—rs, c—m—house and r—v—ue o—rs[1], to seize upon all the little circulating cash of* *our merchants, which may properly be denominated the very life blood of American commerce: It cannot however be very long before distressing sympathy will force its self upon the British merchant and manufacturer, —then, and not till then, may Americans rationally expect full relief from that quarter.*

January 7

This day the Court of Vice Admiralty again sat, and the doors ordered to be shut, when several further interrogations were filed: In examining and *re-examining* witness, the method, in some of its circumstances, appeared so extraordinary to a gentleman who attended as council, that he could not help observing in open court, that the proceedings, he thought, were more alarming than any that had appeared to the world, since the abolition of the *Court of Star Chamber*. It is certainly a matter of great importance to America, that this court should be kept within its *constitutional* bounds. Can it be a question whether its jurisdiction ought to be confined to transactions *upon the seas*, as in England; this seems to be favoured even by the Act of the 4th Geo. III. by which fines and forfeitures may be recovered in the Common Law courts, as well as the Admiralty: If so, one would think the business now before this court, which concerns matters done *on the land*, ought to be tried by the *law of the land*, and the subject would then have the benefit of that inestimable ENGLISH institution, a *jury;*—when there will be an end to the calling of witnesses in this case to support the libels filed, is difficult to determine: Almost every person already, who has the least *connection* with the parties accused, or who can be supposed to have the knowledge of the *secrets of their business*, has been pressed in the service, but to no purpose hitherto. It is justly to be expected that a true state of this extraordinary trial, being the first of the kind in America, will be published to the world: South-Carolina has obliged us with an account of some proceedings of the Admiralty, of that province; wherein the claims of the custom-house officers there, were defeated, and their expectations disappointed by the decree of the

---

[1] Commissioners, custom house and revenue officers.

judge, who it is said has since resigned.—The observations that are made in an appendix to this pamphlet, are so pertinent and judicious, as to have a place in the valuable Boston Gazette, to which we would refer those of our readers, who have not met with the pamphlet itself. The Court of Admiralty again adjourned to next Tuesday fortnight.

A *young* officer in the Admiralty Court, publickly declared yesterday, that G. B—d had positive orders not to summon a General Assembly till May next, and not even then, but upon some conditions. It is probable this may be given out to cheer up the spirts of the sticklers for the present severities; it is certain that it militates with the advices from our friends by the last packet, which give us the strongest assurance of a change, not only of *measures*, but of *men* too.—The following is an extract of a letter to this purpose, from a gentleman in London, to his friend in Boston, Oct. 4, 1768. "Your troops, you may depend upon it, will all be called away in the spring, and the ships, too, Doctor F— has given it as his opinion, that the colonies will obtain all that they can desire or wish for; if they behave with firmness. Your Commissioners stand here exactly in the character that they have established for themselves in America, and its the opinion of every one that the Board will be recalled, and a new Governor appointed for your province; Lord H—gh himself says, he entirely dislikes their conduct." *We are surprised the Commissioners have been continued thus long; as to G. B. he has undoubtedly involved himself and the officers of Government in perplexities,—that cool judgment, extensive views, and upright intentions, would have avoided; and he has now so totally lost the affections and confidence, not only of the C—l and A—ss—y, but of the whole people, that its thought he never can conduct the King's service with dignity and advantage in this province; unless it could be thought favourable to this service, to have the province perpetually embroil'd and made uneasy.*[1]

January 8

The unhappy consequences of quartering troops in this town, daily visible in the profaneness, Sabbath breaking, drunkenness, and other debaucheries and immoralities, may lead us to conclude, that our enemies are waging war with the *morals* as well as the *rights* and *privileges* of the poor inhabitants.

The grand jury for this county, broke up on Friday, having made more presentments than has been known for many years; a considerably part of which has been occasioned by the detentions, assaults, robberies, &c. made by the soldiery, on the inhabitants of this town.

January 9[2]

Among the bills found by the late grand jury; one was against the two soldiers who affronted Mr. Gray a merchant of this town by stopping him for not answering to their challenge, and then putting him under guard, of which mention has been made before; our young K—g's Att—y, refused his assistance in drawing it up, alledging as it is said, that "If a soldier should with his fixed bayonet at the breast of an inhabitant stop and detain him two hours, it would not in law be adjudged an assault." It is hoped a court and jury will otherwise determine it, and that it will no longer be a doubt even in the minds of the most sceptical that the *law of the land* is to yield to the maxims of a *meer oeconomy* of the military, in civil communities.

Upon the arrival of letters here, brought by the October packet, it was given out that L—d H—ls—gh in a letter to G. B. expresses his approbation of the G—r's conduct in not calling for troops to aid the civil power, the last summer, when the Council advised against this measure; but that at the same time his lordship reprehends the Council for giving such advice. This report does not indeed gain credit among sensible people, who cannot suppose that L—d H—ls—gh would take upon himself to reprehend his Majesty's Council who doubtless agreeable to their oaths acted according to their best judgment, tho' from the idea which his lordship at so great a distance had been led to form of this affair, *he* might apprehend them mistaken. Nothing however can be

---

[1] All of the above section in italics is omitted from the *Boston Evening Post*.

[2] Items from January 9 to January 15, 1769, inclusive, are from the *New York Journal, Supplement*, February 9, 1769, pp. 1–2.

plainer, and the Government at home is perhaps before now thoroughly sensible, that this advice of Council, was wise and just, tended to promote the true service of his Majesty, and the peace and welfare of this his province. One cannot forbear however to remark from this report, and the quarter from which it comes, how indiscreetly some people, would represent Lord H—ls—gh as a *mere eccho* to every sentiment suggested *from this side the water*, however *impolitick* and *absurd*. It is not doubted but the Ministry have prudently exerted the utmost of their influence at the first meeting of Parliament, to obtain a parliamentary sanction to the step taken by them in sending troops to America, lest those disagreeable consequences should have followed thereon, as has been predicted by those who disapprov'd of so extraordinary a measure.

January 10

It is said orders have been given by C—re H—d for all his little guarda costas to put out of harbour on a cruise along the coast and in our bays, doubtless by direction or advice of G. B. and the C—mi—rs, who are in hopes that the season of the year may have encouraged some captains or owners to aim at making a few savings, with regard to the new and disputed duties; or whose ignorance may have led them into mistakes, of which they may make advantages upon discovery. We cannot but regret that an officer appointed by the great Mr. *Pitt*, and who during the late war was so successful in destroying the trade of our foreign enemies, should now be so unfortunately employ'd in distressing our own: It is however well worthy the notice of the British merchants and manufacturers; that notwithstanding all the diligence, low arts and severity of the G—r and C—m—rs, supported and assisted by a navy and standing army, not one article has as yet been made prize of, that in the least interferes either with the *growth* or *manufactures* of the mother country.

January 11

We are told that there have been great murmurings and uneasiness among the soldiery, who instead of being paid their sub- sistance money as on their first arrival, have for some time past been obliged to receive the same in beef, which our butchers have agreed to deliver the contractor through the year at one penny three farthings stir. pr. lb. the men alledge, that with their own money they could furnish themselves better provisions at a cheaper rate; beef since their arrival being sold at one penny ½ pr. lb. mutton at a less price, and the offals of both at a mere trifle; and fish so cheap that a cod of 15 lb. weight just out of the water sells for about 9d. sterling, that as geese have been sold at about one shilling sterling a piece, turkeys of the same weight at 1s. 4d. fowls at 4d. rabits 1d. partridges 3d. ½ and other wild fowl in plenty, and the same proportion, they could, had they cash, have now and then an article of this sort, in their mess as well as their officers; but that now they are worse off in the midst of the greatest plenty and variety, than when in Hallifax without it; on the other hand its said, that provisions will probably be higher in the spring, and if the men should have money instead thereof, too considerable a part of it would be converted into *spirituous liquors* rather than eateables, how this matter will end a little time may discover; this may with truth be said, that the inhabitants are far from interesting themselves in this dispute, or doing any thing that may increase the present ferment among the troops.[1]

January 12

The detention of the Portsmouth vessel already mentioned at this season of the year on account of a barrel of wine found on board her, is like to prove very detrimental to a great number of merchants in those parts, who had goods on freight; one gentleman in Kittery has a large ship ready for sailing, waiting only for some necessaries shipt him by said vessel.

A coasting vessel owned at Biddeford having according to custom been sent from thence with a load of boards for New-Port, without being cleared out, was there refused an entry, and seized by the collector agreeable to orders received from the C—m—rs; and notwithstanding it clearly appeared that not the least fraud was intended by the

---

[1] The last thirteen words of this item are omitted from the *Boston Evening Post*.

master or owner, but that his proceedure was wholly owing to a supposition that it would be justified by custom; the vessel was libell'd in a court of admiralty, condemned, and sold by a decree of said court: This is not the only instance of an honest trader's being taken in and ruined, by presuming on a customary indulgence, indulgences which in some places are often given and frequently withdrawn without previous and public notice, whereby to the scandal of office they become means, in the hands of the revengeful and hungry officer to ensnare and entrap the unwary, but honest trader.

It is confidently reported that the A—y G—l on the other side of the water has given it as his opinion, that the officers of the Custom House cannot legally oblige, and ought not to insist upon those vessels who coast it from one part of the province to another, being cleared out as is usual on foreign voyages; but notwithstanding this, there is a greater strictness than ever with regard to such vessels, to the unspeakable worry, and also expence of the concerned; there is however this good grows out of the practice, that the more difficulty and charge there is in conveying and transporting British wares from one town to another, the greater encouragement and stimulus is given the inhabitants to *manufacture for themselves*, or become *more frugal* in the consumption of all foreign articles.

January 13

The present scarcity of money is so great, owing to the destruction of trade, and the monopoly that a large number of revenue officers, place men &c. have made of the same by the instrumentality of the late duties; that some gentlemen among us who have their moneys in the British funds, have given orders to their merchants to withdraw or dispose of the same, expecting greater advantages may be made with those monies, on this side the water; perhaps other reasons operate; stocks had certainly fallen 6 pr. cent: In October last—and advices intimate, that they were like to be still further affected by the measures pursuing.

The honourable House of Representatives of the province of New-York by a *manly, patriotick* conduct on a trying occasion have fully supported the character of an American

Assembly; in the course of their late session they completed a petition to his Majesty, another to the Lords, and a remonstrance to the Commons of Great-Britain, in order to obtain a redress of grievances; and then took into consideration the *circular letters* from the Assemblies of Virginia and Massachusetts Bay, which they *unanimously* resolved to answer in the most respectful manner, and fully to concur with the sentiments of the said Assemblies expressed in those letters; and having entered into a number of spirited resolves in favour of liberty and the rights of their constituents; their governor was then pleased to *honour* them by a dissolution of the Assembly. The speaker of the late House of Representatives for this province, has just received the following letter from the Honourable *Philip Livingston* Esq. late Speaker of the House of Representatives of New-York.

To the honourable Thomas Cushing, *Esq; Speaker of the late House of Representatives for the Province of the* Massachusetts-Bay

31st December, 1768

SIR,

By order of the General Assembly of this colony, I am to acknowledge the receipt of your letter of the 11th. of February last, and am directed to assure you that they are much obliged to your House of Representatives, for freely communicating their sentiments, on a subject so interesting to all the colonies; and are so far from considering it as a desire of dictating to the other Assemblies, that they highly applaud them for their attention to American liberty, and hope the measures they have taken on this important occasion, will fully convince them, that the General Assembly of the colony of New-York harmonizes with those of the other colonies in their representations for redress; they perfectly agree with your house in their opinion of the fatal consequences which must inevitably attend the operation of the several acts of Parliament, imposing taxes and duties in the American colonies; and have therefore prepared petitions to his Majesty, and the Lords Spiritual and Temporal, and a representation to the Commons of Great-Britain, praying relief from the grievances they labour under. They entertain with your house the firmest confidence in his Majesty's known clemency and tender regard for all his subjects, and the candour and justice of the British Parliament; and are not without hopes that the united supplications of all the colonies will prevail on our most gracious sovereign and the Parliament, to grant effectual redress, and put a stop, for the future, to measures so directly repugnant to the true interest of the mother-country and the colonies. In the name, and by order of the General Assembly,

I am, with the greatest respect,

Your most obedient humble servant,

PHIL. LIVINGSTON, Speaker.

P. S. Robert Charles Esq; agent for this colony, at the court of Great-Britain, is instructed to co-operate with the agents of the other colonies in their applications for redress.

At a C—l last Thursday G. B. exhibited another specimen of the inexpressible *littleness* of his mind, and the fullness of its enmity against the people: It seems some boys were the other evening playing at foot ball near the province house when either by accident or design; they threw down one of the centry boxes at the gate; this rude and mischievous behaviour of children, the G—r has represented to the C—l as a serious and important matter, upon which he required their advice or concurrence, in giving orders to the King's Attorney to prosecute them for the same, which we are told has been done; and we doubt not an account of this little rude *boyish* trick, will be transmitted to Administration with such *glosses* and *comments*, as may have a tendency to impress them with the heinousness of the offence; and as another proof of the necessity of regular troops, to keep the inhabitants in order. We cannot but here observe that notwithstanding the many insults offered, and injuries done the inhabitants by our *new comers*, and the danger we have been in from their practices with the Negroes; that the G—r has been so far from taking any steps to secure or relieve us there-from, that he has even suffered them to pass by him wholly unnoticed.

January 14

We have lately been favoured with the King's most gracious speech to both houses of Parliament; wherein his Majesty is pleased to express his concern, that a spirit of faction which he was in hopes had subsided, had again arisen in his American colonies, and in one in particular to a considerable degree.—It is observable that the countenances of our enemies appear very *jocund* upon this occasion, while his Majesty's *loyal* subjects are distressed, that he has conceiv'd such an unfavourable sentiment of the temper of his colonists; who far from the remotest disposition to *faction* or rebellion, are struggling, as they apprehend, for a constitution which *supports the crown:* and for the rights derived to them by their charter and confirm'd by the declaration of his Majesty's glorious ancestors, Wm. and Mary, at that important era, *the Revolution.* We shall make no further observations, but only recite a paragraph which contains the sentiments of truth—"It is a maxim of the English law, and a principle founded in reason, that "the King can do no wrong" and we are ready to apprehend, that in the present case the Ministry have done none; but that the concern which his Majesty has been graciously pleased to express, in regard to the colonies in general, and the supposed disposition of one in particular, is wholly grounded upon the misinformation, and false representations of those, who, if they do not sufficiently revere truth, ought to tremble at the thought of deceiving Majesty, and of plunging the greatest and happiest empire which the sun ever shone upon, into astonishment, anxiety and confusion! Perhaps accounts have been transmitted home similar to those said to have been sent from hence to New-York, Nova-Scotia, &c. in September last, viz. that a certain cas—e was taken possession of, a beacon erected, and thirty thousand men in arms to oppose the landing of the King's troops.—A very few weeks will effect different impressions, in regard to the colonists, and produce very different measures, which we venture to predict, will terminate in the prosperity of the whole empire."

January 15[1]

The friends to a constitutional union and harmony between Great-Britain and her colonies, cannot but hope, and seriously pray, that *wise* and *faithful* counsellors may stand about the King, Men *fearing* God and *hating covetousness;* and that the things which belong to the national peace, may not *be hidden* from the eyes of those who are *entrusted* with the management of the national concern.

January 16[2]

An advertisement of C—e H—d, in this day's paper, would lead the public to conclude, that the inhabitants of this town and province were disposed to encourage the desertion of seamen from his Majesty's ships in this harbour; as he therein informs, "that between forty and fifty had deserted since the 4th of last month, many of which are harboured and concealed in the country, not 20 miles from Boston." From the general character of this officer, we cannot suppose that he has designed unjustly to cast this reflection upon the inhabitants, in order to justify a severe impress for the manning of the ships under his command; but rather that he has been grossly imposed upon by those enemies to truth and the peace of the colonies and nation, which unfortunately for an honest man, is the company he must dispense with for the present: Justice to ourselves however, requires, that we contradict so reflecting an assertion.—We have no crimps in this town or near it, to whom the merchants apply for seamen; and sailors, especially at this season of the year, can be of no kind of service in the country, and their manners and behaviour are too disagreeable to our country people, to permit of their supporting or harbouring any of them: The seamen who escape from what is now too justly term'd in a time of peace, their wooden prisons, immediately make out of the province for safety, and to seek voyages, not being able to remain on shore for want of the wages left behind them: This was notoriously the case in the late war: We were not favoured with one station ship during the whole of it, but were obliged at our own expence to build and man a number of ships of war, for the protection of our trade and coasts; notwithstanding which, the King's ships came from every quarter, in order to get re-manned; those of their companies that could escape, went into the other governments, and our trade was so distressed by impresses, that I assert a truth, in declaring that seamen's wages in this place, were above fifty per cent, higher than in those parts which were not visited by any of the ships of war.

January 17

The desertions from the troops quartered among us, still continue, and it is said increase, the treatment we have all along received from G. B. and the C—m—rs, lead us to apprehend, that it will be represented as owing to the management of the inhabitants: It is known that these troops in general, have been very uneasy, and it is thought, if any large corps was to be sent into the country after deserters, they would leave behind them in the same proportion smaller bodies have lately done; we will not pretend to say whether this disposition to desert, is owing to a disrelish to the service, or a great liking the troops have taken to the country: They observe, that the winter is very moderate, the common people cheerful, hearty, and well clad, and such variety and delicacies in the markets in this town, as lead them to conclude that they are now got into Canaan, a land not indeed, abounding with silver and gold, but a land flowing with milk and honey.

January 18

This day being appointed for the celebration of the Queen's birth, there was a general muster of the troops in the Common; the thin appearance made by the several regiments, fully evinced that their being quartered in this town, was a measure as impolitick as it was illegal.—A gentleman in P——t, when speaking of their arrival in Boston, added, "I am very glad that the trial of N—th A—r—ca and G—t B—n has been made; for those disturbers of the public peace, and subverters of government, are now acquainted both *with* us *and them-*

---

[1] This is "December 15" in the *New York Journal*, an obvious printer's error.

[2] Items from January 16 to January 24, 1769, inclusive, are from the *Boston Evening Post*, March 6, 1769, p. 1, and March 13, 1769, p. 1.

selves."—We are so, and wish we could justly return the compliment: It may not be improper to tell that little S—n,[1] that this province alone, raised four times the number of troops now in town, in less weeks than it has taken months to collect this body of regulars, from all parts of the continent; and that with our troops we took Louisbourg, and thereby purchased a peace for Europe, for a less sum, than the Boston expedition, will cost the nation; and that if the court of Versaillies had foolishly taken it in their heads to have sent twice the number of troops to have taken Boston, as the court of London has sent, as it is said, to support the laws which protect us, the conduct of the Bostonians would have convinced the world, that Americans took a pride to vie with Britons in spirit and resolution upon a justifiable occasion.

Upon the arrival of the King's speech, while a few seemed to enjoy a triumph, the greater part were of opinion, that the warmth and severity of temper against America, to which Administration had been wrought up by cruel misrepresentations from this side the water, would subside, as soon as a fair state of facts could be obtained.— We have the pleasure to find by the arrival of Capt. Scott, that this opinion was not ill-founded; the address of the House of Lords & C—ns on the King's speech, usually a kind of echo of the speech, is somewhat fainter than the original, they speak of us as *fellow subjects*, and not as *rebels* & *traitors* who have *thrown off government*, take notice of our *grievances*, and intimate there will be a *redress*. It seems that the transactions of the town of Boston in Sept. last, in making mention of a law of this province, that requires all the inhabitants to be provided with arms, and in proposing that the several towns should make choice of persons, there being no Assembly, to join in humble petitions to our gracious sovereign, for the redress of grievances, and to prevent *rash* and *violent* measures, at so *critical* a season, were a principal part of those misrepresentations. It is certain that those transactions were not in any degree contrary *to law;* whatever wicked intentions have been basely attributed to those who were in favor of

them, by such as presume to censure and judge the secret thoughts of men, and to attribute the vilest motives to all who oppose their *selfish* views and *dangerous innovations:* Very few can doubt, that *no art* has been unemployed, no *pains* spared by *some men* among us, to represent those proceedings of the town, not only as illegal, but to the highest degree factious and seditious; *one man* in particular, whose *opinion* ought to have *great weight*, if his moderation, judgment and honesty were equal to his *station*, has endeavoured to make it be believed here, that these transactions, taken in their circumstances and connections, amount to *treason* itself, and that they would be regarded in this light on the other side of the water: If any thing could have driven us into violent measures, the base, irritating conduct of the man we are speaking of, must have done it; but our loyalty and tender affection for our mother country, notwithstanding her usage of us, prevented this effect; the sword once drawn, might have been drawn forever;—The vote of the town, respecting being provided with arms, was agreeable to a law of the province, and at a time when a principal officer at Halifax, had wrote up that a war with France was inevitable; the Committee of Convention was not formed, as has been basely represented, upon the plan of 1689,—nor was it an actual assumption of the powers of government; the committee utterly disclaimed all governmental powers and authority, and only considered themselves as persons chosen in a most critical season, to consult and advise for the peace and welfare of the province and nation; *That Government and the people of Britain, now view things in this light, is as much matter of joy to this loyal people, as it is of fear and terror, to the great accusers of the colonies in general, and this province in particular.*

January 19

It seems by the last accounts that complaints have been made at home, among other things, against *two* very *important* charter privileges, as *great defects* in the constitution of this province; the *one* is, the representatives of the people being in part the electors of his Majesty's Council; tho'

[1] Statesman.

the King's Governor may negative whom he pleases, a power which one G—r has for years past exercised in the most wanton manner,—the *other*, that grand juries are chosen by the *townships*, and not by the *sheriff*. *This shews the spirit of some among us, and with what implacable enmity they regard the constitutional rights of this people; not content with having introduced a military power among us, they would have things so modelled, that the authority of the Council and the law itself might be employed only as instruments to promote the measures of arbitrary power.*

January 20

The commissions of the new appointed J—s of Ad—lty, are bro't by Capt. Rowland; what an opinion can we form of the policy of the present M—y, or of the sincerity of their pretended disposition to pursue healing measures, when the most unpopular men among us are the most likely to be rewarded for their pr—f—ns, rather than public services; we are assured that those judges are to have their extraordinary salaries of £660 sterling per annum, paid out of the fines and forfeitures. It is hoped that the *just complaints* of America, against the *extention* of the Court of Admiralty in opposition to the *true spirit* of the English constitution, will *one day* be attended to particularly in giving all causes relating to the revenue, to this court, *without jury*. The Judge of Admiralty, in this province, was formerly paid a commission on the condemned goods, which did not, as it is said, amount to £100 per annum on an average. This, in order to make more and fatter sinecures, was represented home to be a kind of *bribe* against the subject, and it was pretended, this grievance was to be remedied by the *new appointments;* but if the salaries are to be paid out of *fines* and *forfeitures*, will not this be a strong temptation to the judges and other revenue officers, to take special care, that this *fund* do not at any time *fall short* of the *appointments* for which it is appropriated.

January 21

Lord H—ls—gh it appears is now smartly pushed by some leading men in Parliament, respecting his American measures; particularly his mandate to dissolve the Massachu-

setts Assembly in case of non-rescinding, and not allowing another to be called. This step has been severely animadverted on, both in and out of Parliament, as *imprudent* and *arbitrary*, tending to make the people desperate, and to *create confusion*. His lordship we are told in vindication of himself has declared, that he never *prohibited* the calling of a new Assembly, but *expected* this would have been done, soon after a dissolution. It is certain the Massachusetts Commons House, took notice in their reply to the Governor, that his lordship's letters, communicated to them, contained *no such prohibitions;* and we find that the G—r of New-York, after dissolving the Assembly of that province, immediately issued writs for a *new choice;* which perfectly accords to the report of what his lordship has declared. In what manner then will G. B. *account* for his conduct, not only in *forbearing* to convene a new Assembly, but in declaring himself as *not at liberty* to do so, and speaking upon this point in such a manner, as to lead people to imagine, that it was altogether uncertain, *whether ever there would be another:* Has he so thorough a *disaffection* to the people whom he governs, as to lead him, when the measures of administration are *severe* beyond all principles of *policy* and the *constitution*, to go *beyond his orders*, to heighten the severity: Whoever considers the *temper* of his administration, the *ambition* discovered of *forming the ideas of Administration*, respecting American affairs,—and the *attention unhappily* obtained among some leading men in Government, cannot *wonder* at the present *distress* of America; the *convulsions* of this province, and the great *embarrassments* of the British Ministry.

January 22

The common soldiers continue their robberies and violences, and (in the latter) some officers are no way behind them: A constable of this town was much wounded by one of them the other night; a night after, the south watch was assaulted by a number who declared themselves custom-house and naval officers; their language was most profane, their threats high, their abuse to the watch great, and their insult upon the authority of the town audacious; they returned about one o'clock, bringing about

40 regulars, as they said with design to carry off the watchmen, but the officer who commanded those troops gave no offence, unless it was in being witness to such ill behaviour, without informing of or securing the offenders, that they might be dealt with according to the merit of their crimes.

January 23

Two sailors report that they were the last week taken up into a certain J—'s chamber, where they were privately examined, relative to Mr. Hancock's vessel, when questions, to which they had given plain and precise answers, were so reiterated to them, that one of the sailors could not help asking, whether it was really wanted, to have him swear to what he had no knowledge of: *This practice of private chamber examination, seems to be an improvement upon Star Chamber proceedings and must tend to render C—ts of A—y still more detestable to Americans.*

January 24

Last Wednesday night several officers of the army, sallied out of a house in King-street, and meeting with one of the inhabitants of the town, they beat and wounded him very cruelly; soon after this feat, the watch-house in that street, was attacked by them, sword in hand; the watchmen defended themselves bravely, and one of them was so lucky, as with his *bill hook* to twitch into the watch-house one of those *brave leaders*, who they immediately disarmed; the noise and tumult occasioned by this assault reached the ears of the military main guard, who soon after made their appearance, and released *the hookt in officer*, but the watchmen could not be persuaded to part with *his sword*, which they retain'd as a *trophy* of their victory; and for a *proof* against the offender, accordingly the next morning complaint was made to Mr. Justice Ruddock, who by the help of the sword, gained knowledge of the owner, who was immediately brought before him, and dealt with according to the law, made and enacted, for the protection and support of the town watch, while in execution of their duty.

The other evening the *north-watch* was assaulted and much abused by some of our military night arrants, they were not able to seize any of the offenders, but having discovered the name of one of them, a warrant will be issued to bring him before Mr. Justice Ruddock, to answer for his mad behavior.—Another of our military knights, was pleased to draw upon a number of young fellows in King-street, who soon proved too many for him, and had it not been for timely assistance, his rashness might have proved fatal to him. Abuses are daily offered some one or another of the inhabitants, who are generally for seeking redress in a *legal way;* and we cannot but hope that those of the military, who oppose themselves to the *law of the land,* will find the *predictions* of a great lawyer *verified;* "that in so doing, they knaw a file which will break their teeth."

January 25[1]

We hear that *Samuel Venner,* Esq; is by the Commissioners, suspended from his office of secretary of their board.—Various are the reasons (without door) assigned for this event,—some say it is for divulging their secrets in July last, while others, who pretend to know better, hint the true cause to be his not retiring with them last summer to the Castle, in order to help *keep up the appearance* of their service being *obstructed* in the town of Boston: Be it as it may, 'tis said that a great person and the *******, are his *honourable* accusers.—This gentleman, Mr. *Venner,* with his family, has lived pretty much retired in Boston, upwards of 14 months; and by his inoffensive deportment he has rendered himself *personally* respected, by those who knew him, while others of his suit, by a different conduct, and scandalous mean behaviour, are now justly despised by all orders of people.—It may not be unentertaining to remark, that when the four *fugitives,* fled to the Castle last summer, *as it is said,* for safety, the following gentlemen of the suit did not fall in with their plan, but resided *safely* in Boston, and went daily to the Castle to do business—The Hon. Mr. Temple, a Commissioner, Samuel Venner, Esq; Secretary, Charles Stuart, Esq; Receiver-General, John Williams, Esq; In-

---

[1] Items from January 25 to January 29, 1769, inclusive, are from the *Boston Evening Post,* March 20, 1769, p. 1.

spector-General, William Wooton, Esq; Inspector-General, David Lytle[1], Esq; Solicitor-General; Messrs. M'Donald and Lloyd, principal Clerks; to these may be added, the Collector and Comptroller of Halifax, then in Boston, the Collector of Falmouth, the Collector of Piscataqua, the officers of the port of Salem, occasionally in Boston, during the Board's residence at the Castle; the Searcher of Augustine, and all the officers of the port of Boston, at their respective duties, except the collector, who, ('tis said) was, by *positive* order, detained, to keep up the *farce* at the Castle, much against his will. Neither of whom had, even the least insult ever offered them; so that I think it does not appear (however disagreeable the institution was) that this town had any design, illegally to prevent the Commissioners holding their board in the town, whatever reasons they, or their *grand adviser* may have assigned for their *decamping*.

January 26

The *court concert* of the last evening was it seems, turned topsy turvy, as *Joan the Italian's* was a week or two before—Some officers of the army were for a little *dancing* after the music, and being told that G—r B—d did not approve of their proposal, they were for sending him home to eat his *bread* and *cheese*, and otherwise treated him as if he had been a *mimick* G—r; they then called out to the band to play the *Yankee Doodle* tune, or the *Wild Irishman*, and not being gratified they grew noisy and clamorous; the candles were then extinquished, which, instead of checking, completed the confusion; to the no small terror of those of the *weaker sex*, who made part of the company.—The old honest music master, Mr. D—bl—s, was roughly handled by one of those sons of *Mars*; he was actually in danger of being *throatled*, but *timously* rescued by one who soon threw the officer on lower ground than he at first stood upon; the inoffensive Bartholomew Gr—n, who keeps the house for the Commissioners, presuming to *hint* a disapprobation of such proceedings, was, by an officer, with a drawn sword, dragged about the floor, by the hair of his head, and his honest *Abigail*, who in a fright, made her appearance without an head dress, was very lucky in escaping her

poor husband's fate. Whether our G—r will so resent this behaviour of the military, as to *collect affidavits*, and make it *a subject of representation* to Lord H—ls—gh, cannot as yet be determined; be this as it may, Mr. D—s has acted in character, having delivered up the room, which he held from the Commissioners, returned the subscription money, and wisely determined not to give another concert, until he should again have it in his power to preserve order and decency in such an assembly.

January 27

We learn from the late Court Gazette, that poor G. B. finds himself under great difficulties from the constitution of this province, particularly in two points we have before mentioned, viz. The return of juries by *the towns*, and the election of Counsellors, in part, by the *representatives of the people*. A complaint of these difficulties, the Gazette says, was uttered on his behalf, by some friends of the ministry in the House of Commons. It was no doubt *suggested* in his own account of affairs transmitted home; and met with so much *attention*, as to procure a kind of proposal in the House of Commons, for altering the Massachusetts government, in these *important* points. The proposal however was opposed with much energy and spirit, by a number of that house, who observed, that such alterations, instead of *relieving*, would still *further embarrass* the administration of the colonies; that *mild* measures, and a sacred regard to *charter rights*, and some *indulgences*, even to prejudice, would be much more likely to *secure the authority* of Great Britain in America, than *severe* measures (from which the heart must revolt) enforced by a military power, *the last resource of ignorant despotism*. G. B. has had the modesty to profess publickly, that he had a kindness for the people whom he governs, a friendship for their privileges, and an enmity only to disorders and violence. But, the mask drops off, and by proposals among the M—y, and in the House of C—m—ns, which one cannot but suppose, originated from himself, we see his strange dislike to the constitution itself, established by charter. Every one acquainted with the government of this province, knows, that though the General As-

---

[1] David Lesle in the *New York Journal*.

sembly elect the Council, the Governor has a power to negative whom he pleases, and that this power, together with the disposal of offices, civil and military, create at least as strong a dependance in the Council, on the chair, as on the people; but, some men are impatient of *constitutional* restraint, and tho' vested with *much* power, are restless till it becomes *unlimited.* —Had G. B. less affected to dictate and controul the Council, and more encouraged, and regarded their free, impartial advice, it would not have injured either his own honour or repose, while it might have greatly contributed to the peace and welfare of the province. Though the *Council* have been ready to maintain the *constitutional* authority of the chair, and have supported G. B. in *exigencies,* even to the disgust of many, yet they have found themselves absolutely obliged, by *truth* and *justice,* to give their advice upon *favourite* points, not exactly agreeable to his inclinations. They did this particularly, on the question relating to the expediency of introducing a military power into the province, the disorders in Boston, on the 18th of March and 10th of June, and the retirement of the Commissioners to the Castle. In resentment of these and similar acts of Council, it is probable G. B. sent home his complaints, *that the Council chosen by a popular Assembly, tho' intended to support government, became frequently the means of weakening it.* The Council for the Massachusetts, is elected by joint ballot of both houses of Assembly. From the mode of expression in this complaint, which has grown of late very common among us, we cannot but observe what ideas some men have of government. The *Council,* a branch of the legislature, was only intended to *support* government: It is then *no part of* government, much less is the popular *Assembly,* meaning the lower house, by which it is partly chosen; what then is *government,* why the Governor alone. —Good God! what times are we fallen into: *King James's Governor Andros,* never carried his ideas of *provincial despotism higher.*

We have frequently been told, that the leaders of the faction, as the *cant phrase* is, are to be sent home, as *state prisoners.* —It is now said that the accusations against them, have been already forwarded, and

particularly in an anonymous letter to Lord H—, and that his Lordship has *stoop'd so low as to take notice of it,* and transmit it *back, to G. B.* for the proper proof; in consequence of which, every method is made use of in the *inquisitorial court, secretly,* to support the charges against individuals, by evidences taken *exparte,* which is repugnant to law, reason, and common equity. If these things are so, into what times are we fallen! shall we compare them to the infamous times of the *Stuart's reign,* or *the dregs* of the Roman state, when *street conversation* (however innocent) was taken up by *vagabond pimps,* employed and *paid* for their pains and carried to their superiors, who from thence *formed the measures* of the administration! It is well remembered, that within these few years, such wretches were employed to pick up materials of this sort; one of whom swore criminality, against two gentlemen of known reputation, alledging in his affidavit, that he indeed heard not one word they said, but that *"by their looks he was sure they were talking against the G******."* Such were the methods taken against a late worthy collector M—B—s which *caused* his removal, —such methods were taken against the town of Boston, in the well known affair of Capt. Malcomb, and other cases;—and such we have reason to think are the methods *still used against this town and province, and all America,* otherwise it cannot be supposed they could be charg'd in the most public manner, as they have lately been, and this by the *greatest personage* on earth.

January 28

Court of Admiralty again set for the examination of witnesses, respecting Mr. Hancock's vessel; a c—t, as managed in America, *abhorrent* to the *English* constitution; what power is vested in a judge! His decree may be said to be final, as in most cases, an appeal from it cannot be pursued, without involving the appellant in *enormous charges* and the *highest perplexities;* how great a grievance is it that a judge who decides upon *unlimited* sums; is appointed during *pleasures,* and not *good behaviour;* his place therefore *depends* upon the *favour* of a M—r, perhaps his *subserviency* to the views of a designing Governor; this pay of former judges, was a *commission* on condemnations;

It was viewed in the light of *a bribe;* the grievance has been *redressed,* by substituting a *greater;* the present judges salaries are to be paid out of *fines* and *forfeitures,* and is *six times more* upon an average than has been received by all *former judges* thro' the continent.

January 29

The army has been often complimented, as being *the school of politeness;* the practice of *some officers* among us, leads observers to conclude, they are of opinion, that *cards* and *shuttle cocks,* furnish out a more *agreeable* and *becoming* entertainment *for gentlemen on the Sabbath,* than they can find in a church, or in the works of a *Tillotson* or a *Doddridge.*

January 30[1]

Court of Admiralty again set for examining and *re-examining* witnesses respecting the libels against Mr. Hancock, &c. It may perhaps be *tedious* to meet with these accounts, so often in this Journal; how *grievous* then to the subject, to be obliged with his council to dance——such attendance; must it not excite indignation in every American, to be told, that a number of gentlemen shall by order of the C——m——rs be libeled for about £50,000 sterling, and held under bail thus long, when it appears that this was done without their having any proof of the matter of charge *in their hands,* but that the libels were ordered to be laid, with design further to harrass and distress a most amiable and useful member of society, and in hopes that some evidences would be *fished up* in the course of a lengthy trial, which might support those libels.

The C——m——rs affect to mimic high life, not only in their dress, attendants, and in rolling from house to house in their chariots the best of weather; but by an attempt to invert the order of nature; in turning day into night and night into day—one or two o'clock has been the hours for dining in this town, time out of mind; the C——m——rs have pitched upon four a clock as a more *courtly hour,* and it cannot but excite ridicule to perceive, G——n, L. G——r S——y &c.[2] sacrificing their dignity together with their appetites and health in conforming to the mushroom gentry.—The following anecdote may serve to give the public an idea of what these people term *tasty* living,—a lady of character, before the C——m——rs retired to the Castle, made a visit to one of their ladies, between the hours of 4 and 5 o'clock; the visited came into the room, praying the visitor to seat herself, and asking leave of absence to finish her dinner; sometime after she returned, and before the city lady departed she was led to understand that Mr. C——m——r had engaged company who would come at 11 o'clock to spend the evening with him. The unpoliteness of the city lady in breaking in upon a neighbour thus early, was not a little diverting to our stranger, and among other tea table chat soon after, she could not help observing, that one of the natives, awful creature! as she said, had made her a visit before 5 o'clock. At the same time intimating her fears that they must be finally obliged, as to the time of dining to conform to the natives, in order to prevent such unseasonable interruptions.

January 31

At the Court of Sessions now setting, a number of soldiers for hailing, stopping and assaulting the inhabitants, have been tried upon the bills bro't against them by the last grand jury, found guilty and fined—Our young A——y G——l[3] was pleased to enter a *noli prosequi* upon a bill against some soldiers for stopping and detaining several gentlemen who would not answer to the challenges of the guards; which bill he had refused drawing for the jury, alledging that no assault had been actually made upon them—The persons indicted had been bound over to this court, by an old magistrate, *learned in the law,* to whom they had confessed the facts they were charged with. This magistrate being upon the bench animadverted with freedom and spirit upon the conduct of the A——y G——l, who tho' only a

---

[1] Items from January 30 to February 5, 1769, inclusive, are from the *New York Journal,* March 2, 1769, *Supplement,* pp. 1–2.

[2] The *Boston Evening Post* reads *"certain persons"* instead of "G——n, L. G——r S——y &c." The Boston editors were evidently intending to avoid libel suits; besides everyone in Boston must have known who were meant by "*certain persons.*"

[3] In the *Boston Evening Post* this reads "The A——y G——l."

council for the crown, should take upon him in so unusual a manner, to controul the law before he had taken the opinion of those who were appointed the judges. Our Att-y G—l, who is also a J—d A—c—e for the crown, was scarcely known as a lawyer till those offices were conferred on him by a G—r, who has also thro' the c—p—n of the times been able [to] procure him a salery of £600 sterling pr. ann! as a reward for certain services.[1] If such a—t's, without consulting a bench shall wantonly enter his *noli prosiqui* upon bills found by a grand jury; and on the other hand, only by information and complaint, cause a subject to be harrassed with a trial after a bill had been refused; and this trial before judges who are not only appointed *during pleasure*, but also *pensioned;* we say if these things can be done without *violence* to the constitution; our good G— may then make himself perfectly easy, tho' he should not be able to obtain his wish that the return of juries should not be made as they have been, by the *several towns* in the province, but by *sheriffs* of his *own appointment.*

Last evening between nine and ten, a fire broke out in the gaol in this town, which notwithstanding the diligence and activity of the inhabitants was consumed, leaving nothing but the walls standing. It is said that one of the criminals in the prison willfully set fire to it—the distress of the poor prisoners was great, the keeper of the goal having in his fright mislaid his keys, divers of them were in eminent danger of perishing before they could be relieved, and some of them finally escaped very much burnt—The piquet guard were ordered out to attend this fire with their *musquets and bayonets,* and drew up in Queen-street opposite the gaol, but the officer of the guard being told by the firewards (a set of town officers who by the law of the province have the sole conduct on these occasions) that they could be of no assistance in that manner, but were rather an obstruction; that such an appearance was disgustful to the inhabitants; and that he must either draw his men off again, or they must assist in such a way as the firewards should direct, they retired to the main guard

house: After which the gentlemen of the army attended and offered the assistance of the soldiers *unarmed,* as did the navy officers that of the seamen, whose laudable activity and perseverance together with that of the inhabitants, prevented the spreading of the fire which through the whole night threatened great desolation in the very center of the town.

February 1

THIS day at a general Council, the Governor after informing them that he had been able to *persuade* his friend[2] *Commodore Loring* to consent to be an *acting magistrate;* he was pleased to nominate and appoint him a justice of the peace for the county of Suffolk; together with Robert Auchmuty, Esq; the late constituted Judge of Admiralty for this province—As the knowledge of the law cometh not by inspiration, we may conjecture, that the sphere of action marked out for the *Commodore,* has more relation to the *law martial* than the *common law;* Judge Auchmuty who is the *fourth* appointed reforming justice, is a *sterling* acquisition, and G—r B—d cannot but flatter himself that by the exertions of this *meritorious* and *unbashful* judge, the *bench of justices* will soon become as *agreeable* to Lord H—gh and his reforming coadjutors, as any *modern Court of Admiralty* on the continent, we learn that before G. B. left the council chamber he could not help discovering how much he had been nettled, by some late publications; he hinted to some of the gentlemen, his surprize, that his *proposals, reasonings* and *conversation* at the board, should so *find the way out,* and was pleased to intimate that in preventing it, their *own honour* would be consulted rather than *his peace,* as those publications gave him no *personal* uneasiness; we would only remark, that this speech of the G—r's evidences the *exactness* of our relations, and indeed the greatest enemy his *public conduct* has made him, could not better satisfy his *revenge,* than by setting it in its *truest* point of light; the *least deviation* therefrom, must *take off* from that just detestation which as the Philadelphia citizens express it, "this infamous G—r

---

[1] This entire sentence is omitted from this item in the *Boston Evening Post.*
[2] The two words, "his friend," are omitted from the item in the *Boston Evening Post.*

ought to be held in, not only by the citizens of Boston, and the inhabitants of the American colonies, but by every individual whose heart is animated with a *single sentiment* of liberty."

February 2

The following paragraph has appeared in several of our news papers viz. "We hear from Londonderry in the province of New Hampshire that a sergeant and some soldiers having apprehended two deserters, were surrounded on the road about six miles from the place where they first took them in custody, by 100 or 150 armed men, who obliged them to release their prisoners." this relation seems calculated to answer the purposes of a certain party among us; it is therefore necessary to set it right; we have before mentioned that a number of persons were strolling about the country in disguise, who were guilty of such impositions as might be productive of disagreeable consequences; the best and we believe true account of the above release is; that *two men* strangers, were travelling into the country, and made Londonderry in their way. Soon after their arrival, *four* men, in *sailors habits*, entered the town, and in a *hostile* manner *seized* the two strangers, and were carrying them away. This extraordinary behaviour of the four supposed sailors alarmed some of the inhabitants; and *four* men instead of *one hundred and fifty* mentioned, pursued them, determined to know the cause of their *intrusion* and *violent* measures; upon their overtaking the party, a *parley* ensued; and the *prisoners* were released. Had these four men in sailors habits produced a warrant from any *legal authority*, to justify their proceedings, they would not have been *opposed* or *prevented* in the execution thereof: or had they been soldiers, appeared in their *proper regimentals*, and *published* their business, *due respect* would have been paid to his Majesty's messengers; and if requested, *necessary aid* would have been granted: But if any of his *Majesty's immediate servants*, or any *other persons*, shall presume to enter a town *disguised* in such a manner as not to *be known*, and without any *lawful authority* violently seize upon and attempt to carry away, any of the proper inhabitants, or *even strangers* cohabiting with them, *such persons* might reasonably expect *opposition*, and

without satisfaction *suffer* the consequence.

February 3

A vessel that came from Madeira about six weeks ago, which had been entered, and loading again for another voyage, was this day seized by order of the C—m—rs, and one of their officers placed in her who forbid the owner coming on board, without informing him of the pretence for the seizure. No foreign article, has yet been found in any vessel that has been seized or searched, interfering in the least with the manufacture of Great-Britain, but it seems the C—m—rs would have it *appear otherwise;* the libel lately filed against the coasting vessel for having a barrel of wine found on board instead of vinager, also mentions a trunk of silk, which upon enquiry only contains a few made up capuchins and other little articles sent from hence to Salem. *What damage to the mother country as well as the colonies, will the ignorance and malice of this naval b——d occasion.*

February 4

We learn from South-Carolina that writs have been issued for calling a new Assembly, after the dissolution of the last for not rescinding, as has been done by *every Governor* on the continent, excepting ONE, the M—tts, whose ambition leads him to make his administration as *odious* and *distressing* to the people as is possible: Some letters from thence also mention "that as the American Board of Commissioners are determined at carrying all their powers into execution, they shall not be surprised, to hear orders are given to make *another* attempt to oblige all the schooners in that province, that go over the bay to enter and clear at the office." The conduct of the B—d of C—m—rs in this place, cannot but lead us to conclude, that they conceive the *great design* of their institution, is not for the *regulation*, but absolute *destruction* of trade, and *fleecing* of the merchants; the little guarda costas under their directions continue *stopping* and *searching* of *coasters*, and the masters chests do not escape a rummage; and it is as *true* as it is *vexatious*, that even *open boats* from Cape-Ann beech *with sand*, are put to the charge of making an entry at the custom-house, and this notwithstanding the opinion of the Attorney

G—l Mr. D—g. has been sent over, which is clearly against the propriety and right, of their obliging vessels going from one part of the province, to another, to an entry.

We have advice from North-Carolina that the General Assembly of that province, had read and answered the Virginia and Massachusetts Circular Letters, with all due respect, and agreed upon a petition to his Majesty for a redress of grievances. That their Regulators had drove a gang of villains into the back of South-Carolina, where by reason of the CIRCUIT court act, not having been confirmed at home, fresh uneasiness had been given the inhabitants, the consequence whereof they could not pretend to tell; however this may be, we do not hear that *their Governor* desires or has wrote for a *single grenadier* to *protect* and *assist* the civil magistrates in that province in the execution of their duty.[1]

February 5

There has been much talk of an anonimous letter sent from hence to Lord Hillsborough and by him remitted to Governor Bernard: For some time the report was not credited, but now the fact is ascertained, Governor Bernard has shewn the letter to some gentlemen: who waited on him last week, requesting a sight of it but did not allow a copy of it to be taken. It speaks highly of Governor Bernard, &c. but contains the most malignant insinuations against some respectable gentlemen in this town who are mentioned by name. It speaks of deep and dark designs carrying on notwithstanding the peaceable landing of the troops: of an alliance to be formed between Holland and some of the colonists in order to throw off the 'ependance of the latter upon Great-Britain at the first breaking out of a new war, and of 30,000 men between Boston and New-York ready to take up arms, it advises that some leading men should be inveigled over to Britain, and not sent there by force, lest this should make too much noise and occasion resistance. The Governor it is said declared that he made no account of the letter, and should make no account of it in his dispatches—Be this as it may, is it not astonishing, that a letter so palpably base and malicious, so extravagantly false, and without a name, should be so much noticed by a S—y of S—te as to be returned by him to G. Bernard. *Here is a fresh specimen of the methods that have been employed against the rights of the colonists, and those gentlemen that have distinguished themselves in favour of those rights. Had such a letter been written on the other side the question, and so much noticed, what reflections would have been made upon it*!

February 6[2]

We cannot forbear making a few observations on the curious and laboured accounts, of the sentiments of the British Government, and the debates in the House of Commons on American affairs, given in the Court Gazette, of Thursday last. What pains are taken, to make us believe, contrary to the latest and most authentick advices from home, that the affairs of America in general, and particularly of this province, are in a situation almost desperate, only because a few among us have done every thing in their power to make them so, and cannot endure the thoughts of not having their own prophesies fulfilled, their misrepresentations successful, and their malevolence gratified.—It seems that of late, Administration has not only adopted *implicitly* the accounts of facts, but the reasonings upon them, and even governmental matters, as they have been stated, and suggested by a few of its servants on this side the water: Hence the embarrassments of the Ministry, and the perplexity of the nation, from the unnatural contest with the colonies, at a season when the circumstances of Europe, require the most perfect union at home, to give weight to our negotiations, and awe to those, who might wish to disturb our repose.—

The tenor of his Majesty's speech at the opening of the Parliament, as it respects America is easily accounted for, from the *budget*, which about that time was received from hence. The Ministry seem'd to believe, at the first opening of the *budget*, that the proceedings of a certain *town* in America,

---

[1] The last paragraph of the item for February 4 is omitted from the *Boston Evening Post*.

[2] Items from February 6 to February 9, 1769, inclusive, are from the *Boston Evening Post*, April 3, 1769, pp. 1-2.

were not only to the highest degree *seditious*, but nothing short of *treason* itself; and that they had full evidence of all this in their hands.—Tho' the people at a distance from the seat of government, are always under great disadvantages, with respect to a fair state of their case in any disputes between them and the servants of the crown, yet *truth* very soon so far made its own way, that upon a clear inspection into affairs, the charge appeared to be laid too high: Nor is there a person either in or out of Parliament, who has justly stated or proved, one single act of that town, as a public body, to be, we will not say treasonable or seditious, but even at all *illegal:* Nor is it in the power of any man, either on this or the other side the Atlantick, to do it.—

New vouchers we are told, are called for from authority: This is no favourable symptom to the sudden and warm accusers: for we believe there are more than *one*, who may find it an *Augean* enterprise, to support *their own* representation. For it is certainly beyond human art and sophistry, to prove the British subjects, to whom the *priviledge* of possessing arms is expressly recognized by the Bill of Rights, and, who live in a province where the law requires them to be equip'd with *arms*, &c. are guilty of an *illegal act*, in calling upon one another to be provided with them, as the *law directs*. But if some are bold and base enough, where the interest of a whole country is at stake, to penetrate into the secrets of the human breast, to search for crimes, and to impute the worst of motives to actions strictly *legal*, whatever may be thought of their expediency, it is easy to recriminate in the same way; and one man has as good reason to affirm, that a few, in calling for a military force under *pretence* of supporting civil authority, *secretly* intended to introduce a general massacre, as another has to assert, that a number of loyal subjects, by calling upon one another to provided with arms, *according to law*, intended to bring on an insurrection.

It will be equally difficult to prove it *illegal*, for a number of British subjects, to invite as many of their fellow subjects as they please, to convene and consult together, on the most prudent and constitutional measures for the redress of their grievances; or that such an assembly had *actually assumed* the powers of government, when they *actually disclaimed* all such powers, and united in recognizing their subjection to Government, by humble petitions & remonstrances, and by encouraging their fellow subjects in their loyalty, and good order. But the people of Boston are charg'd with "*ingratitude* for the repeal of the Stamp-Act! and because some refus'd to make compensation to the sufferers *in behalf of that act*, and others did it with an ill grace!" What artful confusion is here to make a single town odious? were the people of Boston, ever apply'd to for a compensation? did not the requisition come to the General Assembly; in which there were only four members for Boston? Did not these members unite with the General Assembly in granting *ample* compensation? Was not this a *free generous* act? Could any power on earth *constitutionally* oblige the province or the town to pay the damages done by *unknown rioters?* Has the Parliament done this in the late riots in England? Did Rhode-Island make compensation, tho' call'd upon as this province was? Are Howard and Moffatt, compensated to this day by that colony? What has it suffered for its refusal? It has been complimented for its loyalty and good order in one of Lord H—sb—h's circular letters, *with a view* to induce it to treat with contempt this province, which *had compensated?* But Rhode-Island had sense and virtue to despise the ridiculous lure, and generosity not to withdraw its aid from the *common cause*.—Without saying anything more upon this point, we may venture to appeal to the candid world, where the *ingratitude lies:*

As to the repeal of the Stamp-Act, though the people of this province and America universally regarded this act as an infraction of their constitutional rights, and consequently humbly claim'd the repeal as a point of *equity*, they yet received it with as much *gratitude* as if it had been a *free gift*. They blessed their Sovereign—They rever'd the wisdom and goodness of the British Parliament—They felt themselves happy, till new acts *equally unconstitutional* were made, and severities imposed upon trade, unknown even at the time of the Stamp-Act.—But it seems we are unpardonable for not being thankful for the removal of *one* burthen, after *another* is laid upon us by the same hands, equally hard to bear! How contemptible is such reasoning! What an affront to common sense! We never heard of such discourse in Parliament, till we saw our *Court Paper;* and can these persons be friends to the leading men in Government, who represent *them* as reasoning in such a manner?—

But force is no very suitable means of changing the sentiments of the people! It is rather adapted to rivet and confirm them. Arms ought to be very *cautiously* employed, even against faction, they have often increased rather than quelled.—The present uneasiness in America, has been *falsly* and *insolently* called by this odious name: Can any man suppose, the almost *universal* complaints of a people, to deserve this appellation? As well might the general uneasiness that introduced the revolution by *William* the Third, and that settled the succession in the illustrious House of Hanover, be called a *faction!*

February 7

The Court Gazette before referred to, gives us an account of what was said in Parliament in vindication of the measures of the Ministry, respecting the colonies, and this province in particular, that deserves to be attended to. With respect to the *non presentation* of the petition of the Massachusetts House to the King, the intelligencer says, it was declared the petition had never been given to the S—y of State.—This is not true, it is an undoubted fact, that the petition was offered by Mr. Deberdt to L—d H—sb—gh as he has declared in a letter to the Speaker, so that this could not be the reason why it was not presented, in gross violation of the constitutional right of the subject. And here we suspect that the S—y was led into a scrape by his judicious friend, on this side the water, who formed a plan for the non presentation, such as might be expected, which was not solid enough to bear mentioning in Parliament and so the *whole vindication* was rested on the denial that it had been ever given to the S—y. As to the order to require the Assembly to rescind, that it was said was "*only* to give the Assembly an opportunity to correct a fault of a former Assembly; and

the order to dissolve was a direction for the Governor's conduct in case of non-compliance; neither of them being *addressed* to the *Assembly*, could be deemed a *mandate* or a *threat* to a corporation; the Assembly would of course meet again in May," according to this account the S—y, never designed to *threaten a corporation;* no it was his intention to leave the Assembly *freely* and without any manner of *constraint* and *bias* to correct the error of a former one: The orders not being *addressed* to the Assembly, it seems were not designed to be *shewn* to the Assembly, or to have any *influence* on their decisions; so that either G—r B—d grossly mistakes the *intention* of L—d H—sb—gh, and *rashly* exceeded it, in a point of the greatest consequence; or this is a *quibbling falacious excuse* of his L—p's conduct, said by the authority of our Court Gazette, to have been offered in Parliament. For did not G—r B—d lay before the house, L—d H—sb—gh's letters wherein he was directed to *dissolve the Assembly*, in case of their *non-rescinding?* Had not this letter thus communicated, all the effect upon the deliberations of the house, on this point, as if it had been *formally addressed to them?* Did not G—r B—d declare that he looked upon himself *indispensibly* obliged to comply with the order in this letter? did he not *refuse a recess* to the house, which they requested in order to *consult their constituents*, upon so important a point? Nay when the house took only a *few days*, to deliberate upon this critical affair, did not the G—r express his impatience by a message, requiring them to come to an *immediate* determination, as otherwise he should take their *hesitation* as a *positive refusal?* Did he not according to the order *dissolve the Assembly*, and at the same time declare himself *not at liberty* to call another, *without fresh instructions from the Ministry?* As to the Assembly, meeting of course in May, it is an *artful evasion.* The Assembly cannot *meet then* without *writs being issued from the G—r*, for that purpose. It is true *the charter* provides for the meeting of the Assembly at that time; but people were made to believe that *non rescinding* would *annihilate* the charter, and that there *never* would be another Assembly. It is certain that G. B. and others, spake upon this point in a manner that directly tended to *create* such an apprehension both among the *Assembly* and the *people*.

February 8

The military still continue their extravagances: About six officers coming thro' King-street, some nights past, were hailed by the town house watch; this it seems was taken as such an affront, that no language was bad enough for the watchmen; they even formed a sort of a blockade to the watch-house, which was continued for about three hours; but having learned caution by the misfortune of one of their corps, not long since, they neither of them chose to come within the reach of the watchmen's bill-hooks.—As several others were passing the streets one evening, they were heard to express their wishes that the town might be burnt down; and cast very abusive reflections on the Select men, threatening, to give them all a severe whipping, before three months had expired. —This evening as a sober inhabitant was returning home with his wife, they were overtaken by several officers of the navy; who accosted 'em in a very indecent manner, and swore that the woman should go on board the man of war, upon her expostulating with them for this rudeness in the presence of her husband; they d—n'd him, and swore she should go on board with them; one of them laid hold of the husband while another was pulling the wife along with him; her screams, soon brought up a gentleman, who having a lanthorn with him presently discovered one of the criminals to be a L—t of a King's ship, and we hear the injured party intends prosecuting him, for this audacious attempt.

February 9

One of our coasting shallops, which lay at Hubbard's wharf the last week, was examined by one of our new sea custom-house officers; he happened to find a small quantity of bad fish on board, the vessel not having been entered out, and he informed the skipper of this discovery, in such a manner, as caused him immediately to put out of harbour with his vessel, for fear of a seizure. —Other skippers bound to different parts of the province, have had their vessels stopt, and even libelled for having things on board not cleared out, this has given such alarm that even the skippers of open boats do not care to take so much as a loaf or two of sugar on board, until it has been reported, and as this cannot be done without the sugar boilers making oath respecting the sugar, the trouble given the masters and freighters in this, and innumerable like cases is inexpressible; the detention of coasters by means of the novel formalities, is very detrimental to the owners, and vexatious to those, who depend upon receiving their family supplies by water. In short almost every step taken since the arrival of the C—m—rs, appears to have a direct tendency to embarrass, if not totally to annihilate the trade of the province.

February 10[1]

Letters from Georgia, dated the 28th December last, give us to understand; that the Assembly of that province, have fully harmonized with the Assemblies of their sister colonies, by asserting their constitutional rights in a number of spirited resolves, and in petitioning their gracious sovereign for a redress of American grievances, as also in the respectful notice they have taken of the Virginia and Massachusetts Circular Letters. The patriotick conduct of this Assembly, does them the more honour, as their Governor, has been pleased to tell the world, that *more than ordinary pains* had been taken, to *prevent* their receiving and shewing countenance and support to the *Boston letter*, and that notwithstanding this, they had suffered themselves to be influenced by the conduct of other provinces, and thereby deliberately laid him under the necessity of dissolving the Assembly: Those members who have thus dared to maintain the constitutional rights of their constituents, tho' threaten'd with political death, by the mandate of a M—r, have justly merited the grateful acknowledgments of every American; and that their names should live for ever, in the annals of their country. —Governor Wright's speech upon this occasion may lead us to imagine that he

---

[1] Items for February 10 to February 19, 1769, inclusive, are from the *Boston Evening Post*, April 10, 1769, pp. 1–2.

would not have L—d H—h conclude that G—r B—d, is the only governor upon the continent, who could reason with *propriety*, upon the justice and policy of American measures, but the good gentleman ought to be borne with, as his speech is *quite dispassionate*, and does not, like some others, discover the *basest ingratitude* and the most *inveterate enmity* against the people of his government, or that he was *vain enough* to fancy himself *capable* of forming the measures of Administration.

February 11

The summoning of new witnesses, respecting the libels against Mr. Hancock still continues. A clerk of that gentleman, was this day, brought to Judge Auchmuty's chamber, and closely examined; when this trial will end we know not; as long as it continues, we shall notice their procedure, that the friends of liberty, on the other side of the water, may be able to form some idea of an American Court of Admiralty.

February 12

The prevalency of vice and profaneness, the robberies, thieving, house-breaking, &c. which have been committed since a certain set of men were sent among us, as we have been told by L—d H—h to assist the civil magistrate, must greatly affect every member of the community, who views those licentious proceedings, either in a moral or political light: The faithful magistrate at such a day, has it in his power to testify his regard to the honor of the Supreme Lawgiver, and his love to his country, in his endeavours to discountenance and suppress them: Those who have exerted themselves herein, have justly merited the applause, and esteem, of the wise and virtuous; and when any one instance comes to our knowledge of the late appointed justices, having acted up to the *true* character of *reforming* magistrates; we shall with pleasure record the same in this Journal.

February 13

We have had more of winter since Feb. set in, than in all of the preceeding months; the ice having opened new passages out of town for the soldiery, desertions are more numerous than ever; notwithstanding all

the care the officers, and vigilance of the military guards, which almost surround the town: the practice of sending out sergeant's parties in disguise, still continues, but we do not hear of any one deserter being brought back, excepting poor Ames, whose execution is thought to have been as *impolitick* as it was illegal; it deters those country people from making discoveries, which the prospect of a reward might tempt them to do, as they now apprehend, that this cannot be done without involving themselves in the guilt of blood— We wish those statesmen, on the other side of the water, who were in the measures of sending troops, could but look into Boston, and see the present state of the regiments quartered among us; if all upon the British and Irish establishments were now in America, and were no fuller than the former, it has been conjectured, that the number of British troops would not, in such case, exceed twenty thousand effective men. What policy must have been adopted by the British M—y! The sure hold, Britains once had of Americans, by having their *affections*, has been *wantonly* thrown away, for the *precarious* one, which a body of *troops* can only obtain; a few regiments placed in Boston neither of which can be trusted without the walls, lest the greater part should disappear, or kept together within them, even by a discipline hitherto exercised only in an enemy's country, is the goodly power which has been thought sufficient to keep a whole continent in subjection. It was certainly a shrewd conjecture made by one in the House of C—ns, upon the first news of the troops being *peaceably* landed in Boston, that we should now be better acquainted with *ourselves* and with *them*.

February 14

In the papers bro't us by the last post, we have seen with pleasure, the petition of the Pennsylvania Assembly, to his Majesty and both houses of Parliament, in which that Assembly fully concur with those of the other colonies in *asserting* with great decency and loyalty, and a manly firmness, the *natural* and *constitutional* rights of Americans, not to be *taxed*, but by a representation of their *own*; a right, *essential* to a British subject, and *inseparable* from the idea of a free government. It is now evident beyond a doubt, that *one sentiment* upon the grand point, runs thro' all the *colonies*, not excepting the infant settlement of Georgia, which tho' it must be supposed under particular discouragements from *asserting* this right, has yet dared to do it.

This union is the *safety* of colonies, and a pleasing *omen* in favour of the great American cause, which patience and a persevering firmness, must at length bring to an happy issue, both to the parent country and the colonies. It is certain that the *right* of taxation is the *cause* of the present controversy between them; and the colonies not *conceding* this right to the British Parliament, is what has alarmed and offended Administration: An union among the colonies in this point, is what they principally dreaded, and endeavoured to avoid—Hence the *impolitick* dissolutions & prorogations of the colony assemblies, adopted rather to *confirm* than *change* the sentiments of the people; the liberal spirit of the Massachusetts Assembly, and particularly the Circular Letter, were considered as strongly *leading* to such a *union*.—The warm attachment of the citizens of Boston to the *rights of America*, and the patriotick conduct of their representatives were looked upon, as having no small influence upon the *Assembly;* this is the *true source* of that high displeasure, expressed by the Secretary of State, for the American Department; and by other leading men at home, against the Massachusetts Assembly, and particularly the *town of Boston.* Hence the misrepresentations, and aggravated accounts of disorders here, transmitted to Administration, and too easily credited, to form a *pretence* for treating this town with particular severity, and for placing so large a body of troops in its very bowels; from an *absurd opinion* that if the spirit of liberty was once thoroughly quelled *in this capital,* it must not only be *extinguished* through the *province,* but in all the *colonies.* Vain imagination! *One spirit* animates all America; and both the *justice* and *importance* of the cause is so plain, that to *quench* the spirit, *all the colonies* must be absolutely *destroyed.* What has contributed to *distinguish* this province, *is the residence* of the Commissioners among us—and the *uncommon exertions* of G. B. & others in favour of power, and to promote the most disagreeable measures of Administration; exertions that have however been so *ill directed,* that they have happily *embarrassed* rather than *promoted* the intended plan— Being pushed *first,* and more *violently* than our neighbours, we were *early* and *vigorous* in the opposition, and do not therefore arrogate upon this account, any undue merit to ourselves—We rejoice to see the colonies in the great point of right, *completely united.* Severe measures towards *any one,* or on the whole, must tend to *confirm* the union. The *tighter* the cord of unconstitutional power is drawn round this bundle of arrows, the *firmer* it will be; and the *hand* that can *forceably break it,* in such a cause *must be strong enough* to break the *pillars* of the British constitution, and *overturn* the whole nation.

February 15

The coasting vessel which we have before told had been seized by a guarda coasta for having a barrel of wine in the run, which had not been cleared out; has been since libelled and *condemned,* at a Court of Admiralty, together with some New-England tobacco, which was found on board upon unloading her:—It is proper to observe, that the *only pretence* for stopping this vessel was the *cask of wine,* but the *cause* of the condemnation was the *tobacco* found on board: we must therefore leave it to the world to judge whether this, or like circumstances can justify the conduct of those captains of our guarda coastas, who upon most frivilous & slight pretences, shall take upon themselves to expose the owners & freighters of coasting vessels to the charge and damage of having their vessels detained and unloaded, in order to search and rummage out a pretence for their condemnation.

February 16

A concert hall is again opened to all who have, or may commence subscribers to such musical entertainments. We are told proper concessions have been made Mr. D—bl—s, and that G— P—y, has engaged that the o—ff—rs of his core, shall for the future behave with decency, and agreeable to the regulations of such assemblies.

February 17

There has been within these few days a great many severe whippings; among the number chastised, was one of the negro drummers, who received 100 lashes, in part of 150, he was sentenced to receive at a Court Martial;—It is said this fellow had adventur'd to beat time at a concert of music, given at the Manufactory-House.

A Court of Admiralty held yesterday, when the witnesses brought by Mr. Hancock, relative to the libels, entered against him on account of the Madeira vessel, were examined:—The court then adjourned to Tuesday next.

February 18

One H— lately T—e W—r, was sent for by the Com—rs and closely examined by them, in hopes of finding out some matter which might support the libels against Mr. Hancock:—It is said one B— followed the said person from the C—m—rs chamber, and hinted to him, that if he would bring out any thing to purpose against Mr. Hancock, he might be again *restored* to his place, and otherwise find it to his advantage.

February 19

To condemn a person before he is acquainted with the charge laid against him, and allowed to answer for himself, is plainly repugnant to the principles of equity: But it is certainly an higher act of injustice to treat a community in this manner: None doubts that heavy charges against the town of Boston have been laid before Administration, which must affect the interest of the *whole province*, and remotely *of all the colonies*, in their present critical situation.— What has been alledged against the town we *know not*, nor consequently in what manner we are to make our defence: It seems but just that the servants of the crown here, from whom an account of things is expected, should communicate to the people such *representations* of facts as may be supposed to operate against them with the Government at home, that so they may have an opportunity of vindicating *themselves*, as far as they can, before they feel its displeasure. Instead of this, these accounts are *concealed* with great care; and the first intimation the people have of them, is by their *effects*, who are left to guess at

them, by the influence they have *actually had* upon governmental measures.—This has certainly been the case with the town of Boston; to the astonishment of all who are acquainted with its transactions; it has been represented as in a state *subversive of all law and government*, when not *one instance* can be produced, of the interruption of justice, in any of our courts, not so much as those held by only a single magistrate, nor even in the *Courts of Admiralty*; and the *duties* exacted by the laws of trade, have *been paid*, at least as punctually as ever they were.— The town has an undoubted *right*, and has been solicitous to know, the *particular facts*, upon which this general and heavy charge *has been founded*; accordingly the *Selectmen* from a tender regard to the welfare of the inhabitants, have waited upon the Governor last Friday, with the following address.

May it please your Excellency,

At a time, when artful and mischievous men have so far prevailed, as to foment and spread divisions in the British Empire: When mutual confidence, which had so long subsisted, with mutual advantage between the subjects in Britain and America, is in a great measure broken: When means are at length found, even to excite the resentment of the mother state against her colonies; and they are publickly charged with being in a state of disobedience to law, and ready to resist the constitutional authority of the nation: The Selectmen of this metropolis, cannot be the unconcerned or silent spectators of the calamities which in consequence thereof have already fallen upon its inhabitants.

To behold this town surrounded with ships of war and military troops even in a time of peace, quartered in its very bowels; exercising a discipline, with all the severity which is used in a garrison, and in a state of actual war, is truly alarming to a free people. And what still heightens the misfortune is, that our gracious Sovereign and his ministers have formed such an idea of the present state of the town, as to induce a necessity of this naval and military force, for the aid of the civil magistrate in the preservation of its peace and good order.

Your Excellency can witness for the town, that no such aid is necessary: Loyalty to the sovereign, and an inflexible zeal for the support of his Majesty's authority, and the happy constitution, is its just character: And we may appeal to the impartial world, that peace and order were better maintained in the town before it was even rumoured that his Majesty's troops were to be quartered among us than they have been since. Such a measure then we are persuaded, would never have been ordered by the wisdom of the British administration, had not the necessity of it been drawn from the representations of some of his Majesty's servants in this province.

Your Excellency will allow us to express our opinion, that the public transactions of the town, and the behaviour of some of its individual inhabitants have been greatly misapprehended by his Majesty's Ministers. We therefore in duty to the town we have the honor to serve, respectfully wait on your Excellency, and pray that you would be pleased to communicate to us such representations *of facts only* as you have judged proper to make since the commencement of the last year. And as there is a prevailing report, that depositions are and have been taken *ex parte*, to the prejudice of the town and particular persons, may we not assure ourselves that your Excellency will in justice cause to be laid before us such other representations as may have come to your knowledge, that the town knowing clearly and precisely what has been alledged against it, may have an opportunity of vindicating itself.

Attest, WILLIAM COOPER, *Town Clerk*.

February 21[1]

A Court of Admiralty, for the trial of the libels entered against Mr. Hancock, for treble damages sat this day, being the time assigned by the judge, *for hearing the arguments* on the cause, the witnesses brought by the *defendant* having been examined last Thursday. It was expected that this trial, which has been as *lengthy* and *vexatious* as it is *new* and *unprecedented*, would now have been finished; but to the astonishment of the publick, and as it is said, even to the judge himself, the Com—rs acquainted the court, that they had other witnesses, to be interrogated; accordingly a master of a vessel owned by Mr. Hancock, his wharfinger, and one or two others attended by summons, were examined, and the judge has allowed the C—m—rs the whole of this week to produce their other witnesses. It is conjectured, that the C—m—rs are apprehensive, that the evidence given into court by the defendant is fully sufficient to *invalidate* or set aside the testimonies of those persons they had brought on the part of the crown; which has prompted them to ask a further time for them and their emissaries to hunt up other evidence.—When this trial will end, we cannot say; perhaps not before every townsman has been summoned, and given in their testimony; and if the C—m—rs should be still unlucky, they may continue the trial, until every seaman that has sailed out of this port shall be return'd and examined.—We shall omit making reflections on the treatment that Mr. Hancock has met with: Those who have the least spark of humanity cannot but feel for him. *O Britons!* turn your eyes upon poor America, and you may behold a J—e of A—y, appointed only *during pleasure*, whose salary of £600 per annum is to be paid out of *fines* and *forfeitures*, and whose *continuance* in office must depend upon the representations of such *a set of men* as constitutes the American B—d of C—s—ms!

February 22

Some lines in verse appeared in Messrs. Edes and Gill's Gazette of last Monday, being a few lively remarks on a song handed about in manuscript, in which the characters of some young ladies in town, were treated with great indelicacy; the same day one L—t S—, of the 14th Regiment, came with another officer to the printers, and pretending that he was some how pointed out therein, as the person who had satyrized those ladies, and demanded the author's name; which was not given him; he returned the next morning and claimed a promise of one of the printers that he should have it.— The printer then told him, that he should not comply with his demand, as it would be an infringement of the liberty of the press,

---

[1] Items from February 21 to February 25, 1769, inclusive, are from the *Boston Evening Post*, April 17, 1769. pp. 1–2.

which should be as free for him as for any other.—Or that if he still thought himself injur'd, the law was open, and he might seek his redress, upon which he uttered many threatenings, and swore that he would come the next morning, and if *satisfaction* was not then *given him* he would *take it himself*, of the printer; he accordingly kept to his promise in the first particular, but prudently broke it in the second; otherwise he would soon have been convinced, that there were some persons among us, who could as well defend the liberty of the press, as they had before maintained the *rules* and *orders* of a *coffee-house*.

February 23

A number of coasters with grain and other provisions, arrived from the Vineyard, have had two custom-house officers put on board them, to inspect their unlading; another novel practice introduced by the C—m—rs. The master of a vessel which had been froze up at the Vineyard for some time, finding his cargo of corn almost spoiled, adventured to dispose of some of it to the inhabitants, who were in want; for this offence his vessel was seized on her arrival here.

A small boat from Braintree a town *in our harbour;* but a few miles from Boston, coming up here as usual, with candles and oil from the spermaceti works, was stopt by a guarda costa, when an officer came on board, and demanded the *clearance, letters* and *invoice;* the boatman answered that he had no *clearance,* &c. the officer then told him that he must seize the *vessel,* and he accordingly put an officer on board, with strict directions not to let them *unload;* but not thinking one man sufficient for the weighty charge of guarding *the boat,* he returned with another hand, with *swords* drawn, and *pistols* loaded, and gave orders that they should defend *themselves* and the *vessel* and *cargo,* and not suffer any thing to be taken out, till further orders. We are told that upon application made to the Com—rs by the owner, the Hon. Thomas Flucker, Esq; they have ordered the officer of the guarda costa to take off his men and release the boat.

February 24

This day came on in the Court of Admiralty an argument, upon a question which serves to show the *strange uncertainty* to which this unhappy country is reduced by *the modern code* of revenue laws.—The advocates for Mr. Hancock, offered evidence to prove that a witness, who had been before examined for the proponent, was a *fugitive* from his native country, to *avoid the punishment* due to a very *heinous crime.*—The advocates for the crown objected to this evidence as improper, urging that by *common law,* nothing could be proved against a witness, but his general character for falsehood. The advocates for the respondent, replied, that the Court of Admiralty proceed according to the *civil law,* whereby a witnesses whole life and conversation ought to be examined.—And they insisted upon knowing by what law their client was to be tried. The Stat. 4 G. 3 gives jurisdiction of a crime to Courts of Admiralty in America: If therefore the court is to adopt the common law, because the jurisdiction was created by act of Parliament; it ought to adopt it as a system, and *summon a jury* accordingly, *to try the facts,* especially as a trial by jury is not *expressly taken away,* and in general to conform to all the *other rules* of the common law, thro' the whole trial. But if the court is to proceed by the civil law, the respondent ought to have the advantage of all the beneficial rules of that law, particularly to examine into the whole life and conversation of the witnesses, to except peremptorily to all persons, who are related to him, within the degrees mentioned in the civil law, and to all persons under 20 years of age, and finally to be convicted only on the testimony of two unexceptionable witnesses.—Or will it be said Americans are to be tried by an hotchpotch mixture of common law, and civil law! If so, who is to determine? Does it lie wholly in the discretion of the judge to pick and choose out of each such rules as please him? If this is to be the case, we must be allowed to be in a very precarious situation indeed. *Misera servitus est.*

February 25

The Selectmen received from Governor Bernard last Saturday evening, the following reply to the address presented to him last Friday noon.

Gentlemen,

The propriety of your addressing me upon public business I shall not now dispute; but in my answer I shall confine myself to such part of your address as relate to you as the Selectmen, or to the town as a body. I have no reason to think that the public transactions of the town have been misapprehended by his Majesty or his ministers, or that their opinions therein are founded upon any other accounts than those published by the town itself.

If therefore you can vindicate yourselves from such charges as may arise from your own publications, you will in my opinion have nothing further to apprehend.

FRA. BERNARD.
Province-House, Feb. 18, 1769.

It is evident at first view, that in this reply, the Governor evades an answer to the proper and decent request of the Selectmen; which could not mean, as he would insinuate, that he should inform them what were the *public acts* of the town meeting; *but how facts have been stated,* and what depositions or *testimonies* have been given, relative to the behaviour of the inhabitants, out of town meetings, and considered as individuals, that might lead Administration to think they were in a *state of opposition to all law and government,* when no instance can be brought, in which the cource of justice has been violently interrupted, *in any court,* not before even a *single magistrate;* and when the Council have published their testimony, the most authentic one that could be, that the town was far from being in such a state, and that the *civil authority* did by no means *want the aid of a military power.* The town knows not in what manner facts have been stated, to convey so unjust and injurious an idea of it, as has certainly been entertained; and consequently, is at a loss how to proceed in its own defence: No one can suppose the Governor *to be ignorant* of the state of facts *transmitted* to Administration; and certainly candour and common justice would have led him to communicate this to the town, in order to its own vindication. Instead of this, the application of the Selectmen upon so important an occasion is insinuated to be impertinent.

With respect to testimonies and deposi-tions taken *exparte* against *the town* and *particular persons,* and *industriously concealed from them.* Had the Governor not *known* or not *believ'd* the truth of this, he had here so fair an occasion of declaring it, and such a declaration would have been so much to his *own honour,* as well as the satisfaction of the town, that we cannot suppose he *would have omitted it:* His silence therefore upon this head, *and studied evasion* of so important a request, must *confirm* the general apprehension, and be considered as a *new proof,* that such kind of evidence has *actually* been taken. The world will from hence judge what kind of treatment the town of Boston has received.

The Governor in his reply, has, however, publickly declared his opinion, that the town has *nothing* to *apprehend* from any part of his conduct, except *its public acts* in town meeting. Here is then a *testimony in favour of the town,* a testimony that no man can object to, that the disorders that happened on the 18th of March and 10th of June, which have been so greatly magnified, and of which such use has been made for the worst of purposes, cannot, or ought not *in his opinion,* to affect the interest of the town, for he says, if the town can vindicate *its own publications; that is its own acts,* which are *all* that it has published, it has *nothing further* to apprehend—Whether his Excellency, really intended so far to *vindicate* the town of Boston, I pretend not to say, but am glad to find, such is the *force of truth,* that he has *actually done it* in this public manner.

The town has never yet been convinced that any of its public acts were *illegal,* it indeed has been said in general of their illegality by some persons, but *no one* has undertaken to shew what laws *they have infringed.*—The Selectmen, with the decent boldness of conscious innocence, have requested the Governor to do the town *this favour,* but he has declined it; which will appear from their second address, and his reply: which are as follows,

May it please your Excellency,
The Selectmen of the town of Boston, beg leave once more to wait on your Excellency, hoping you will excuse this further trouble as it is upon a matter of the greatest importance to the town.

In your answer to our late humble request,

your Excellency was pleased to say, that "you have no reason to think that the public transactions of this town have been misapprehended by his Majesty or his ministers; or that their opinions thereon are founded upon any other accounts than those published by the town itself." And "that if we can vindicate ourselves from such charges as may arise from our own publications, we shall in your opinion have nothing further to apprehend."

As the town has published nothing but its own transactions, in town meeting legally assembled; it gives us the greatest pleasure to find your Excellency, in your reply to us, thus vindicating it from any just cause of apprehension, from the general character of its inhabitants, considered as individuals: If therefore the town has suffered, on account of the disorders which happen'd on the 18th March or the 10th June last, by persons unknown (the only disorders that have taken place in this town within the year past) we take your Excellency's declaration to us, to be a full testimony, that in your opinion, it must be in consequence of some partial or false representation of those disorders to his Majesty's ministers. And we rejoice to find your Excellency's sentiments, as expressed in your reply, so far harmonizing with those of his Majesty's Council not long ago published. We have in this case, the most authentic evidence that can possibly be had, the joint testimony of the Governor and Council of the province, that the town has not been *in a state of opposition to order and government*, and such *as required a military force to support civil authority.*

With regard to the public transactions of the town, when legally assembled, from which *alone* in your Excellency's declared opinion, the town could have any thing to apprehend, we beg leave to say: That after the most careful retrospect, and the best inquiry we could make, into the nature and import of those transactions, we are utterly at a loss, in what view they can appear to have militated with any law, or the British constitution of government. And we en-

treat your Excellency would condescend, to point out to us, in what particular respect, they either have been, or may be viewed in such a light; that either the town may be made sensible of the illegality of its proceedings, or, that upon the most critical examination, its innocence may appear in a *still clearer* light.

Your Excellency's high station in the province and the regard you have professed for the interest of the town, we humbly apprehend, must give propriety to this, as well as our former address.

Attest, WILLIAM COOPER, *Town Clerk.*

The Governor's Answer,

As in my answer to your former address I confined myself to you as Selectmen and the town as a body, I did not mean to refer to the disorders on the 18th of March or of the 10th of June, but to the transactions of the town meetings, and the proceedings of the Selectmen in consequence thereof.

FRA. BERNARD

Feb. 24, 1769

February 26[1]

This reply (*See the Governor's reply to the second address of the Selectmen, in our last Supplement.*)[2] is either wholly unintelligible, or a flat contradiction to the former one. The Governor in that, had publickly declar'd that in his opinion, the town had nothing to apprehend but from its own public acts, and the conduct of the Selectmen in their publications. If any thing may be gather'd from this last reply, it is, that he did not *mean* to say, the town had nothing to apprehend from some *other* transactions.— But whatever he meant, this he certainly did say.—It is not easy to know, what the Governor means by *confining himself* in his reply, to the town as a body, and to the Selectmen: Is not the town interested in every representation, of the conduct of its inhabitants that must greatly affect its welfare? Has it not already suffered, and greatly too, by a representation of the transactions in March and June last, that must from its effects, have been essentially differ-

[1] Items from February 26 to March 3, 1769, inclusive, are from the *New York Journal, Supplement,* April 6, 1769, p. 1.
[2] This comment by the newspaper editor is omitted from the *Journal* as reprinted elsewhere.

ent from that publish'd by his Majesty's Council.—And is it not like to be still farther injur'd by depositions and testimonies, taken in the most conceal'd manner? It must however, sooner or later, find a sure redress of these wrongs, in the justice of our gracious sovereign, and the British Parliament.

February 27

Our former predictions of what would be the unhappy effects of quartering troops in this town, have been too fully verified: They are now most wretchedly debauched, and their licentiousness daily increasing; a particular enumeration of instances thereof, would be as tedious, as it is painful.—Two women the other evening, to avoid the *solicitations* and *insults* of a soldier, took refuge in a house, at the south end of the town; the soldier was so audacious, as to enter with them: The cries of distress, brought the master of the family into the entry with a candle; and before he could know the occasion of the noise, he received, a stroke from the soldier with his cutlass, which brought him to the ground, where he lay senseless for some time, and suffered the loss of a quart of his blood.—Another woman not happening to please some soldiers, received a considerable wound on her head with a cutlass; and a 3rd. woman presuming to scream, when laid hold of by a soldier, had a bayonet run through her cheek: A number of persons passing the north watch house, were hailed by the centry; on their refusing to answer, the watchmen went out, when they perceived three officers with drawn swords, who with bad language grossly insulted them. — Two other officers passing by the dock-watch, being hailed were so very profane and abusive in their language, that the watchmen went out to them, when one of those officers drew his sword, and swore he would run the man through that should come near; they soon came to blows, by one of which the spear of a watchman's pole was broken, however the officers soon fled, and the watchmen could not overtake them, neither have they been able to make a discovery who were the assailants. But a still more extraordinary insult upon the citizens, was made the other night: It seems that it was wrongly apprehended, that an officer's dog had been shot by one Mr. Hemmingway, living near Winisimmit Ferry: To revenge the death of this animal, upon the supposed murderer, Lieutenant M—t of the 14th. Regiment, with a number of armed soldiers, entered Hemmingway's house, which they searched and ransacked, threatning to be the death of any man they should find there, to the no small terror and distress of the women and children of the family: Those offenders have been apprehended, and taken before Richard Dana, and John Ruddock, Esqrs. two of his Majesty's justices of peace, and have by them, been bound over to the Court of Assize, to be held next month, then to answer to the charges which shall be brought against them—But notwithstanding those offenders were thus dealt with! It did not deter some soldiers the next, and several succeeding nights, from insulting said house with stones and brick bats, firing off guns, &c. thereby renewing the terror of those belonging to the family, and greatly disturbing the whole neighbourhood.

February 28

We have advice from Halifax, that G—r C—p—ll, having returned from Boston without success, Mr. Frankland, their Lieutenant Governor, has sailed from thence for England; and that the chief design of this voyage at this season, is to make representation to Government, of the distressing circumstances of that province, occasioned by the withdraw of the King's troops, and ships of war, and also personal application that those ships and troops, may be replaced by others, in order to prevent the settlers from leaving that colony, and to secure the town of Halifax, against any sudden surprise, upon the breaking out of a new war, which they are very apprehensive of.

March 1

IN Messrs. Mein, and Flemming's paper of the 20th instant, there is this article. "That the centinel stationed near Oliver's dock, on the night of the 14th inst. saw the men who its supposed broke into Mr. Gray's store, making the attempt; But his orders being not to challenge any person unless an attack was made upon himself or on the house, at which he was stationed; like a good soldier he acted agreeable to his orders."—The intent of inserting this, was without doubt, to *insinuate* how *useful* our military guards might be for the protection of the town in the night, and the impropriety of disputing their right of challenging the inhabitants, which has occasioned its being laid aside. It is but just however to observe, that the centry mentioned above, was actually taken off from the house at Oliver's dock, in the morning of said day, and no one has been placed there since; and that it is notorious that there has not lately been a robbery or house-breaking in town, in which some soldiers were not either the principals or accomplices.

March 2

A Court of Admiralty relative to Mr. Hancock's libels, sat yesterday.—It is said the judge has given his decree upon the question mentioned, in our last Journal.—And it is said that the purport of it is, that considering the usage of the court, and the inconveniences that would attend the introduction of the rules of civil law, in cases of this nature, he decreed the question to be withdrawn.— As to the *usage* of the court, it might be observed, that there can *be none established* because there never was *such a case* in any Court of Admiralty, in the world; nor in *any other court*, for it is confidently affirmed that no prosecution for penalties and treble damages, was ever known in England even in the *Exchequer;* the officers there *contenting themselves* with the confiscating of ship and cargo if they can catch them; which is no doubt the most natural punishment of illegal importation—So that it is not easy to comprehend, by what usage this question is determined. As to the *inconveniencies;* these have not been sufficient to deter the court from introducing *interrogatories,* into such cases, which are *unknown* to the common law, and are odious to Englishmen; from setting at one place and another, at one time or another as pleasure directs, or policy, or convenience dictates, without any such *regular adjournments,* as in all courts of common law, are necessary—from issuing *compulsory* citations against witnesses—From ordering persons to be *arrested* and held *to high bail* to answer before the court *immediately,* without any number of days allowed as at common

law, to *compromise the suit* or prepare *for defence:* in all these cases, the court has adopted the rules of the *civil law,* in trials of matters, the jurisdiction of which is given it by act of Parliament.—Now where is the *criterion* but in *the judge's will,* to distinguish which rules of the civil law *shall,* and which *shall not* be adopted by the court?—If the *inconveniencies* have not been sufficient to prevent witnesses from being examined upon *interrogatories,* and the party from being *compelled* to take the oath of calumny, as in the case lately at S— Carolina; if a case should happen that should require it, or if the C—n—rs should give their mandate to the court, supposing them *hereafter* to get a judge fit for the purpose, why might he not gently put *parties* or *witnesses* to the torture, and extend them on the rack? Donec eorum rumpuntur nervi, et venae in sanguinis fluenta prorumpunt. It is reported that the advocates for Mr. Hancock, had no solicitude about the question they put to the witness, but they thought that if the court would proceed by such rules of the civil law, *as pleased the officers of revenue,* they had a right to *such rules* of the same law, *as made in favour of Mr. Hancock.*

March 3

The last month was inserted in this Journal, the votes and resolutions of the Assembly of Georgia, which reflect much honour on themselves and give great satisfaction to the friends of liberty; as they hereby perceive the union of the colonies to be complete; an event which must in a short space of time be productive of the happiest consequences. The speaker of the late House of Representatives for this province has just received the following letter.

Georgia Commons House of Assembly Dec. 24, 1768.

SIR,

In obedience to the resolution of this House, of which I inclose a copy, I have the satisfaction to acquaint you, that this House, truly sensible of the importance of the matters contained in your letter to them of the 11th of Feb. 1768. and of the motives which induced your House to communicate them by that letter, entirely approve of the measures pursued by your House to obtain redress of our common grievances and also of the method by them taken to communicate those measures to the other provinces on the continent. Having thus fulfilled the orders of the House, I shall only add that I sincerely wish and hope our most gracious sovereign, by equitably attending to the united representations of his American subjects, will remove every impediment to that harmony and union which ought to, and I trust ever will subsist, between our mother country and the colonies.

Signed, M. JONES, Speaker.

March 4[1]

A gentleman from Swanzey, writes,— Being a spectator, at the setting of the Assembly at Providence, I had the opportunity, of hearing the publick letters read,— among others, one in particular excited my curiosity; I therefore took it down in characters, from which I wrote the whole at large, and having heard the same read a second time, you may be assured the following is a correct copy: As it is of a pretty extraordinary nature, you are requested to insert it in your useful paper.
March 3d. 1769.   Yours.

No. 11. Circular, Duplicate.
Whitehall, September 2d. 1768.
Gentlemen,

The King having observed that the Governors of his colonies have upon several occasions, taken upon them to communicate to their Councils and Assemblies, either the whole or parts of letters, which they have received from his Majesty's principal Secretaries of State: I have it in command from his Majesty, to signify to you, that it is his Majesty's pleasure, that you do not upon any pretence whatever, communicate to the Assembly, any copies or extracts of such letters, as you shall receive from his Majesty's principal Secretaries of State, unless you have his Majesty's particular directions for so doing.

I am gentlemen, your most obedient, humble servant,

HILLSBOROUGH

Governor & Company of the
Colony of Rhode-Island.

One cannot but observe, that this letter intended for the direction of the Governor's conduct alone, and requiring him not to communicate upon any pretence whatever, to the Assemblies, copies or extracts of letters from the Secretaries of State, without special leave, is directed to the Governor & Company. And it might perhaps have been no *disservice* to Government, and no *dishonour* to the Secretary for the American Department, if some of his letters had been totally and forever *concealed*. His letter to G—r B—d requiring him *to dissolve the Assembly* of the Massachusetts in case of *non-rescinding*, had better have been *kept secret*.—The Secretary was charged in Parliament, with *threatening a corporation* in order to *command* its decisions; even Mr. *George Grenville* spake of this order, in the House of Commons, as an *unwarrantable stretch of power*. Had this letter never been communicated to the Massachusetts House, this charge on the Secretary of State, would have been avoided, and much trouble saved *to himself, as well as to his friends*, in their attempt to vindicate it. They said it was never *designed* to be communicated, and was a direction only for the *Governor's* conduct, being directed to *him*, and not to the *House*.—But it was laid before the *House*, by the Governor, and so became a menace *in form* to a *free* assembly, as full as if it had been directed to *them*: Tho' through the virtue and never to be forgotten firmness of the members, it had not the intended effect. How far G. B. *mistook* or *exceeded* the intention of the Secretary, I pretend not to say, but leave this *dark* point to be settled *between themselves.*

It is to be wish'd, that the letters from the great officers at home were more carefully attended to, and founded upon a more *accurate* knowledge of the *constitution* of the colonies, their *true* state & temper, and the *methods* by which they might be made *most serviceable* to the parent country. —We have heard that L. H. gave orders to the G—r of P—a, in case the Assembly of that province did not act *conformably* to his pleasure, *immediately* to dissolve them. Whereas it is an inherent privilege of that House, to sit on its *own* adjournments, and not in the power of *any Governor* to dissolve

---

[1] Items from March 4 to March 7, inclusive, are from the *Boston Evening Post*, May 1, 1769, p. 1.

them. —Such mistakes, and many others of much greater importance, that have taken place, shews the *wisdom* of the British government, in *granting* originally to the several colonies, a government among themselves, founded upon its own happy model. —A government, tho' *subordinate*, yet *sacred* and *inviolable*, and not to be *controuled* in its grand principles. —For if the colonies, are bound to make no laws *repugnant* to those of Great-Britain, it is at least equally reasonable that Great-Britain should make none for the colonies, *inconsistent* with their essential rights, as British subjects, and *repugnant* to the spirit and first principles of the British constitution.

March 5

Letters from South Carolina, mention, That if the revenue acts, *for the repeal whereof, this whole continent have earnestly and unanimously petitioned*, be not speedily repealed, the generality of the people of that province, will strictly adhere to several resolutions they have lately entered into, for establishing oeconomy, incouraging provincial labour, and keeping more money in the colonies; amongst which, are the following. 1st. Not to purchase or cause to be purchased, any goods whatever imported from G. B. except hard ware. 2d. To go heartily to work in manufacturing their own, and Negroes clothing. 3d. To avoid as much as possible, the purchasing of new Negroes. 4th. To give all possible encouragement to the importation of such goods (not prohibited) as are manufactured in other of his Majesty's colonies. 5th. Totally to disuse all kinds of mourning, &c.

We have also the pleasure of being advised from Philadelphia, that their merchants were about signing articles, not to import any more English goods, and that there was no doubt of their abiding by them. The friends of America on the other side the water, having clearly pointed it out to them, as a measure absolutely necessary to be *immediately* taken, if they would hope for a full redress of our present grievances.

March 6

The quartering troops upon British Americans, in time of peace, is quite repugnant to the Bill of Rights, and a measure that always has been considered as an intolerable grievance, by a free people—Bold and daring as the present M—rs have shewn themselves, in the rapid inroads they have made upon the British constitution; they have yet modestly aimed at saving appearances, with respect to the troops that have been cruelly intruded upon this town.—A pretence has been framed, that the aid of the military was absolutely necessary to preserve order in the town, and support the civil magistrate in the execution of his duty; and the M—y have declared to the world that they were to act no otherwise than as their assistants. This covering, which the M—y have endeavoured to wrap themselves in, has proved too scanty for the purpose; and the cloven foot is visible to every American. Preceding articles in this Journal, evince what friends the military have proved to the peace and order of the town, and the following relation, among others, will satisfy the publick, what kind of support the civil magistrate can reasonably expect from such a quarter.

As some sailors were passing near Mr. Justice Ruddock's house, the other night, with a woman in company, they were met by a number of soldiers, one of whom, as usual with those people, claimed the woman for his wife; this soon bro't on a battle in which the sailors were much bruised, and a young man of the town, who was only a spectator, received a considerable wound on his head; a great cry of murder, brought out the justice, and his son, into the street; when the former who is a gentleman of spirit, immediately laid his hands upon two of the assailants, and called out to one who pretended to be an officer, and all other persons present, requiring them in his Majesty's name to assist him as a magistrate, in securing those rioters; instead of this, he was presently surrounded with thirty or forty soldiers, who had their bayonets in their hands, notwithstanding the unseasonable time of night; some of whom endeavoured to loose his hold of the persons he had seized, but not being able to do it, they then made at him with their fists and bayonets; when he received such blows as obliged him to seek his safety by flight; they struck down a young woman at his door holding out a candle, and followed him and son into the entry-way of his house with their bayonets, uttering the most profane & abusive language, and swearing they would be the death of them both; upon the first assault given to the magistrate, one of the persons present posted away to the Town-House, and acquainted the commanding officer of the picquet guard, of what was taking place; but it seems that officer did not apprehend himself at liberty to order a party out to secure, or disperse those riotous drunken soldiers. Due enquiry is making for the discovery of those daring offenders, in order to their being presented to the grand jury, a bayonet wrested from one of the pursuers in the entry, may lead to a knowledge of the owner, and be a means of procuring proof. — This magistrate who has before shewn himself to be an enemy to every kind of riot and disorder; has had many threats lately thrown out against him, and suffered no little insult and disquiet: The other evening a petty officer of one of the ships of war, who had knocked down a married woman of this town, as she was quietly passing the streets, was bro't before him; and being reproved for his indecent speech & behaviour, on trial, he swore that he would run his jack-knife thro' the magistrates heart, whereupon the justice committed him to goal: soon after as several fishermen were coming out of a tavern in the same part of the town, they were assaulted by a corporal and some soldiers, who wounded one of the fishermen very grievously, they were soon apprehended, and brought before the said justice, who was kept up the chief part of the night on the occasion. In short, disorders and violences, are so increasing, that it is said this magistrate is intending an application to his Majesty's Council, for their countenance and assistance, in raising and arming such a number of the inhabitants as may be sufficient to secure himself and the inhabitants from receiving any future insults from Lord H—b—gh's *military peace preservers*.

March 7
The inhabitants of the New England governments really seem in earnest to promote industry, by encouraging home manufactures; for this we are under the greatest advantages, having wool, flax and other raw materials in plenty, and the quantity annually increasing; new and skilful artizans are daily multiplying upon us, and may already find full employ.—In Rhode-Island, it's now expected that gentlemen in office recommend themselves to their constituents, by encouraging and patronizing their own manufactures, and so earnest are many of the inhabitants to save their country from ruin, that they have resolved not to give their votes for any of the candidates at their ensuing election, who do not appear principally clothed in cloth manufactured either in that, or other American colonies.—Connecticut is in a like respect, become an example worthy of imitation, their clergy and those in office among them, pride themselves in being clothed by the industry of their wives and children, with the wool and flax of their own growth.—The people of New-Hampshire, are making progress in their manufactures, and it is with as much pleasure, as truth, we can tell the world, that the inhabitants of the Massachusetts, already provide themselves with the chief part of their necessary clothing.—Several well approved schemes are now on foot in Boston, for the employment of our poor, under very able direction,—a great number of suits of homespun cloth are subscribed for, by its principal gentlemen.—The clergy and men in office through the province, countenance and encourage this spirit of industry; and the man, be his family or estate ever so distinguish'd, is now more respected with an honest home made garment, than if he were clad with the most gaudy attire of the East. These are some of the happy effects, flowing from the injudicious burdens and restrictions laid upon our foreign trade; and the resentment which Americans have taken, at having their assemblies dissolv'd for not complying with the mandates of a M—r, and at the steps taken to *dragoon* rather than *reason* us into a submission to the late measures of A—d—n.

March 8[1]
The following letter from a gentleman in Connecticut, does in a sprightly manner

---

[1] Item for March 8 is from the *Boston Evening Post*, May 8, 1769, p. 1, which also contains the items for March 9 to March 15, inclusive, and most of the item for March 16.

convey the sentiments of the judicious in the several colonies, respecting the late violent and affrontive measures of Ad—n, and their hopes of the happy tendency they may finally have to promote the trade and establish the liberties of North-America.

"I am glad the troops are come and, believe their arrival will be for the health of this country.—There is a great deal of oratory in the glitter of arms; and a few ships of war contain all the arts of persuasion. A cannon ball carries with it, solid and weighty arguments; and a thrust in the side with a bayonet, will give conviction in a moment. I imagine we are now convinced of the necessity of leaving off trade with the people of Great-Britain, and the danger of meddling with their manufactures till they are in a better humour, and will rescind their resolutions of taking our money out of our pockets without our consent: We have paid dear enough for being infatuated with this destructive trade, it is the source of almost all the mischiefs and confusion, that has happened in the land; and it is time the inchantment was broke, and our attention turned upon the productions of America; we are able to live within ourselves, and have business enough at home, without gadding abroad after every knick knack, and trinket that is worked up in Great-Britain, and as we can't be persuaded into such a wholsome practice by lenitive and moderate means, we must be brought to the exercise of reason by vigorous measures, and the point of the bayonet becomes necessary to fix the conviction. Preparations of steel and surgical instruments, when lenitives fail, often times produce wonderful effects, and are frequently used in opening the eyes of the blind.—If we were not a dull stupid race of mortals, and had seasonably relinquished the trade to Great-Britain, the operation of cutlary ware, and the rhetoric of red coats, would be of no service; but as matters now stand, the eyes of many want couching, and these surgical operations must take off the film, and bring us to our senses, and to measures that are so confessedly for our interest.

To speak without a metaphor.—The troops are highly necessary to clog, em-barrass & obstruct the importation of British manufactures, and to give us clear and distinct conceptions of the nature and tendency of the late revenue acts; and herein I think they will apparently co-operate with the measures we are pursuing, promote the cause we are pleading, and be a means of fixing our attention upon the only means of our safety. America is greatly indebted to the troops, and highly obliged to the sagacity and fore-sight of that incomparable politician G—r B—d for procuring them. And for my part, I cannot but consider the military parade, and every insult and abuse which the people of Boston meet with from the soldiery, as a comment upon the Farmer's Letters, a confirmation of his observations, and I believe they will serve as an expositor, to illustrate & set his reasonings, if possible, in a more clear, conclusive & striking light, and convince Americans of the inestimable worth of liberty, and establish them in the lasting enjoyment of it.

March 9[1]

The procedure of G. B.[2] the C—m—rs, &c. with respect to the trade of this province is such, that the most just and impartial representation thereof must be the greatest reproach on their official conduct and characters: The appearance of guarda coastas, and custom-house boats in our harbour, and the parade of tide waiters, land waiters, surveyors, searchers, and we know not what other kinds of custom and revenue officers, on our wharves, is useless, and is extravagantly ridiculous, as is that of the troops in our streets and commons.— All this may indeed lead foreigners to conclude, that the chief part of our commerce is really detrimental & ruinous to our mother country, and that it is intended wholly to annihilate it.—The error of the former part of the conclusion, may be pointed out hereafter, but the verity of the latter must appear from the following relations,—A small schooner from Maryland, with a load of corn, when coming into the harbour, was at different times, boarded with no less than four boats from our guarda costas, and searched and rummaged by those marine

---

[1] Items from March 9 to March 18, inclusive, are from the *New York Journal, Supplement*, April 13, 1769, pp. 1–2.

[2] *The Boston Evening Post*, omits "G. B." from its item for this date.

custom-house officers; and no sooner had she touched the wharf, than four land and tide waiters, &c. took possession of her, for another search, and to inspect her unloading: Our other provision vessels have been dealt with in much the same manner. A sloop from the West Indies, last from the Vineyard, was no sooner arrived in the harbour, than one Manwaring,[1] lately brought from Quebec, as a suitable person to answer the purposes of the C—m—rs, came on board, bringing a number of other officers as assistants, who with dark lanthorns, gimblets, spears for the piercing of casks, spits and other implements of modern introduction, made a thorough rummage and search of the hold and cabbin, when happening to find a small case which contained scarce six quarts of foreign spirits, part of the captain's sea stores, this faithful officer tho't himself obliged to carry off the same to his employer; the master then reported at the custom-house, all the molasses which came in her from the West Indies, together with 40 lb. of indigo upon oath; informing at the same time, that having received damage to his rudder, while at the Vineyard, he was obliged to take out part of this molasses, in order to repair the same; this it seems was construed by the C—m—rs as breaking bulk before an entry, and the vessel actually seized for the same, and the owner thereby obliged to make a journey to Boston, of above one hundred miles, at this difficult season for travelling; the cargo has been since released, but the owner is not yet certain that his vessel will not be libelled in a Court of Admiralty.

March 10

A ship from Lisbon with a load of salt, owned as it is said by Mr. Lane, of London, which has been arrived for some time, was the other day seized, and taken possession of by order of the C—m—rs. It seems one of the sailors had acquainted an emissary of the B—d, that while the ship was froze up at the Vineyard, part of the cargo had been sold: Upon the strictest enquiry it appears that the captain, had disposed of a few lemons, not more than 1500, and that this is the only pretence as yet made for

the seizure and detention of said ship and cargo.

March 11

A vessel from Maryland, loaded with corn and other grain, had a number of custom-house officers placed on board her, so soon as she got to a wharf, who proved that they were more sagacious, than the marine officers, who had rummaged her hold before them; for in their searches they actually found about forty pounds weight of refuse tobacco, stuffed near the masts, scarce worth four shillings sterling, to prevent the grain running into the bilge water, which has by the C—m—rs and their abettors, been thought a sufficient breach of the acts of trade, to justify their seizing and taking possession of said sloop—Whether more tobacco, or anything else may be turned out, when she is unloading that has not been reported at the custom-house, neither we nor the C—m—rs can as yet pretend to say: That vessels should be seized and taken from their owners upon such slight pretences in order to search for articles, upon which a libel may be founded, and a condemnation obtained, we may venture to affirm, is a practice not countenanced even in old countries, and a grievance that affords the American merchant a just cause of complaint.

March 12

Several vessels which had been seized and detained from the owners for a considerable time, to their very great damage, have been released to them again: One that had been libelled, has been cleared by a decree of the Judge of Admiralty, and some cargoes, which had been taken possession of by the custom-house officers, have been delivered up to their owners, while nothing has as yet been determined by them, with respect to the vessels—Those who are still concerned in trade, are continually distressed or alarmed, and know not how to conduct themselves; scarce a vessel enters at the Customhouse from a foreign voyage, but the captain is reminded by one or another of the custom-house or revenue-officers, that some omissions had been made in his papers of clearance, &c. for which he was liable to a seizure; and such advantages have been

---

[1] This name was written M—nw—g in the item as published in the *Boston Evening Post*.

taken by the C—m—rs of the little mistakes made by a master or the merchant, that shipping is now become the greatest burden, and our navigation is daily decreasing, which must be severely felt by the nation in a future war, an event which may too speedily take place—The seas cannot then be spread as they have been, with our private ships of war, and though the pockets of Americans, may then be forceably opened by a British M—r, he will certainly find, that preceding ones have drained them to the very bottom.

March 13

The Raven transport, one of the ships with troops from Ireland, parted with the rest of the fleet in distress, just before they arrived here in the fall; there was no intelligence of her for months after; happily she found the way to the West Indies.—The following letter contains some diverting particulars of her arrival there.

Nevis, Jan. 8, 1769.

Dr. Sir,

Some of his Majesty's forces arrived here that were design'd for your place *to keep you in good order*, the Colonel is a member of Parliament; full of expectations of your being a resty people, but he has been told here, that he will be made so happy in Boston, that he will forget the trouble Government had given him, by his jaunt to America to quell a rebellion that never had existence: Whilst I think of it, I must hand you a curious anecdote.—The night this transport, that was blown from North-America, turn'd the point of Nevis, (it being Christmas times, and martial law in force) some little mistake happened, and an alarm of five guns was fir'd from the fort: By the carelessness of the gunner, some of the shot were not drawn, and one or two whistled among the Raven's rigging.—The soldiers were mustered.—Some say with bayonets fixt, and "all rebels, both island & continent by G—d," was the word.—A boat with an officer, are said to have come on shore, to know whether this was *intentionally* against a ship in his Majesty's service.—By the return made by the officer, it was found there were no more signs of a rebellion there, than ever had appeared at Boston."

March 14

G—r B—d's picture has been lately returned to Harvard-College to be *hung* up in the library: Our American limner, Mr. Copely, by the surprising art of his pencil, has actually restored as *good a heart* as had been taken from it; tho' upon a near and accurate inspection, it will be found to be no other than *a false one*.—There may it long remain *hanging*, to shew posterity the true picture of the man, who during a weak and w—d Ad—n, was suffered to continue in the s—t of G—m—t, a sore scourge to the people, until he had happily awakened a whole continent to a thorough sense of their own interest, and thereby laid the foundation of American greatness.

March 15

Last Monday there was a meeting of the freeholders, and other inhabitants, of this town, for the choice of town officers, &c. when a number of respectable gentlemen were appointed committees, "To consider what was proper to be done relative to the trespasses which have been made by the soldiery, on the town's land, and to prevent like trespasses, for the future; or what steps may be necessary for the town to take in addition to what has been already done by the Selectmen, for vindicating the character of the inhabitants, and obtaining the knowledge of such representations as may have been made to their prejudice.—As also of the measures that can be taken to check the progress of vice, and immoralities, now breaking in upon the town like a flood; and of some suitable methods for employing the poor of the town, whose numbers and distresses are daily increasing, by the loss of its trade and commerce; which committees are to report to the town at the adjournment of the meeting on Tuesday the 4th of April next.

March 16

Being Thursday, we are informed orders have been given out to the soldiery, that they keep in their barracks from Friday 9 o'clock until the Lord's day following; and that every man be provided with six rounds of powder & ball: The picquet guards were also ordered to hold themselves in readiness to turn out at a minute's warning.—Various are the conjectures of the inhabitants on this occasion; some think that it is in order to restrain their men from all extravagance upon the morrow, which is Saint Patrick's day, while others are of the mind, that it is in consequence of some reports which have been propagated, that there are to be effigies hung upon the Tree of Liberty, on the Saturday, being the anniversary of the repeal of the Stamp Act, and that great disturbances are then like to take place; it seems the G—r would have it thought so, or he would not have told his C—l not long since, that he had been informed of such intentions, and that he gave them this advice, that they might consider before hand the part they had to act, as he should certainly call upon them for their advice and assistance in case it should so happen.— We apprehend such reports are only propagated by the cabal to answer certain purposes of their own, and that the behaviour of the Sons of Liberty on that day will be still, as it ever has been, such as cannot reflect any dishonour upon themselves, or in any respect tend to create the least disturbance among us.

March 17

Instances of the licentious and outrageous behaviour of the *military conservators* of the peace still multiply upon us, some of which are of such a nature, and have been carried to so great lengths, as must serve fully to evince that a late vote of this town, calling upon the inhabitants to provide themselves with arms for their defence, was a measure as *prudent* as it was *legal;* such violences are always to be apprehended from military troops, when quartered in the body of a populous city; but more especially so, when they are led to believe that they are *become necessary to awe a spirit of rebellion*, injuriously said to be existing therein. It is a natural right which the people have reserved to themselves, confirmed by the Bill of Rights, to keep arms for their own defence; and as Mr. Blackstone observes, it is to be made use of when the sanctions of society and law are found insufficient to restrain the violence of oppression.—We are however, pleased to find that the inhabitants of this town, under every insult and outrage, received from the soldiery, are looking up to the laws of the land, for redress; and if *any influence* should be powerful enough to *deprive* the meanest subject of *this security;* the people will not be answerable for the *unhappy consequences* that may flow therefrom.

March 18

A woman of this town, was struck down the other evening near the rope-walks, and much abused and wounded by a soldier; another woman, when passing the streets, was served in the same brutal manner, and then robb'd of a bundle of linen she had under her arm; as was also a pedlar coming into town, from whom they took about forty dollars.—And a still more daring attempt was made the Monday before last. When the post-rider, with the mails for Rhode-Island, New-London, New-York, Philadelphia, &c. &c. &c. was assaulted on Boston Neck, just after sun-set, as he was setting out on his journey, by four or five persons, who appeared dress'd as officers, one of them took his sword from his belt, and with the small end in his hands, struck the rider on the head with the hilt, that it forc'd the sword out of the scabbard, and went to a considerable distance:—The rider recovering himself, inform'd them that he was on his Majesty's service, whereupon they all ran off. The rider would have returned to town, but as there had been stoppages lately, occasioned by the bad travelling, he was determined not to be the means of the mail's returning out of season, he went on, and at the first stage had his head bath'd, which was considerably swelled with the blow; he reached New-Port on Wednesday, from whence he employed another person to perform for him the last week.

March 19[1]

But while the persons and properties of the inhabitants, are suffering such repeated injuries from the soldiery: G. B. and the C—m—rs go on, exercising their severities against the merchants.—A vessel belonging to this town, just returned from the West-Indies, has been seized and taken possession of by a party of the revenue officers; the only pretence therefor, being this; that while the vessel lay at the Vineyard wind bound,

---

[1] Items for March 19 to March 24, inclusive, are from the *New York Journal, Supplement*, April 27, 1769, p. 1.

one of the seamen took the liberty to dispose of his adventure, which was not more than half a barrel of molasses: This information, it is said was obtain'd through the instrumentality of one of their gang, who it seems had found means to influence a common sailor to make this notable discovery.— Some hogsheads and barrels of molasses, which came from Newbury, have also been seized and carried off to the custom-house store; a most extraordinary procedure! the captain of said vessel, having declared, when he reported this cargo at the custom-house, that he could not ascertain the exact quantity taken on at Newbury, as the mate's and seamen's adventures were unknown to him, and therefore requested that it might be noted, that he desired a post entry, those adventures were therefore not taken out of the vessel, but only hoisted upon deck at noon-day, where they were to have remained until the captain had made the proposed entry, had they not been taken from thence, as above recited.

March 20

Saturday last being the anniversary of the repeal of the Stamp Act, the same was noticed as has been usual. The British flag was displayed on Liberty Tree, and at noon a number of gentlemen met in the hall under the same, where a number of loyal toasts were drank, and the greatest order and decorum observed by the company.

The confinement of the soldiery to their barracks upon Saturday, together with a wicked report, which was spread among them by our enemies, that the Sons of Liberty had intended, to expose the effigy of St. Patrick, upon the Tree of Liberty, on said day, so provoked our military, that numbers of the three companies, quartering at Murray's sugar-house, determined to sally forth that night, and cut down the Tree of Liberty; accordingly, just before 11 o'clock the signal was given by firing a gun, as was intended, over the guard house, when by carelessness they fired a brace of balls through the same, but happily hurt no one; immediately thereupon every man was out with his arms complete; and also axes and saws, to demolish the Tree of Liberty; one soldier in his freak, fired a ball from one room to another, and shot the tail of a sergeant's shirt off, but did no other damage:

The officers were immediately alarmed, and by their intreaties and promise of pardon; the soldiery returned to their barracks, and remained quiet through the night.

March 21

We are advised from Providence, that on the 18th of March, a day auspicious to American freedom, early in the morning a paper appeared on Liberty Tree, and another in the most public part of the town, of the following contents,

To the SONS of LIBERTY.

DEARLY BELOVED,

Revolving time hath brought about another anniversary of the repeal of the odious Stamp-Act—an act framed to divest us of our liberties, and to bring us to slavery, poverty and misery. The resolute stand made by the Sons of Liberty against the detestable policy, had more effect in bringing on the repeal, than any conviction in the P—rl-m—t of G—t-B—n of the injustice and iniquity of the act.— It was repealed from principles of convenience to O—d–E—d, and accompanied with a declaration of their right to tax us. And since the same P—t have passed acts, which, if obeyed in the colonies, will be equally fatal.—Although the people of G—t-B—n be only fellow subjects, they have (of late) assumed a power to compel us to buy at their market such things as we want, of European produce and manufacture; and at the same time have taxed many of the articles, for the express purpose of a revenue; and, for the collection of the duties, have sent fleets, armies, commissioners, guarda costas, judges of admiralty, and a host of petty officers, whose insolence and rapacity have become intolerable.—Our cities are garrisoned—the peace and order which heretofore dignified our streets, are exchanged for the horrid blasphemies and outrages of soldiers—Our trade is obstructed—Our vessels and cargoes, the effects of industry, violently seized; and, in a word, every species of injustice that a wicked and debauched ministry could invent, is now practised against the most sober, industrious and loyal people, that ever lived in society.—The joint supplications of all the colonies have been rejected, and letters and mandates, in terms of the highest affront and indignity, have been transmitted from little and insignificant servants of the Crown, to his Majesty's grand and august sovereignties in America.

These things being so, it becomes us, my brethren, to walk worthy of our vocation—to use every lawful mean, to frustrate the wicked designs of our enemies at home and abroad—and to unite against the evil and pernicious machinations of those who would destroy us. I judge that nothing can have a better tendency to this grand end than encouraging our own manufactures, and a total disuse of foreign superfluities.

When I consider the corruption of G—t-B—n—their load of debt—their intestine divisions, tumults and riots—their scarcity of provision—and the contempt in which they are held by the nations about them; and when I consider, on the other hand, the state of the American colonies, with regard to the various climates soils, produce, rapid population, joined to the virtue of the inhabitants, I cannot but think that the conduct of O—d-E—d towards us, may be permitted by divine wisdom, and ordained by the unsearchable providence of the Almighty, for hastening a period dreadful to G—t-B—n.

A SON of LIBERTY.

Providence,
March 18, 1769.

The above among other articles of a like tenor, have been inserted in this Journal, with an honest intention, to convey to the people of Britain, the unhappy tho' powerful tendency of the late measures, respecting America, to alienate our affections and excite such resentments, as must be productive of the most unhappy consequences to Great-Britain; consequences which we are surprised, that the weakest states-man and most short sighted politician, should not have fully apprehended.

March 22

Governor Bernard, has published a proclamation, for a general fast to be kept the 6th of April next.—It has been observed, that in all the proclamations of his predecessors on such occasions, they never once omitted, the following supplicatory article, viz. "That God would be graciously pleased to continue to us, the enjoyment of all our invaluable privileges, of a civil and religious nature." But that our present Governor has not once inserted such a clause.—We are not at a loss however, to account for said omission.—This gentleman had not been long among us, before he discovered a *dislike* of our constitution, and a *disposition* to get the same *new modeled,* as soon as an opportunity presented, this accounts for all his conduct, relative to the Stamp Act, at which time his speeches and letters, as well as his conversation clearly discovered, that he was making the most daring attempts to effect his detestable purposes; may the people of this province, unite in their supplications on the approaching fast, that those inestimable privileges may still be preserved, and transmitted *inviolate* to the latest posterity.

March 23

We have before mentioned the spirited resolves, which had passed the Assembly of North-Carolina, they carry in themselves, the best compliment, to the good sense and patriotism of those worthy members.—The speaker of the late House of Representatives for this province, has just received the following letter.

North-Carolina, Newbern, 10th Nov. 1768.
SIR.

The House of Assembly of this colony being prorogued to the 3d instant, prevented my sooner laying before them your very important letter of the 11th of February last, the purport of which they proceeded immediately to take into their consideration. And I am directed to inform you that they are extremely obliged to the Assembly of the Massachusetts-Bay, for communicating their sentiments on so interesting a subject; and shall ever be ready, firmly to unite with their sister colonies, in pursuing every constitutional measure, for redress of the grievances so justly complain'd of.

This House is desirous to cultivate the strictest harmony and friendship with the Assemblies of the colonies in general, and with your House in particular.

With you we entertain the strongest confidence of his Majesty's clemency and justice; nor do we doubt but that the dutiful and united supplications of his loyal American subjects, will meet with his most gracious favour and acceptance.

This House have therefore taken the earliest opportunity permitted them, of pursuing measures for obtaining redress, similar to those adopted by your's, and have directed their agent *Henry Eustice McCulloh*, Esq; to join the agents of the other colonies in obtaining a repeal of those oppressive acts of Parliament imposing duties on paper, glass, &c. in America.

The Assembly of this colony will at all times receive with pleasure, the opinion of your house in matters of general concern to America, and be equally willing on every such occasion to communicate their sentiments, not doubting of their meeting a candid and friendly acceptance. In the name, and by order of the House of Assembly.

I am, with great regard,

Sir, Your most obedient humble servant,

JOHN HARVEY, Speaker.

To the Hon. Thomas Cushing, *Esq;* late *Speaker, &c.*

The above letter completes the answers to our Circular Letter.—The colonies no longer disconnected, form one body; a common sensation possesses the whole, the circulation is complete; and the vital fluid returns from whence it set out.—If this circulation is kept up, its constitution will be firm and durable.

March 24

Not long since, there was a promise given in Messrs. Fleet's paper, by a person unknown, of a *full* answer to the Farmer, in a series of letters; it was never imagin'd that this large promise could be fulfill'd; tho' it excited some expectation.—At length the mountain brings forth,—and there appears in the Evening-Post, as strange, awkward, uncouth a figure of a writer, as ever thrust himself into public view; without any traces of parts or education, reason or humour, strength or fancy, taste or even grammar: He opposes himself to a writer possessed of all: The expectation he had rais'd, was soon changed into ridicule, and the public laugh at this *misshapen object*, whose *malignity*

against the rights of America, fully justifies what might otherwise appear an *inhuman* diversion. This wretch however, has tho't himself qualified, (and perhaps for once he has tho't right) to make a panegyric, upon one of the principal authors of the troubles of America, and the perplexities of Britain. No one can doubt, that like other late prostitutes, he writes for a large fee, and if it should bear any proportion to the public *scorn*, which falls to his own share, and that of the cause in which he is engag'd; it must be a *large* one indeed.

March 25[1]

A number of resolves, said to be the resolves of the H—e of L—ds respecting American affairs have, made their appearance in all our newspapers.

The resolves, lately published in our papers as the Lord's, it is said were introduced into the House by L— H—h, and seconded by the D. of B—d; but were opposed, among others by the Duke of R—d and Lord Sh—ne.[2] Lord Sh—ne said he had his sentiments of American affairs, which he reserved to the time when those affairs would come before the house in a more important view. The Duke of R—d spoke strongly against the resolves, and appealed to their L—ps whether it was equitable, or could tend to the honour of that august body, or give to the Americans at this critical season, an advantageous and respectful idea of the British Government, to decide upon such important questions, when the accounts that lay before them, were all from one side, and whole realms were to be condemn'd unheard; without being allowed any opportunity of refuting or alleviating the charges laid against them, or even knowing what those charges were.—This weighty objection, it seems, did not prevent the passing the resolves; though we cannot find that any lord offered any satisfactory reply to it, from the principles of reason and equity, or the spirit of the British constitution, so favourable to the subject, and mild to the accused.

The M—y greatly wanted, and no doubt strenuously exerted themselves, to procure a s—h[3] at the opening of Parliament, and

---

[1] Items for March 25 to March 27, inclusive, are from the *New York Journal, Supplement*, May 4, 1767, p. 1.
[2] Duke of Rutland and Lord Shelburne.
[3] Speech.

such resolutions from both Houses, as might prove a sanction to their own impolitic and violent measures respecting America. To whose misrepresentations, these ruinous measures to both countries, are principally owing no one is at a loss to determine. A dark cabal here, have left no means unemployed, to beguile the leading men in the British Government, into these measures, and to create a pretence, a very false one indeed, for enforcing them by a military power. A—n is fallen into the snare; and ashamed to confess its own weakness; and not knowing how to make an honourable retreat, fly to P—t for protection. It is certain that among sixty papers, laid before the Lords, which are also to come before the Commons, more than thirty are letters from G—r B—d to the Secretary of State.

Some among us are of opinion that these resolutions, as we have seen no copy published by authority, must be spurious, for they cannot suppose that a majority of the House of L—ds wou'd ever so severely condemn the Circular Letter of the Massachusetts House of Assembly, which implies nothing but a right in British subjects to unite in humble supplications to the throne. Good God! If this is denied us, this last refuge of the miserable, what have we left!

It is also deemed highly improbable that any one should dare, so far to impose upon such an august assembly, as to lead them to call the letter of the Selectmen to the several towns, a PRECEPT, when it assum'd no shadow of authority; and to condemn a large number of as loyal subjects as any in the British Empire, for meeting together to recognize and strengthen the authority of Government, to petition their sovereign under their grievances, and to promote order and a good temper among their fellow subjects, towards all which salutary purposes their meeting was known to have a happy influence at a very critical season. Whatever grounds there may or may not be for suppositions, we are told by our friends on the other side the water, that some of the resolves of the Lords will meet with opposition in the House of Commons. But even the copy of them that has appear'd here is far from being pleasing to the cabal! They suppose that all the resolutions, except the last, are design'd to lie in the Journals, and

have all their effect there; they find nothing said of disfranchising the town of Boston, of annulling the constitutional assemblies of the several towns, of vacating provincial charters, and appointing the Council of the Massachusetts by the King, &c.—This is the game at which they have play'd, and in which they are greatly disappointed.

The last resolve, which all the foregoing were design'd to introduce, perplexes and chagrins them: There is a formal address of the Lords beseeching the King, to require the Governor of the Massachusetts to do, what is not only his indispensible duty, but that of every good subject. According to this resolve it seems their Lordships, with all the artful and agravated accounts of G. B. before them, cannot as yet find any satisfactory evidence of treason or misprision of treason.—They appear to have expected this, but *the proof fails*. They therefore supplicate his Majesty to require Governor Bernard to make *further* enquiry— This is particularly distressing to the *cabal:* Their whole force now lies before Parliament, and so far are they from being able to make any addition to it, that plain and indisputable facts, if attended to, must invalidate what they have already offered.— When we reflect upon the treatment America in general, and this province in particular has receiv'd, and trace the methods by which the great have been abused, and the *whole empire shaken.*—What bosom burns not in its country's cause?

March 26

The new commission, constituting Robert Auchmuty Esq; Judge of Admiralty, &c. was read in *open* Court of Admiralty, and upon a motion made by the King's advocate, the prosecutions which have for many months past been carrying on against John Hancock, Esq; and other gentlemen of this town were dropt—We cannot help remarking at present, that one of the witnesses summoned on the part of the crown in these vexatious prosecutions, stands presented by the grand jury of the county for perjury, in this very instance; but we shall defer a full narration of the infamous steps taken by the C—m—rs without the least shadow of proof, to harass and if possible, to ruin the fortunes, as well as reputations, of gentlemen of the most distinguished and unblemished character; until we shall have leisure to make it the particular object of our attention.

March 27

The grand jury for the county of Suffolk, broke up last week, having sat a longer time than usual; among other bills found by the said jury are one against Capt. J—n W—n, for stirring up, exciting, and encouraging the Negro slaves in Boston to a conspiracy against their masters; one against Lieut. M—r, of the 14th. Regiment, quartered in this town, and a number of soldiers, for forceably breaking open and entering the dwelling house of Mr. John Hemmingway in the night, with design to revenge the murder of a favourite dog; another against a number of soldiers, for way-laying, assaulting, and smiting, some inhabitants of the town in the night, —another against a number of soldiers, for assaulting with drawn cutlasses and bayonets; smiting and wounded, John Ruddock, Esq; one of his Majesty's justices of the peace, when suppressing a riot at the north part of the town, late at night, in which they were actors; and another bill against one Joseph Muzzele for perjury in the case between the King and John Hancock Esq; lately pending in the Court of Vice Admiralty—Mr. Att—y then laid before the jury, a recognisance of one S—s B—r of Connecticut, to answer at the court of assize, to the charge of enticing soldiers to desert from the regiments quartered among us, but there not being any kind of proof produced to support said charge.— No bill was found against him.—The behaviour of the K—g's Att—y while attending the jury was in their opinion, no other than might be expected from one who had lately received so many lucrative court favours through the instrumentality of a G—r, to whose views he had for some years past rendered himself quite subservient.— What treatment the bills referred to, will meet with when laid before the C—t, a little time must determine.—If the dignity of a b—ch of j—s, and the peace and security of the subject, are to be sacrificed to the perverse will and evil intentions of a G—r

and C—rs. The province is then, in a pitiable case indeed.

March 28[1]

The charge and vexation of clearing out vessels coasting from one part of the province to another, is a growing evil.—The master of a vessel, owned at Duxbury, a town in the port of Boston, to which harbour the coasters go and return in about a fortnight, having taken some necessaries on board for the people dwelling there, was, as all others are, obliged to clear out, &c. The charge of which amounted to three dollars; a large tax upon the English merchandize transported from port to port, in the course of a year, and a great discouragement to our trade and navigation,—Sufferances must be obtained at the custom-house, before shot, powder, rum, sugar, molasses and any triffling articles are taken into a coaster: A brazier of this town put a bar of steel on board one of these boats for a customer, and offered to swear it was English; this was not satisfactory, unless he would swear to the very vessel this bar was imported in; this could not be done by him, as the steel in his store had been mixt; the skipper was therefore prevented from receiving it on board, and obliged to return it back to the brazier: A merchant of this town, was put to the like difficulty, respecting a box of Bristol glass, and another relative to a chest of English tea: And we are told, that in consequence of orders from the C—m—rs, it is required at the custom house, when a barrel of sugar, rum, and a few pounds of coffee, &c. &c. &c. are reported for shipping to any place even in this harbour, that instead of the usual certificate from the merchant, that those goods were legally imported and had paid the imposed duties, the vender of such articles must make oath, as to the vessel it was imported in; and also the *purchaser*, that they are the same; and even the *truckman* is to give evidence that such goods have been put on board those coasters.—*The confusion which must be occasioned by such before unheard of requirements, in a new country, whose settlers are scattered along an extensive sea shore, and are constantly needing supplies, are as obvious, as the illegality and impolicy of*

---

[1] Items from March 28 to April 2, inclusive, are from the *New York Journal, Supplement*, May 11, 1769, p. 1.

those and such like proceedings of the American B—d of C—rs.

March 29

By the number of vessels, brought into this, and other American harbours, by our little guarda costas, we might be ready to conclude, there had been a formal declaration of war against the trade and navigation of this continent, and that in the manner of pursuing it, the G—r and C—m—rs were determined to make it as distressing as possible.—A vessel owned in the colony of Connecticut, having received on board, several hogsheads of rum at the island of St. Christophers, for which a clearance could not be produced, was taken possession of by an English guarda costa, near the Vineyard, and is now brought into this harbour,—another vessel belonging to a gentleman in this town, returning from the West-Indies, being met with by a guarda costa at no great distance from this place, she was stopp'd and searched; and a trifle of coffee being found on board, she was seized; and the captain instead of bringing her into the port she was bound to, thought proper to carry her into Rhode-Island harbour.

March 30

It was early conceived, by the most sagacious and knowing nations, that a number of females had always determined the condition of men, by means of their spinning wheels: And Virgil intimates, that the golden age advanced slower, or faster as they spun.

"Talia saecla, suis dixerunt, currite Fusis
—— —— —— —— —— — Parcee."

And had the ladies, in every age since, ruled in this laudable way, perhaps some nations would be in a far better state than they now are, but be that as it will; I presume there never was a time when, or a place where, the spinning wheel could more influence the affairs of men, than at present, in this and the neighbouring colonies;—or sooner produce a golden age. The following relations and instances amongst a multitude of others, in all the colonies, of the industry and frugality, of American ladies, must exalt their characters in the eyes of the world, and serve to shew how greatly they are contributing to bring about the political salvation of a whole continent.

A gentleman at New-Port writes—"As I am a very great lover of liberty, of beauty, of music, of my country, and of all those who endeavour to promote and establish, by good oeconomy its wealth, peace, prosperity and tranquility, and being at the sign of Pitt's Head in this town, on Tuesday last, was extremely pleased by having admittance into the company of eleven of the Daughters of Liberty, ladies of character, and lovers of British freedom, and industry; each being laudably employed in playing on a musical instrument, called a spinning wheel, the melody of whose music, and the beauty of the prospect, transcending for delight, all the entertainments of my life. I was still more pleased with the ladies company, (when by inquiry) I had learnt more of their love of liberty, and strict attachment to their country's welfare, and of their determination of persevering in such laudable exercise and good oeconomy, as is a credit to the fair sex, and an honour to America.

For I found that, as these Daughters of Liberty, delight in each others company, they had agreed to make circular visits to each of their houses, and in order to excite emulation in serving their country, promoting temperance and industry, had determined to convert each visit into a spinning match, and to have no entertainments but what is the produce of their own country; and to appear as much as possible clothed with our own manufactures, and that more especially which is the effects of their own labour—The above-said ladies spun between 6 o'clock in the morning, and 6 o'clock in the evening, 37 skeins and 15 threads, which upon an average make three skeins five knots and five threads.

March 31

A gentleman in James-Town, also writes—as a proof that the Daughters of Liberty, in this town are not less zealous in promoting American manufactures, and the cause of constitutional liberty, than those of New-Port. I can assure you that eighteen ladies, of good fashion and character, of this town, and two from New-Port, met on Monday last at the house of Mr. James Carr, Junr. in order to try their dexterity, at a spinning match: And notwithstanding one was but eleven years old, and another left off at about two o'clock, they spun between sunrise and sun-set 78 skeins and nine knots of choice linen yarn; each skein containing 15 knots, and each knot 40 threads.—I will only observe to the honour of the above mentioned twenty in particular, and the fair sex in general.—That were the gentlemen really as sincere, and as much in earnest in promoting frugality, industry, and all other virtues, as the ladies are, there is not the least doubt, but we should soon free ourselves from the burdens with which we are now oppress'd, and lay the foundation of American liberty on a basis not to be shaken by any power on earth!

We are informed from North-Kingston, that last Friday, eleven neighbouring young ladies met together, at the house of John Congon, Esq; in this town, upon a spinning match; where they began to spin about sun-rise, and spun about forty six fifteen knotted skeins of good linen yarn, and left off about five in the afternoon of said day; when about as many young gentlemen, as there were ladies, came to said house, and opened a fine ball, as a recompence to the ladies, for their industry.

And from New-Port, that lately eleven ladies met at the house of Mr. Stephen Tripp, on the Point, and spun 34 skeins and seven knots of good linnen yarn,—Though the quantity they spun, was not so great as has been produced by some spinning matches, consisting of the same number; yet I believe it may with truth be said, that it exceeded in firmness, as the whole weighed but 4 lb. 5 oz. which is eight skeins to the pound.— To the honour of those ladies, it ought to be mentioned, that they refused the regale of the destructive Bohea, and were most of them dressed in clothes of their own spinning, and the others are resolutely determined to follow the laudable example as soon as possible.

April 1

WE are also advised from Huntington on Long-Island, that very lately a company of young ladies belonging to that town, to the number of sixteen, met to spend the day together, not in idle dissipation, (as is too often the case,) but with a truly laudable design of promoting industry, for they had no sooner met together, but to divert themselves, they each took their spinning wheels and applied themselves so closely and with that dexterity that at the close of the day, they had spun one hundred and seven skeins, in each skein were ten knots, which made in the whole one thousand and seventy knots, weighing thirty two pounds of very good linen yarn. The ladies were all decently clad in homespun, the manufacture of their own town; who like true female patriots, shewed by their conduct, that they despised to dress with the manufactures of a country that is endeavouring to enslave us.—It also appeared, that a female patriotism was predominant in their conduct, when the tea table was introduced; for instead of making use of any foreign tea, (which is become more nauseous since loaded with an unconstitutional tax,) they substituted a tea the growth of that town, called *Ever-Green*, which for its pleasant flavour, and many excellent qualities, is prefered by many to the best green tea.

April 2

There are shameful instances of some persons in all towns, who esteeming money the chief good, are not unwilling to dispense with troops being quartered among them, provided their gains may be thereby increased; the wise and good, who prefer the public prosperity to their own little interests, are very differently affected by such an occurrance; knowing that vice debases, and must finally work out the ruin of the most flourishing societies; they cannot but be deeply affected, with the prevalency of it in this town, more especially since the troops came among us; The exertions of the most faithful magistrates are not sufficient to stop the progress of every immorality: The air is contaminated with oaths, and blasphemies; violences are in the midst of us; and the sun as well as the moon and stars, witnesseth to the shameful prostitutions, that are daily committed in our streets and commons.

April 4[1]

This day the freeholders, and other inhabitants of this town, met by adjournment at Faneuil-Hall, to receive the reports of several committees; when among others, the following were accepted, viz. The report of a committee relative to employing the poor, in which the overseers had a grant of £500 lawful money, to be apply'd for the procuring of spinning wheels, &c. for such women and children as are unable to purchase them. —Another report, pointing out the most likely methods to check the progress of vice, and immortality! wherein it was observed, that nothing would better contribute to bring the proposals to effect, than agreeing upon some effectual scheme for employing the numerous poor of this town. —And another, directing, and empowering, the Selectmen to bring such actions as they may judge proper to prevent or remove any trespasses upon the town's lands, and for obtaining damages for the same.—

April 5

The committee, to consider what was further necessary to be done for vindicating the character of the inhabitants, and obtaining the knowledge of such representations as may have been made to their prejudice; Reported the draft of a humble petition to his Majesty, which was unanimously accepted, and ordered to be transmitted to the Hon. Col. Isaac Barry, a member of the British House of Commons, with the desire of the town, that the same might be immediately presented. —In this petition, the town express their grief and astonishment, to find that such accounts had been laid before the House of Lords, as to induce them to pass a resolve, that they had been in a state of disorder and confusion for some time past. —They assure his M—y that none of his subjects in the town, can be justly charg'd with disaffection to his person, family, or government, or the least disposition to oppose the due restraints of law, or constitutional authority, —And that the only instance that could bear a representation of disorder in the town within the year past, was in a great measure occasioned by the misconduct of some of the servants of the crown; who by exercising a power not warranted by acts of Parliament, or beyond their direction, had irritated the minds of some individuals; but that the disorder was immediately discountenanced, and suppressed by the body of the inhabitants, That his Majesty's Council however, the next morning began an inquiry into the disorder, and the persons active in it, but were stop'd in the process by G. B. himself, who chose *in his own way and manner*, to take depositions, and transmit them, *such as they were*, without giving the town the least notice of what they contain'd, or the knowledge even of the magistrate before whom they were taken? They complain to his Majesty that their public transactions have been represented as springing from undutifulness, disaffection, and even the principles of rebellion; the unhappy effects of which they feel in the ordering a *military* force, under a supposed necessity of them to aid *civil* authority and preserve the peace, while the town is kept in total ignorance of the matters alledged against them. —They represent to his M—y, that they had particularly waited on G. B. and intreated him to point out in what respects the public transactions of the town had militated with law, but could not obtain such a favour. — They beseech his Majesty with hearts full of affection and duty, and at the same time, with the warmest attachment to their own constitutional rights, liberties, and privileges, to allow them to declare those accounts to be ill grounded, which have represented them as held to their allegiance and duty, only by the hand of terror, and the force of arms; and they supplicate the removal of a military power, —a power unnecessary, — a power unfavourable to commerce, destructive to morals, dangerous to law, and tending to overthrow the civil constitution. —They fly to the justice as well as the clemency of the s—n, and pray that they may be favour'd with copies of Governor Bernard's letters (*some of which have since come to hand,*) the memorials of the Commissioners of the customs in America, and other papers, that affect their most im-

---

[1] Items from April 4 to April 12, inclusive, are from *The New York Journal, Supplement*, May 18, 1769, p. 1. Apparently there was no item of the *Journal* for April 3, 1769, as it is missing from the *New York Journal* and the *Boston Evening Post*.

portant interests, that they may have the opportunity of vindicating themselves: And they conclude with declaring, that they doubt not their being able to make their innocence appear to the satisfaction of their s—n, and the shame of their accusers.

April 6

In the appointment, of acting justices for every county, too much care cannot be taken, that they be not only persons of the *best morals*, but of a spirit which will lead them to act up to the true character of *reforming* magistrates: This town has been so happy in times past, as to have a number of such magistrates; men who nobly exerted themselves, for the suppression of drunkenness, Sabbath-breaking, profaneness and other immoralities; and it is cause of thankfulness, that the present day still offer'd instances of such faithfulness—However, it seems G. B. is of opinion, that a reform of the magistracy is become absolutely necessary for making better times; but dispairing of having the consent of his C—l, for displacing any of the present justices; he has seen fit to add a number to the bench, who are to labour in this salutary work.—The people might reasonably have concluded, that a suppression of the immortalities enumerated, would have been the main object of their pursuit, but it seems nothing less is intended,—a reform of *government* and not of *the manners* of the people, is the service allotted them; and this reform is to consist in a bracing up of *government*, which has been represented to be in a much more *lax state* than are our *morals*. A *foreigner* has been pitch'd upon to take the lead in this arduous undertaking, of *bracing up government*, the plain English of which is, *strengthening and aiding the measures* of an avaricious, arbitrary G—r; but the service has proved too fatiguing for even a S—ch[1] constitution, —he often reels and staggers under his load of service,[2]—Poor gentleman, some persons were passing his house the other night, as he was coming to his street door with a large taper in his hand, to light one of his clan into the street, when they observed his knees to smite one against another, which

presently after buckled under him, and this reformer received a fall, which excited the *pity* rather than *laughter* of the beholders.— It is to be hoped some proper help will be speedily afforded him, as it cannot but excite ridicule, to perceive a *lax unbraced* magistrate, employed in *bracing* up government.—*It is a serious truth, that if magistrates are vicious and immoral, the people will soon be so; and if in those appointments, so little regard is paid even to political characters, as that t—s, and r—s,[3] may be entrusted with the execution of the laws, provided they will act in subserviency to the views of a selfish, arbitrary, G—r, the rights, as well as the morals, of such a people, must be in the most deplorable situation.*

April 7

The resolutions of the merchants of Philadelphia, not to import any more foreign merchandize, while the present restrictions, burdens, and impositions, upon the trade of North-America are continued, gives high satisfaction to the true friends of the colonies in this province, as does the conduct of the merchants in New-York, in appointing a committee to inquire into, and inspect all European importations, in order to a strict compliance with their agreement, respecting a non-importation of foreign wares; which committee is to correspond with the merchants of other colonies.—Measures which we hope will be adopted by all their neighbours and be productive of the most salutary effects to a whole continent.

April 8

The capacity of a Hottentot at this time of day, is sufficient to discern, that our ruin can come only from ourselves: And that our fellow subjects in Great-Britain, can't deprive us of our rights if we *mind our own business* and let *theirs alone*. The truth is, we have *no occasion* for British manufactures, they are *rank poison* to the constitution of this country. We live in a land that flows with milk and honey, and with suitable culture, will presently yield us the necessaries and conveniences of life in rich abundance.

We have had line upon line, and lecture

---

[1] Scotch.
[2] The remaining part of this item was omitted by the *Boston Evening Post.*
[3] Probably "traitors and rogues."

upon lecture, to shew us the *importance* and *necessity* of disusing as fast as possible *European articles*, and attending to those that are fabricated and manufactured *in America*, as the only way to unrivit the chains, and burst asunder the bands of iron that are fastened on us.

Those persons who for the sake of a little foreign pelf, directly or indirectly, encourage or connive, at the importation of articles pernitious to the constitutional rights of this country, ought to be look'd upon as men destitute of reason, civility, and common sense. The people of Great-Britain, by the burdens and impositions on trade, and by their coersive and vigorous measures, abundantly intimate that our trade in those parts is *disagreeable*, and that it would be well to forbear, at least for a season.—It must therefore be *unmannerly* and contrary to the rules of reason, and good breeding, to keep haunting them, after their actions have amounted almost to a flat denial.

Let us all my countryman, resolve to be constitutionally free, and not barter away our birth-right privileges, for that which profiteth not. Let us *save our money* in order to *save our country;* let the business of *importation*, already thick set with difficulties, and dangerous to pursue, *come to a period*, and those who promote it to the disadvantage of the cause of liberty, be looked upon with an *eye of contempt:* Let us by no means promote or esteem those, who are pursuing interests diametrically opposite to the interest of the public, and who to gratify their avaricious cravings, would sell their country, and compass sea and land to obtain articles, which if obtain'd tend to involve America in *irretrievable ruin.*"[1]

April 9

There have been great disturbances not long since, in the barracks at New-Boston, and some tumults in the street near them, occasioned by the insults and outrages of the drunken soldiery, in which several of the inhabitants, as well as the soldiers were wounded.—*Violences must be expected from soldiers, who have a raging appetite for spirits, and whose barracks, are encircled with distilling-houses and dram shops.*

April 10

Two soldiers the other evening, left the guard on the Neck, and were making off into the country; one of them who had been much in liquor, on coming to his senses, thought it most expedient to return, and throw himself upon the mercy of a Court Marshal;[1] by this court, we are told, he was sentenced to have *only* eight hundred lashes, three hundred and eighty of which, he received in part, and was then carried off to the hospital, to all appearance a dead man.

April 11

There was very severe whippings the day before yesterday; a grenadier having received about two hundred lashes, in part of a Court Marshal's[2] sentence, the doctor as it is said, advised to his being loosed from the halberts, it being his opinion, that a greater number might endanger life. He was accordingly unloosed, when he fell upon the ground senseless, but upon pouring some water down his throat, he soon came to himself; this encouraged the humane officer, to order his being again tied to the halberts, and that the drummers should proceed in executing the sentence; he accordingly received about fifty more lashes, as seemingly *insensible* of the strokes as would have been a *statue of marble:* He was then taken down and conveyed away to the hospital, a seeming corps.

April 12

Yesterday morning it was confidently reported to the inhabitants, by several of the soldiers, that the grenadier whipped the day before, was actually dead. —The minds of people were agitated with this news; the circumstances of his punishment, could not but greatly affect them: They applied to the two coroners in town, who discovered that they needed no stimulus, to discharge their duty. —Thomas Daws, Esq; immediately proceeded to the hospital in the Common, and would not be satisfied with any information of doctors, &c. until, he had seen the man, and was assured that he was living; soon after Mr. Pierpont, the other coroner, made a legal inquisition; he also informed the inhabitants, that the man was alive, but that he appeared to him to be in a

[1] The beginning of this quotation is omitted in this item in the *New York Journal.*
[2] The spelling in the *Boston Evening Post* is "martial."

most hazardous condition. *We hope he may recover, or in case of his death, that it may be manifested to the world, that the town of Boston in New-England, as well as the city of Winchester, in Old-England, has its worthies, who can never rest until they have taken all proper and legal methods, to clear the land of the guilt of that blood, which would otherwise lie upon it.*

April 13[1]

Yesterday a vessel from Barnstable came into the harbour in order to fit out for a whaling voyage. —The crew seeing a man of war's boat in chase, thought proper to consult their own safety, by taking to their whale boat; by dint of superior dexterity, after rowing near three miles, they landed upon an island, before the King's boat could reach them, and ran a shore, leaving their boat to the mercy of their pursuers, who greedily seized it together, with several bundles of clothes, and other necessaries, belonging to the whale men, and return'd with their *plunder*, to their ship, from whence they came.

April 14

Some free, tho' honest publications, have it seems, given great offence to the *cabal*, in this town, who cannot bear to have their *public* conduct animadverted upon in the prints, or their *private* machinations, to serve themselves, at the expence of their country, laid open to the public eye. —We are therefore not surprized, to hear that the H—ble R— A—, Esq; Judge of Admiralty for this province, &c. has forbid Mr. E. P. the Deputy Register of the Court of Admiralty, from putting any of his advertisements, relative to seizures, &c. in Messrs. Edes and Gill's Gazette, or the Boston Evening-Post, published by Messrs. John and Thomas Fleets.

April 15

A young woman lately passing thro' Long-Lane, was stopt and very ill treated by some soldiers, the cry of the person assaulted, brought out another woman into the street, who for daring to expostulate with the ruffians, received a stroke from one of them, and would probably have been further abused, had not her husband, and some

other men came up timely to her assistance; the soldiers were then soon beat off and the young woman whom they had seiz'd as their prey, rescued.

April 16

The owner of the sloop from Barnstable, who had his boat, &c. taken from him the other day, by some people belonging to one of the men of war in this harbour; waited upon Commodore Hood, the 13th inst. to desire restitution of his property; when, as we are well informed, the Commodore was pleased to say, that tho' he had suffered much by the frequent dissertions, and wanted a number of men to complete his compliment, he was yet determined not to man the King's ships by hurting the trade, that the men would have been immediately released, had they been impressed, as they were bound on a whaling voyage, he being determined not to impress either fishermen or coasters. The Commodore then gave him an order to the captain of the ship which had made the seizure, by which the owner obtain'd his boat, &c.—*If instances of a due regard to justice, and tenderness to the merchants, should become more frequent, they will occur the oftner in this Journal.*

April 17

Advices have been received from the different colonies, on this continent that the anniversary of the repeal of the Stamp Act, on the 18th of March 1766, has been kept as a day of festivity, and celebrated by the friends of liberty, with the usual formalities. —The following are the principal toasts, drank upon the memoriable occasion. The King, Queen, Prince of Wales and royal family, the Earl of Cahtham, Marquis of Rockingham, Earl of Dartmouth, General Conway, Col. Barry, Mr. Bourke, and every other generous assertor of American rights, Alderman Wilkes, John Dickenson, Esq; author of the Farmer's Letters,—James Otis, Esq; author of the Rights of Colonies.— The spirited Assembly of the year 1765— The 92 members of the Boston Assembly, who voted against rescinding —The patriotic Assembly of Connecticut, Rhode-Island, New-York, Pennsylvania, Maryland, N. and S. Carolina, and Georgia, unanimity, fidelity

---

[1] Items for April 13 to April 23, 1769, inclusive, are from the *New York Journal, Supplement*, June 1, 1769, p. 1.

and perseverance to the Sons of Liberty in America, a perpetual union and harmony between Great-Britain and her colonies,— Success to the American manufactures, the liberty of the press, and disappointment to those who endeavour to subvert it, success to that uncorrupted patriot General Paoli and the brave Corsicans.

April 18

In most parts of the continent there are ladies, which continue their noble exertions, to encourage a spirit of industry, and manu-facutres.—A gentleman on Long-Island, informs the public, that three young ladies, namely Ermina, Liticia and Sabina, having met together, agreed to try their dexterity at the spinning-wheel; accordingly the next morning, they set themselves down and like the virtuous woman, put their hands to the spindle, and held the distaff; at evening they had 26 skeins of good linen yarn, each skein containing four ounces, all which were the effects of that day's work only.—And adds.—It is hoped that the ladies of Connecticut, and Rhode-Island, who have shewn their skill and industry, at the spinning-wheel, will be sincerely pleased to find their laudable example, so well imitated, in Huntington, and that it has kindled a spirit of generous emulation in the ladies of New-York government; we hope the same spirit will spread through the continent.—That the ladies, while they vie with each other in skill and industry, in this profitable employment, may vie, with the men, in contributing to the preservation and prosperity of their country, and equally share the honour of it.

April 19

In the Superior Court at Boston, begun in March last, Daniel Mertier, gentleman, Peter Robinson, John Newton, John Bromfield, John Ashley, and Joseph Annis, all residing in Boston, (being soldiers) were indicted for riotously entering the house of one Joshua Hemmingway, (in Boston) armed with swords and bayonets, and for assaulting the said Joshua Hemmingway, Elizabeth Ridley, Rebecca Hemmingway, and Moses Hemmingway, threatening them, and putting them in fear of their lives, &c. the said Peter Robinson, John Newton, John Brom-

field, John Ashly, and Joseph Annis, appeared and pleaded not guilty; but were informed that if they would plead guilty, and throw themselves upon the mercy of the court, it was not doubted but the punishment would be very small; a motion was then made by their council, that they might have leave to retract their former plea and, plead guilty, which was permitted; and so those persons then said they would not contend with our lord the King, &c. and afterwards a *nolle prosequi*, was entered in behalf of the King, by Jonathan Sewel, Esq; his Majesty's Attorney General, on the back of the said indictment, but no entry of the said indictment was ever made in the court minute book, nor doth it any where appear that the said Daniel Metier, ever appeared in the said court according to his recognizance, or was ever call'd upon to appear, no minute or order thereof, being found, though carefully sought for.

April 20

Capt. John Wilson, being under a recognizance, for an appearance at the said Superior Court, to answer an accusation against him, for wickedly soliciting the Negroes of the town, to abuse their masters and cut their throats, &c. as has been heretofore related, came into court and took a seat *upon the bench* together with a number of military officers; after sitting some short time (Judge Auchmuty his council, being about to move the bench in his behalf) beckned to him to come down, which hint was with difficulty taken—after he was upon the floor, Mr. Auchmuty, informed the court that Capt. Wilson, was attending there, in compliance with his recognizance, and that as his client did not know how soon he might be ordered away upon the King's service, he was now waiting the orders of the court,—whereupon the court asked the Attorney General whether he was ready for the trial—who answered he was *not ready*, tho' all the witnesses lived in Boston.) Captain Willson's council, in order to save his recognizance, then moved that his appearance might be minuted; which being done, he had leave to depart, with directions to attend the court whenever he should be called upon, he departed accordingly, and has not been notified to give his attendance during the term, and it is probable never will appear, the court having adjourned without day, the 17th of the last month.

April 21

It was expected that the tryal of a number of soldiers for assaulting and resisting with drawn swords and bayonets, John Ruddock, Esq; justice of the peace for this county in the execution of his office, would now have come on, but to the surprise and disappointment of many, it was not brought on, nor has any thing been done upon it, as we can yet learn.

April 22

One Maysel, against whom a bill of indictment was found, for being guilty of perjury in the Court of Admiralty, upon a libel there against John Hancock, Esq; for landing part of a cargo of Madeira wines, without paying the duties, could not now be brought to his trial, as this fellow, to whom a post has been given by recommendation of the Commissioners, on board the sloop Liberty, late Mr. Hancock's, now a guarda costa, is upon a cruise in said sloop.

April 23

These proceedings are as unusual, as they are alarming.—Perhaps Mr. DeBerts letters, may lead us in some measure to account for them, being there informed, that L—d H—b—gh told him, he was advised from hence that a number of law suits (meaning no doubt, some of those recited above) had been commenced against certain persons which evidenced, that *an ill temper* still remained among us: It is possible this young S—y may have thought that throwing a discouragement upon prosecutions of this sort may be one way of *bracing* up Government and *supporting* its dignity. Be this as it may, we are fully of opinion, that a *delay* of justice in some cases amounts to a *denial* of justice, and that if ever the time should come, when justice shall be only suspended in complaisance to the military; and soldiers instead of supporting the civil magistrate,

in the legal execution of his office, shall be the persons who may obstruct and terrify them with impunity when thus doing, the law of the land will then be set afloat, and wretched indeed must be the circumstances of such a people.

April 28[1]

At the Superiour Court held at Charlestown, application was made by the Custom-House officers, for a full supply of writs of assistance, which were accordingly granted. By the late acts the officers of the customs are "empowered to enter into any house, warehouse, shop, or other place, in the British colonies, or plantations in America, to search for, or seize prohibited or uncustomed goods."—A dreadful power indeed! And if we can recollect instances of such a wanton use of this power, even in Boston, as that a magistrate should be threatened and his house rummaged, by an officer in resentment at his being fined for breach of law; what may we not fear at a time when Spanish policy has been so far adopted, as that the most ignorant, hair-brain'd, and extravagant persons in commission on board the ships of war are converted into custom-house officers? If we only reflect that the judges of these American courts, are appointed *during pleasure*, and that one purpose for which money is to be levied upon the colonies by a late act is, that they may have adequate provision made for them, which is to continue, *during their complaisant behaviour*, what an engine of oppression may this authority be in such hands! We are well aware that writs of this kind, for searching houses in England, have been granted under the seal of the Court of Exchequer, according to the statute, which seal is kept by the Chancellor of the Exchequer: it should however be remembered that the custom-house officers, at home are under certain checks & restrictions, which they cannot be under here; and therefore the writ of assistance ought to be look'd upon as a different thing there, from what it is here. In England the Exchequer has the power of controuling them in every respect; and even of inflicting corporal punishment upon them

---

[1] Apparently there were no items of the *Journal* for April 24, 25, 26, 27. The publication of the *Journal* in the *Boston Evening Post* was continuous at this period. So far no items for the above dates have been found. Items for April 28 to May 2, inclusive, are from the *Boston Evening Post*, June 26, 1769, p. 1.

for mal-conduct, of which there have been instances; they are the proper officers of that court, and are accountable to it as often as it shall call them to account, and they do in fact account to it for money receiv'd, and for their behaviour, once every week. Do the officers of the customs here account with the Superior Court, or lodge money received in the hands of that court; or are they *as* officers under any sort of check from it? Will they concede to such powers in the Superior Court? Or does this court, notwithstanding there are powers belonging to the Exchequer,—notwithstanding it is said to be vested with all the powers belonging to the Exchequer,—and further notwithstanding this very writ of assistance is to be granted as a power belonging to the Exchequer, will the Superior Court itself assume the power of calling these officers to account, and punish them for misbehaviour? We know not of one instance of this sort, but on the contrary, have we not seen not long ago, an inferior custom-house officer, who has since swelled into a C—m—r of the B—d of C—s—ms, refusing to account to any power in the province for monies receiv'd by him by virtue of his office, belonging to the province, and which we were then assured by the joint declaration of the three branches of the legislature, was unjustly as well as illegally detain'd by him?

But notwithstanding writs of assistance issued in Britain are guarded with such restrictions, "The greatest assertors of the rights of Englishmen have already strenuously contended that such a power was dangerous to freedom, and expressly contrary to the common law, which ever regarded a man's house as his castle, or a place of perfect security.—If such power was in the least degree dangerous there, it must be utterly destructive to liberty here. For the people of England have two securities; against the undue exercise of this power by the crown, which are wanting with us.— In the first place if any unjustice is done there, the person injured may bring his action against the offender, and have it tried before independent judges who were *no parties in committing the injury.—Here* he must have it tried before dependent judges, being the men who granted the writ."

April 29

We are well informed, that the officers of the customs applied the last year to the Chief Justices or bench of judges, in several of the colonies, for granting them writs of assistance but that those justices from a tender regard to the constitution, and the rights of American freeholders, did actually refuse a compliance with those demands.— The C—l—r of the port of New-London in Connecticut, has lately applied a second time to the Superior Court there for such writs; at the same time laying a letter before them, which he had received from one of the crown lawyers in England in answer to one wrote upon the subject, in which letter, a great compliment was paid to the Chief Justice of the Massachusetts, for the proof he had given of a right understanding of the law, and of his zeal for his Majesty's service, by so readily granting those writs, upon the application made by the custom-house officers; and his example was recommended as worthy of their imitation. The court did not however, think proper to show a like complaisance, but chose to refer this request, to the consideration of their General Assembly at the approaching session.

April 30

The quartering troops in the body of a town is as ruinous to the soldiery as it is distressing to the inhabitants; every day furnishes out instances of their debaucheries and consequent violences.

As an aged woman at the north part of Boston; was setting the other evening in a lower room, having no person in the house with her: a soldier came in and seeing her have a Bible on the table before her; he expressed his approbation of her piety and attempted a kind of exposition upon some parts thereof, but soon dropping this discourse, he acquainted her that he had a bad swelling on his hip, and should be glad of her advice; but while the good woman was attending to his relation, this abandoned wretch, seized her, by the shoulders, threw her upon the floor, and notwithstanding her years, attempted a rape upon her, which was prevented by the resistance and screams occasioned by his brutal behaviour; he thought proper to hurry off, taking with him a bundle of shirts and other linen, which had been just before sent into the house for washing, and ironing; a business which the person followed to obtain a livelihood.

May 1

A CAPTAIN of a vessel lately arrived from Halifax, passing the streets last evening, in company with two married women, were met by some soldiers, who immediately accosted them in a rude indecent manner; the captain tho't proper to inform them, that those women were married, and also to reprove them for such behaviour; but for taking this liberty, he was presently knocked down, and had like to have lost an eye by a blow receiv'd.

May 2

On the other night past 11 o'clock several officers and one soldier, meeting with two of the town's watchmen, they began to curse and damn them, and soon after the soldier struck one of the watchmen, who returned the blow, which laid him in the gutter, then the two officers came up, and were as free with their blows as the soldier; the noise and racket soon brought other watchmen to the assistance of those who were assaulted, when one of the officers drew a bayonet, and damning them, said stand off, or I will run you through; the watchmen not being intimidated, gave him a stroke on the arm which obliged him to drop the bayonet; when they seized him and carried him off to prison, the watchmen were followed by another officer, with a drawn sword or cutlass under his arm, but being told that if he did not leave them, they would endeavour to secure him also, he thought proper to sheer off. Several officers came at different times, and offered the watchmen drink or money, if they would release the prisoner, but to their honor they refused those offers, & entered a complaint against them, to a magistrate the next morning.

May 3[1]

Last Lord's day some assemblies in this town, were greatly disturbed during divine service, by the rattling of drums and play of the fifes.—A party of soldiers with those noisy instruments passed one of those assemblies twice in the space of half an hour: As there has been lately no disturbances of this sort in the time of service, it is to be hoped, that this behaviour was accidental, and rather owing to the inattention or wildness of the officer who commanded the party, than to a design of again bringing up the practice.—It has also been noticed by some persons, that the sawing of wood at the barracks, is more heard on the Sabbath, than on week days; perhaps this may be pleaded for a work of *necessity* and *mercy*, the service the troops are engaged in, being so *important* as not to permit any other leasure time being allotted them for this business.—Col. Mackay, in the Ravin transport, with the remainder of the 65th Regiment arrived from St. Christophers on the morning of said day.

May 4

The following relation of what lately happened on board the brig Pittpacket, Capt. Thomas Power, belonging to Marblehead and bound in there from Cadiz; we may venture to assert, is a more just and impartial one, than what appear'd in Messrs. Mein & Flemming's newspaper, the day after Governor Barnard, Commodore Hood, the Lieut. Governor, Secretary, and Robert Auchmuty, Esq; Judge of Admiralty condescended to go on board the Rose man of war, to make enquiry into the matter.

This brigantine when within seven leagues off Cape Ann, was met with by the Rose man of war, Capt. Caldwell, who boarded her and took out two men he had impressed; but these being for some reasons released, Mr. Panton the Lieut. of the Rose, with a number of men, again boarded the brig with design to take some other of their hands, who four in number, had secured themselves in the fore-peak, there determining to defend themselves with the weapons they had procured, against any illegal attack, upon their liberty; such an attack was then actually begun by the Lieut. He at first used many persuasive arguments, to induce them to surrender themselves, offering in that case, to take but two of them, and afterwards only one of them, but finding all his endeavours ineffectual to induce them to come

---

1 Items from May 3 to May 10, inclusive, are from the *New York Journal, Supplement*, June 22, 1769, p. 1.

up: The Lieut. then informed them that he was determined to make use of force; and the sailors as resolutely protested, that they would defend themselves to the last extremity: A pistol charge of powder was then fired at them, which wounded the face of one Michael Corbett; and soon after another of the men received a pistol shot in his arm, which broke the bone and occasioned a great effusion of blood.—This outrage of the press gang, so far from intimidating, increased the resolution of the men to die, rather than surrender themselves to such a lawless banditti; and indeed their whole conduct, seemed to manifest an abhorence of being forced on board a man of war, and that they preferred death to such a life as they deemed slavery.—They repeatedly declared, they would kill the first man that offered to approach them: And a man the Lieut. sent in to begin the attack upon them, was considerably wounded, on which he retreated.—The Lieut. then told them that he would lead the way to them himself: Corbett answered him, with the most solemn protestations, and called Almighty GOD to witness, that so sure, as he advanced one step farther, he should instantly lose his life. The Lieut. told them he had seen many a brave fellow; should take a pinch of snuff and then consider of it, which having deliberately done, he began to step towards them, when Corbett, agreeable to his promise, struck the Lieut. with a harpoon near his throat which cut the jugular vein; he only had time to say, that they had taken his life; and, gasping three or four times, fell and expired.

The sailors still continued to defend themselves, notwithstanding there was a large number of marines at this time on board the brig; but having provided themselves with a quantity of liquor, all but Corbett became so intoxicated therewith, that they were soon pulled out; he continued to defend himself for three hours and a half after he killed the Lieut. and it is thought would have been killed on the spot, rather than have been taken, if he had retained the use of his limbs; but being also overcome with liquor, was by that means taken.

May 5
The captain of the Rose, after this tragical affair, thought himself obliged or rather presumed to take charge of the brig, as well as the men belonging to her, and has brought them into this harbour, together with the corps of the lieutenant.—The inhabitants were not a little alarmed to learn that those who were the aggressors, and acted in defiance of an act of Parliament, are left at liberty, while the men who only stood upon their defence against an illegal attempt upon their liberty are confined in irons, on board the man of war, in order to their being put upon a tryal for life; and that proper application for their being brought up to town, and treated as the law prescribes has been hitherto ineffectual; but they are quite astonished to hear that C—m—r R—b—n and others of the cabal have given out that Lieut. Panton was not on the business of pressing men, but only executing the duty of a custom-house officer on board the brig by endeavouring to search out and secure contrabrand goods; and that he was therefore opposed and slain, while in the due execution of that trust.—We shall only remark upon the above account, that if the captains of our men of war have it in their power to stop vessels at sea and impress the seamen; as also to detain such vessels in order to break open hatches and make a search for uncustomed goods; that then the floating property of the merchants lies at their mercy: Or if such officers can assume on board a merchantman at sea, the shape of either marine or custom-house officer as best suits them, in order to their laying hands on our seamen; that then a kite is made of a most solemn act of Parliament, provided, and enacted, for the security of the persons of that class of his Majesty's leige subjects in America, whether by sea or land.

It is said the Lieut. of the Rose was the person who not long since fought a duel with an inhabitant of this town, who generously gave him a life, which he has since sacrificed to his rashness.

May 6
The merchants of this town met according to adjournment, on Thursday last, when the committee appointed to make enquiry relative to the importation of goods, by the vessels lately arrived from Great-Britain,

reported, and then adjourned their meeting to the Tuesday after.

For the satisfaction of the friends of liberty, in this and the neighbouring colonies, they are acquainted that there has not been imported in all the ships from *England*, more woollen goods than would fill a long boat,—that the agreement of the merchants has been strictly adhered to: Such of them as have had goods sent them, having freely engaged to deliver them up to the Committee of Inspection.—A few traders have taken advantage of the virtue and public spirit of the merchants; their names may soon be made public through the continent, and transmitted to posterity with infamy, in the annals of their country.

May 7

The merchants and traders of Salem, Marblehead, Cape Ann, Ipswich, New Plymouth, Nantucket and other towns in this province have discovered a like firmness and virtue, such an union among the mercantile interest, of this and the neighbouring provinces, relative to a non-importation, &c. as at present subsists, cannot finally fail, of freeing the trade of the colonies from its present intolerable embarrassments, and causing it to be put on its old footing, which must prove as beneficial to Great-Britain as it will be advantageous to America.

May 8

Last week three criminals, sat upon the gallows and received twenty stripes each under the same, agreeable to their sentence of the Superior Court, for setting fire to the county gaol.—It seems the guard of soldiers at the fortification gates had orders to stop all persons going through, who appeared like sailors; some of the inhabitants being stopt among them, it gave great uneasiness, and was so resented, that had they not been released, and those orders countermanded, it is apprehended a great tumult might have been the consequence.

At the above execution the conduct of—— was tho't calculated to promote an appearance of resistance to the civil authority; a number of inhabitants suspecting this, offered their assistance to the sheriff, to prevent an escape of the prisoners which would have afforded a noble subject for G— B— and his cabal, to build a representation to the Ministry upon. It is however a fact that the inhabitants of this province in general and this town in particular, are determined to support the execution of justice at all events, without any regard to the quality or station of the offenders.

May 9

The report of his Majesty having conferr'd upon G— B—, the title of a baronet, is supposed to have occasioned the following congratulatory address.

To Sir ——

As an individual inhabitant of this province, tho' obscure and mean, I beg leave to present my congratulatory compliment to your —— on the high honour you now sustain, of a baronet of Great-Britain. This is a promotion which the friends of Government, or which is the same thing, your own friends have long thought you justly merited: And even your enemies, and the factious leaders themselves, must confess that, the eminent services you have done for the present M—y have been such as my L— of H—, that patron of true worth, could not fail to set forth in the most distinguishing point of light.—Your promotion, Sir, reflects an honour on the province itself: An honour which has never been conferred upon it, since the thrice happy administration of Sir Edmond Andros, of precious memory who was also a baronet; nor have the unremitted endeavours of that very amiable, and truly patriotic gentleman, to render the most substantial and lasting services to this people, upon the plan of a wise and uncorrupted set of M—rs, been ever parralled till since you adorn'd the ch—r. —Your own 'etters will serve to convince the world, and the latest posterity, that while you have constantly preserved a sacred and inviolable regard to punctilious truth, in every representation, which you have made of the people of you G—, you have carefully endeavoured to give the most favourable colouring to their conduct and reputation. And the tenderness which you have ever remarkably felt for their civil rights, as well as their religion, will not admit of the least room to question, but that were the influence you have evidently employ'd with success to introduce a military power, and the unwearied pains you took to get them quartered in the body of the town, sprang from your piety, and benevolence of heart,—Pity it is that you have not a pension to support your title But an assembly well chosen, may supply that want even to your wish. Should this fail, a late letter, said to have strongly recommended a tax upon the improved lands of the colonies, may be equally successful with the other letters of the like nature, and funds sufficient may be rais'd for the use and emolument of yourself and friends without a dependance upon a "military establishment supported by the province at Castle William." I am, Sir with the most profound respect, and with the sincerest wishes for your further exaltation, the most servile of all your tools,

A Tory.

May 10

The policy of the present day is totally different from what it was in former times, that those governors who discover a capacity for that trust by conciliating the affections of the governed, and carrying favourite points for Administration, without alarming the people, do not seem to stand in so fair a way of receiving C—t favours, as they do who render themselves quite obnoxious, and are so happily successful as to throw, not only a single province, but a whole continent and kingdom, into anxiety, confusion, and distress.

☞Notwithstanding the publication of J—s M—y, the late new made justice, in all the papers of this day; the facts contained in the Journal cannot be controverted, and the Journalist will take proper notice of the late abusive attack, in the course of his observations; he thinks for very obvious reasons, that 'tis best he should remain concealed, tho' absolutely certain that every account published in the Journal is strictly agreeable to truth. Many occurrences therein mentioned he was perfectly acquainted with, being an accidental spectator of them.[1]

May 12[2]

On the first instant the freeholders, and other inhabitants of this town, met for the choice of Representatives for the ensuing General Assembly to be convened on the last Wednesday of this month, agreeable to the royal charter.—It is very probable that G— B— wou'd have been glad to have had the calling this Assembly further postponed, as it would have served two purposes, viz, the continuance of the present extraordinary state dissolution, and more especially the subversion of the present constitution of the province, to which as appears by his late letters, he has discovered a pretty thorough aversion.—But such a step would perhaps have caus'd a convulsion which would have afforded additional matter of weighty representation on the part of the people, which he would have found it difficult to have answered,—previous to this election the Selectmen of the town, attentive to its true interest, waited on the commander of his Majesty's troops quartered in this town, and acquainted him, that it was expected that the town should be in the full enjoyment of their rights of British subjects upon this important occasion, agreeable to the Bill of Rights, which declares, *that the election of members of Parliament ought to be free,* upon which the General acquainted the Selectmen, that he would not any further conform to their expectation, than by confining the troops to their barracks during their election, which was accordingly done.—The town received this declaration as a concession of the justice of their expectation, but by no means adequate to the extent of their constitutional right, to have the troops removed from the town, and therefore postpon'd the election till they had protested that the residence of an armed force in the town at the time of election of members of the General Assembly, was a high infringement of their constitutional rights, and that their proceeding under such a circumstance, was wholly from necessity, and not to be considered as a precedent at any time hereafter, or construed as a voluntary receding from their incontestable right. —After the election, they appointed a committee to prepare instructions for the members they had chosen, and adjourn'd to the 8th instant.

---

[1] This last paragraph, with a hand to call attention to it, is omitted from the *Journal* as published in the *Boston Evening Post.*

[2] Items from May 12 to May 19, inclusive, are from the *New York Journal, Supplement,* June 29, 1769, p. 1.

May 13

At the adjournment on the 8th instant, the committee appointed for that purpose, reported a draught of instructions which were accepted by the town *nemine contradicente.*—in these instructions, the town direct their representatives when in General Court assembled, to endeavour that the debates may be free, by the removal of the cannon, and guards from before the Court-House, and every thing that might carry the least appearance of an attempt to awe, or intimidate; after which, that enquiry be made into all the grievances we have suffered by the military power: Why they have been quartered in the body of the town, contrary to the express words and manifest intention of an act of Parliament. Why the officers, who have thus violated our rights, have not been called to account; Whether Governor Bernard's appointing an extraordinary officer to provide quarters for the troops, was not an invasion of the act of Parliament for billeting, &c.—The professed rule of their conduct, with design to elude the clause of said act, purposely provided for the convenience of American subjects and their security against an excess of military power; why the repeated offences and violences committed by the soldiery, against the peace, and in open defiance and contempt of the civil magistrate and the law, have escaped punishment, in the courts of justice: And whether the Attorney General has not, in some late instances, unduly exercised a power of entering "nolle prosequi," upon indictments, without the concurrence of the court, in obstruction to the course of justice, and to the great encouragement of violence and oppression, and as the quartering troops here has proved the occasion of many evils, they earnestly desire them to use utmost endeavours for a speedy removal of them.—They enjoyn upon them in the most solemn manner, by no means to comply with any requisition that may be made for the defraying the expence of barracks, and necessaries for troops, pretended to be sent among us for the aid of the civil magistrate, at the same time that his Majesty's Council and the other civil magistrates, the Governor excepted, had declared that they neither required, or needed their assistance, and which appears to be sent among us to awe

and controul the civil government of this province.—They recommend to them another object of great importance, and which would require their earliest attention, the late flagrant and formal attack made by the *Governor of the province*, upon the *constitution* itself. An attempt, not only to deprive us of the liberties, privileges, and immunities of our charter, but the rights of British subjects, clearly appearing in a few of his letters to Lord Hillsborough, authentic copies of which have been received, and they declare it as their expectation, that our representatives, use the whole influence they may have, that the injurious impressions which they have unhappily made, may be removed, and that an effectual antidote may be administred, before the poison shall have wrought the ruin of the constitution.

May 14

They observe, that it is unnecessary for them again to repeat their well known sentiments, concerning the revenue which is continually levied upon us to our great distress, and for no other end, than to support a great number of very unnecessary placemen, and pensioners; nor their expectation that they pursue with unremitted ardour, every measure that may tend to procure us relief; never yielding their consent to, or connivance at the least incroachment upon our rights.

The town declare, that next to the revenue itself, the late extensions of the jurisdiction of the Admiralty, are their greatest grievance,—and that the American Courts of Admiralty seem to be forming by degrees, into a system, that is to overturn our constitution, and to deprive us intirely of our best inheritance, *the law of the land;* that, it would be thought in England, a dangerous innovation, if the trial of any matter upon land was given to the Admiral: It would be thought more threatning still, if the power of confiscation, over ships and cargoes, for illicit trade, was committed to that court: But if forfeitures of ships and cargoes, large penalties upon masters, and such exorbitant penalties as the treble value of cargoes, upon every person concerned in lading uncustomed goods, were by act of Parliament, to be tried by the Admiral, the nation would think their liberties *irrecoverably lost;* that this however, is the miserable case of North America.

In the 41 Sec. of the statute of the 4th of George III. Chap. 15 we find that "all the forfeitures and penalties inflicted by this, or any other act of Parliament, relating to the trade and revenues of the British colonies, or plantations in America, which shall be incurred there, may be prosecuted sued for, and recovered in any Court of Admiralty, in the said colonies. —That this hardship is the more severe, as they see in the same page of the statute, and the section immediately preceding, "That all penalties and forfeitures, which shall be incurred in Great-Britain, shall be prosecuted, sued for, and recovered in any of his Majesty's Courts of Record in Westminster, or in the Court of Exchequer in Scotland." A contrast that stares us in the face! A partial distinction, that is made between the subject in *Great-Britain*, and the subject in *America!* The Parliament in one section guarding *the people of the realm*, and securing to them the benefit of a trial by jury, and the law of the land, and by the next section *depriving Americans* of those important rights.—That this distinction is a brand of disgrace upon every American? A degradation below the rank of an Englishman? And with respect to Americans, a repeal of the 29th Chapt. of Magna Charta? "No freeman shall be taken or imprisoned, or disseized of his freehold or liberties, or free customs, or outlawed, or exiled, or any other ways destroyed, nor will we pass upon him, nor condemn him, but by lawful judgment of his peers, or the laws of the land."—The town also declares, that the formidable power of these courts, and their distressing course of proceedings, have been severely felt within the year past, many of their fellow citizens have been worn out with attendance upon them in defence against informations for extravagant and enormous penalties: And that they have the highest reason to fear from past experience, that if no relief is obtained for us, the properties and liberties of this unhappy country, and its morals too, will be ruined by these courts, and the persons employed to support them.—They therefore earnestly recommend to them by every legal measure, to endeavour that the power of these courts

may be confined to their proper element, according to the antient English statutes; and that they petition and remonstrate against the late extensions of their jurisdiction: Not doubting the other colonies and provinces, who suffer with them, will cheerfully harmonize in any justifiable measures that may be taken for redress.—They conclude with giving it, as their clear opinion, that the House of Representatives in any one province, has an undeniable right whenever a just occasion shall offer, to communicate their sentiments upon a common concern, to the Assemblies of any, or all the other colonies, and to unite with them in humble, dutiful and loyal petitions for redress of general grievances.

May 15

Yesterday, *but before divine service began*, part of the town had opportunity of hearing NANCY DAWSON from a most elegant band of music, the French horns certainly were inimitable.—It is some time since we have had such a Sunday morning's regale, the drums and fife, being the common entertainment, and 'tis uncertain to whose taste we owe this: Some think it the fancy of Madam G—m, while others think that the Justice himself conceived it might be an agreeable relief to the *wardens* under the burthen of their duty.

May 16

A girl at New-Boston, was lately knock'd down and abused by soldiers for not consenting to their beastly proposal; a gentleman hearing the cry of murder, ran to her assistance, one of the villains, immediately made off, the other the gentleman seiz'd, tho' upon his stiffly denying the fact, and charging it upon the other soldier, the gentleman suffered him to depart; presently after the same men assaulted a young gentleman of character supposing him to be the person who had rescued the girl from their violence; their oaths, and insults brought several people out of their houses, upon which the soldiers made off, but return'd a few minutes after with a number of others, and a sergeant at their head, calling out a riot! A riot! They then drew their bayonets upon the people, and with many oaths and execrations, threatning to confine them in the barracks if they did not immediately disperse, accordingly, they began to put their threats in execution by seizing one of the company and drag'd him towards the barracks, but the rest being resolute, the soldiers were obliged to quit him; upon which the whole dispers'd.

May 17

A woman at the north end enter'd a complaint with Mr. Justice Ruddock against a soldier, and some others for a violent attempt upon her, but a rape was prevented, by the timely appearance of a number of persons, for protection; when the soldier made his escape.

May 18

The public highly resent the conduct of those persons in this town, who by an importation of goods from Britain, contrary to the general agreement of the merchants, have preferr'd their own supposed private advantage to the common good of all North America; some of them have been turned out of the fire societies they belonged to, and also warned out of their stores, the owners fearing a backwardness of the people to assist in case fire should break out near them,—a number of their best customers in the country, have declined a trade with them, and taken their supplies of those who have discovered a public spirit in this time of danger.—Our merchants in general, are displeased with those in Britain, who have answered any orders from hence, and some of them have wrote their friends, that they shall withdraw their business from them, if they are guilty of a like inadvertency; and there are of our principal traders, who have refused selling their wares to those who have had any dealings with our late importers.

May 19

Some thousands of the following address have been dispersed in hand billets thro' this and the neighbouring colonies.

Fellow Citizens and Countrymen.—Inasmuch, as some persons among us have in a case of the utmost importance, preferr'd their own supposed private advantage to the welfare and freedom of America, it is highly proper you should know who they are, who have at this critical time sordidly detach'd themselves from the public interest.—May this disgraceful, but necessary, publication of their names, lead them to reflect on the baseness of their crime; and when they find themselves slighted and shunned by their neighbours and acquaintance; when their shops are deserted, and they feel their fortunes miserably impaired by prosecuting the plan of purblind avarice; when their guilty consciences have rendered this life insupportable; may they seriously attend to the concerns of another: And altho' they must suffer the punishment due to their parricide in this world, may a humble and sincere repentance open the way to their forgiveness in the next.

The misguided men who have imported goods from England, since the late agreement of the merchants of this town, are,

Messrs. Natha. Rogers, Jona. Simpson, Wm. Jackson, T. & E. Hutchinson, J. & R. Silkridge, J. Taylor,[1]

May 20[2]

We have before mentioned that one Samuel Fellows who lately commanded a vessel belonging to a merchant in Cape-Ann, having behaved in such a manner in the West-Indies, as to make it difficult for him, to render a fair and just account of his transactions chose an easier way of settlement, by informing the custom-house officers upon oath, that more molasses had been landed, than was reported; for which the vessel, &c. was seized, to the almost ruin of his owners. —So flagrant an instance of baseness and perfidy, could not but intitle him to the favour of such a set of men as G——B—— and the B——d of C——m——rs, in consequence of which, he had a command given him, in one of our little guarda coastas, and was also furnished, as other such infamous and inconsiderate marine officers have lately been, with a commission, constituting him an officer of the customs, with the power of making seizures.

Thus commissioned, and empowered, he soon commenced hostilities against the merchants, by stopping such vessels, as he

---

[1] The remaining names in the list were blurred in the *New York Journal* for June 29.

[2] Items from May 20 to May 28, inclusive, are from the *New York Journal, Supplement,* July 6, 1769, p. 1.

met with in cruises, rummaging and searching them, for pretences for a seizure, impressing men &c. &c. —Frequent advices of his extravagancies of this sort, have been received, but the account we have of his behaviour at Cape-Ann, is really astonishing, and among many other instances of a similar nature, may serve to convince Americans, what plan has been adopted by L——d H——ls——gh, for the bracing up of government, and what treatment we are to expect, so long as we are held under a military government.

The inhabitants of Cape-Ann, had spirit and strength enough, to have immediately taken, punished or secured, a wretch, who had shewn as little regard to their lives, as to the laws of the community; but prudence got the better of their resentment, and we have this affair fully related in a memorial which Mr. Jacob Parsons, the deputy sheriff, by their desire, presented to the Governor and Council of this province. — Representing that on the 25th instant, he had in his custody, having duly taken by virtue of a process of law, one Josiah Merril, as a prisoner: That while he was in the due execution of his office, one Samuel Fellows, a commander of one of his Majesty's armed cutters, then in the harbour of Cape-Ann, with four of his men with fire-arms, cutlasses, &c. came on shore in a boat, and said Fellows, immediately accosted the said Merril, by asking him, "What he did there? Upon which, said Merril replied that, "an officer had taken him, and had him in custody for debt. "That in consequence of this reply, said Fellows, commanded said Merril, to come away to him, and that he would protect said Merril: That on this encouragement, said Merril broke away from the deputy sheriff, and ran towards said Fellows; whereupon the deputy sheriff, commanded in his Majesty's name, several persons to assist in seizing and stopping his prisoner; whom they obeyed and seized, and held said prisoner; that while this passed, said Fellows, who was within four rods from the deputy sheriff, and his assistants, ordered his four men to fire: Whereupon two of Fellow's men leaped upon the beach, and ran towards them, until they had got within two rods, when they presented their arms directly to the deputy sheriff,

and his assistants, and then fired; the shot and ball scarcely missing them, and entred a store within a few inches of where they stood: The prisoner taking advantage of the consternation they were in, broke away and ran towards said Fellows's boat. That during the whole of this time, said Fellows, and his men, although they were repeatedly told, that the deputy sheriff was a King's officer, kept a constant round of oaths, and imprecations upon the deputy sheriff, and his assistants; damning the King's officer, and all who belonged to him; swearing, he would blow the brains out, of the first man who offered to touch said Merril, or come towards the boat; that they would take better sight the next time, and the like; that as said Merril, came nearer to the boat, said Fellows and his men, kept firing at the deputy sheriff, till said Fellows commanded his men not to fire any more yet; but to keep a reserve for any who should attempt a retaking of said Merril. And that after said Fellows and his men, had fired six or seven times, by which the deputy sheriff and his assistants were in the most imminent hazard of their lives, the said Fellows and his men yet defending said Merril, retired on board the boat, and still kept firing as they left the shore; and the sheriff has not since been able to retake the prisoner, or bring said Fellows to justice.

The memorialist then, implores his Excellency and Honours, to take the affair into consideration, and to act thereon, as they shall deem most for the advancement of justice, and the preservation of peace, order, and good government, &c.

May 21

In consequence of the above representation, his Excellency the Governor, and his Majesty's Council, taking the said memorial into consideration: His Majesty's Council advised and ordered, that the King's Attorney, make strict inquiry into the affair, and prosecute in law, the supposed offenders. And also ordered, that a copy of said memorial be handed to Commodore Hood, which was accordingly done, and the Commodore was pleased to signify that he would give immediate orders for inquiring into the affair, and do all in his power to secure the person offending in so notorious a manner, to appear and answer for his conduct in a court of justice.

May 22

It has been justly observed. "That the colony trade is in a measure, a system of art and restriction; yet the very principle may be destroy'd by multiplying to excess, the means of securing it." The present trade of America has of late years, been embarrassed beyond description, with the multiplicity and intricacy of regulations and ordinances; our late M—n—rs, from whom we must exclude the Rockingham Administration, seem to be possessed with something hardly short of a rage, for regulation and restriction, they have extended to us their several acts of Parliaments, calculated to prevent a contraband trade with their French neighbours, multiplied bonds, certificates, affidavits, warrants, sufferances, cockets, &c. and every species of custom-house officers, both upon the land and water; have supported the new regulations with such severe penalties, and extended them without the least consideration of circumstances to so many objects, that American commerce is expiring under them. Upon the first appointment of an American Board of C—s—ms, it was trumpetted to the merchants, by the tools of power, that it was an institution calculated to *retrieve the trade* from many of its present embarrassments; and that some of the colonies agents in London, were so well satisfied, that the residence of the C—m—rs in any trading province would be greatly advantageous to its commerce, as to offer in behalf of their constituents a large sum of money, to obtain the preferrence. — Our merchants however, were by no means disposed to hearken to such delusory insinuations; they considered the project of an American revenue, to be wholly founded upon anti commercial principles; and that a set of men sent among us to support this project, and riot upon its produce, must become as obnoxious, as the exercise of their power would be distressing. — Their conjectures were soon realized; to say nothing of the haughty imperious, indelicate behaviour of the B—d as men, their whole official conduct has been such, as lead people to consider them as the greatest political curses that could have been sent among us. — This B—d soon gave being

to such an innumerable train of under officers, &c. that the whole revenue raised by the late duties, has been scarcely sufficient to satiate their craving appetites; but the monies drained from our merchants, distressing as it has been, is the least part of our sufferings; they have, with the advice and assistance of G— B— and the cabal, gone into every measure that has appeared to us most likely to cramp and lessen both a provincial and foreign trade, by which we have been so impoverished; that thro' necessity, as well as resentment, our farmers and mechanics, are lopping off many articles of superfluities, and going into such manufactures as may be carried on here to the greatest advantage.

We have before adduced many instances of the wanton, cruel, and strange behaviour of our modern revenue, naval, and custom-house officers, all of whom are under the influence or direction of G— B— and the C—m—rs, also noticed the injuries included in them. What follows carries the same complexion.

May 23

The brig Industry, which loaded in London, and cleared out at the Custom-House there, for Nantucket, where she arrived, as the winter was setting in, applied to the naval officer, there being no custom-house officer fixed upon the island, who gave him a permit to unload, which he did accordingly, and then took on board part of another cargo, for London, and intended to Boston, there to fill up his vessel; he had also on board some chests of oyl, owned in Boston, which were imported in the same bottom; but before sailing, an officer of the customs, appointed by the C—m—rs arrived; upon which the Capt. of the brig immediately applied to him, with the cockets brought from London, in order to pay duty on some tea, which was the only dutiable goods he had brought from London; he was accordingly cleared for Boston, being first obliged to give bond for paying the duty of said tea on his arrival there, the cockets were also sent for the inspection of the Custom-House, where he applied for an entry on his arrival, but was told they should not enter her, but gave him a permit to take out the oyl brought from London; immediately after, by order of the C—m—rs they seized his vessel, and what cargo she had on board, and kept her in possession ten days, to the great damage of the owners, but after being petitioned several times, said vessel and cargo was delivered up to the owners.

May 24

The master of a coasting vessel, bound to Casco-Bay, in the eastern parts of this province, took in by sufferance, about four hundred of iron, and a few coils of cordage, for the landing of which, on his arrival there, and the producing certificates thereof, he was obliged to give two bonds at the Custom-House office.

May 25

Capt. Durphey, master of a vessel, owned in the southern part of the province, on going from Rhode-Island, to Connecticut, with a load of fire-wood, took on board two casks of molasses, without clearing them out, the molasses having been legally entered, and the duties paid upon them; but being met with by one of our English guarda coastas, they seized and detain'd the vessel, and thereby obliged said master to make a long and expensive journey to this town in order to settle for this extraordinary breach of the acts of trade, with the honourable the B—d of C—m—rs.

May 26

Capt. Dean, in a brig from Green-Island in Jamaica, was brought to and searched on his passage, not by a Spanish, but by an English guarda coasta; the captain of which, on finding that the mate of the brig had omitted clearing out his little adventure, was pleased to seize, and take possession of the vessel, as well as the mate's adventure.

May 27

A petty officer of the Custom-House came on board Capt. Freeman's ship, lately arrived from London, and behaved in the same insolent manner this set of men are accustomed to; upon finding a barrel of New-England rum, which was sent on board for the refreshment of the people at work in unloading, he threatened as if the ship should be seized; they not having, as he told them, a right to receive and keep on board a larger quantity than six gallons.

May 28

The captains of several vessels, lately arrived in different parts of this province, report that, they have been stopt and detained at sea by English guarda coastas and their hatches, &c. opened, in order to search for uncleared, or contraband goods, and that some of their seamen had been impressed and taken from them before they were near the land.

May 29[1]

It is thought there are as many patriotic members return'd for the General Assembly, which is to meet on the thirty-first of this month, as ever appeared in any former House; and they are not like to be disgraced with the company of above three or four, out of seventeen of those unhappy men of the last House, who are branded by their countrymen, with the title of Rescinders; and the return of some of these, is said to be owing to honest confessions, deep repentance, and solemn assurances of a more cautious, circumspect behaviour, for the future, in their public capacity.

Salem, Marblehead, Ipswich, Newbury and many other towns besides this capitol, have given instructions to their several representatives, for their conduct at this alarming crisis; such of them as have been published in the news-papers, are specimens of the others, and may serve to convince the world, that the present manly and rational opposition to the late violent attempts upon our rights and privileges, is not confined to a single town, but includes the whole province.

We have also the pleasure to learn, that the modern practice of dissolving such Assemblies, as could not be made subservient to the views and designs of the Ministry, has been so far from abating the spirit of the people, in the cause of liberty, that it has rather served to raise and invigorate it; the complexions of all the Assemblies, lately chosen in New-England, and the other colonies, are full as agreeable and promising, as were those of former years. The rights of Americans, are not now left to be defended by a single province; a whole continent is united in the glorious struggle.

---

[1] Items from May 29 to June 12, inclusive, are from the *New York Journal*, Supplement, July 13, 1769, pp. 1–2

May 30

The protest of the inhabitants of this town, against the residence of a military power among them, on the day for the choice of gentlemen to represent them in General Assembly, has already been inserted. — It seems the members who compose his Majesty's Council for this province, agreeing in sentiments with the town, on this point; made timely application to the Governor, that the cannon and main guards which had been placed directly against the Court-House, might be removed before the day arrived for the election of a new Council; but we apprehend the application will be unsuccessful, as the G—r was pleased to read to one of his Council the paragraph of a letter, said to be wrote by General Gage, in answer to one on the subject, "That he did not conceive what influence the mouths of cannon could possibly have in the choice of a speaker, for the House of Assembly:" — and it is said a certain officer wittily observed, upon the complaint of one relative to the cannon's being directly pointed at the Court-House; "that if the mouth of cannon was offensive to the Assembly, they would turn its breech to them."

May 31

On Tuesday last his Majesty's commission, for the trial of piracies, robberies and felonies on the high seas, was read, and a court formed for the trial of Michael Corbett, and three others, charged with being concerned in the murder of Lieut. Panton, of his Majesty's ship Rose: A motion having been made on behalf of the prisoners, that they might have the privilege of a trial by jury; the court was adjourned to the Thursday following, when they again met and adjourned to the 29th instant; when it was determined, that said prisoners were not entitled to a trial by jury. The prisoners then, by their council, filed a plea against the jurisdiction of the court; and it having been thought proper by the court, to take the same into consideration, they adjourned to the 14th of June next.

It was with difficulty, that this court was formed, a great part of the gentlemen named in the commission living at a distance; and the inhabitants had the mortification to perceive, that the whole of his Majesty's Council of this province, who had been included in all former commissions, was excluded from the present; while, not only the Council of a neighbouring colony, but even pro. temp. collectors, helped to constitute this court. For such an indignity thrown upon this ancient and loyal province, it is known we are obliged to the generosity and prudence of G—r B—d: The particular motive which influenced to the exertion of those virtues for so laudable a design, is thought to be this. Towards the close of the late war, when burdens were very heavy upon the people, they learnt that considerable sums of money due to the province, by decree of the Court of Vice Admiralty, as the thirds of forfeitures upon seizures, were unjustly detained; upon which a number of the inhabitants, petitioned the General Court, that measures might be taken for the recovery of those dues; upon which a committee was raised of both houses, to consider said petition, who reported; that wrong had been done the province, and that the treasurer should be empowered, and directed to demand payment, and on refusal thereof, to bring an action, or actions at common law, for recovering the sums due, for the use of the province; this report was accepted by the House, and concured by the Council, and after several messages had passed, consented to by the Governor, though sorely against his inclination. — In consequence hereof, a suit was commenced against his favourite, and manager, C—s P—x—n, Esq; M—sh—l of the C—t of A—l—y;[1] but by some means or other, which might with more truth than prudence be related, all the measures for recovery were baffled, and the monies still rest in other hands than those of the province treasurer. — The Council through this whole affair, were too just, to prefer the interest of a favourite, to that of a whole province, and thereby brought upon themselves the resentment of a B—r—d; and the first discovery of its effects was made in the next commission for a special Court of Admiralty, from which the whole Council was

---

[1] Charles Paxton, Esq.; Marshal of the Court of Admiralty.

excluded, and only the names of a L—t G—r, S—c—ry and J—e of A—y appeared.

June 1

ON the 21st of last month, Capt. Willson with the detachment of the 59th Regiment, sailed for Halifax; that officer is now out of the reach of the laws of this province; but the conduct of the King's Attorney, relative to the military in that and other instances, has been highly disgustful to the people; and the representatives of Boston, and other towns, are instructed by their constituents, to use their influence, that a parliamentary enquiry may be made into those matters.

June 2

The next day, when the 14th Regiment were mustered in King-Street at roll-call, a fray happened between two little boys about seven years old, which as usual, gathered a crowd of people; several persons going through the street were oblig'd, in order to avoid the crowd, to pass near the right wing of the regiment; for which daring intrusion, four persons were successively struck down by a drummer. — The battle of the boys naturally produced a larger one between some of the inhabitants, when a constable interposed, to preserve the peace; — one of the soldiers gave the word to *hustle the constable*, immediately upon which, his hat and wig were struck off, and he was toss'd about from one to another, tho' he repeatedly cried, he was a King's officer in the execution of his duty; some of the inhabitants being near, he called to them for their assistance, and many of them readily went to his assistance; upon which the battle became general, and the constable, and his assistants were much abus'd by the soldiers. Some of the officers of the regiment were present, none of whom offered to interpose, till Col. Dalrymple came into the street, and being told what had happened, he quickly dispers'd the soldiers, — since which they have not met in King-Street, but in the Common for the business of roll-calling. — It is said one of his Majesty's Council perceiving the first reforming magistrate in the street when the quarrel began, went to him, and motioned his taking proper measures to quell it; but the reformer only shruged his shoulders, and went off.

June 3

On Wednesday the 28th of said month, all endeavours to bring about a private composition having been honestly rejected, a warrant was issued by his honour the Chief Justice, against Samuel Fellows, mention'd in this Journal, for having forcibly rescued a prisoner from the sheriff of Gloucester. The day after the deputy sheriff of this county had received the warrant, he with the complainant, waited upon Commodore Hood, to acquaint him with it, and desire he would permit him to serve it upon said Fellows, who was then on board the Commodore's ship. The Commodore told him he would order said Fellows ashore, and desired him to wait upon him again at a particular hour, which the sheriff did. The Commodore then told him, he had sent for said Fellows, and that he desired a longer time, in order to procure bail; and further told him, if he would wait upon him again the next day, he would have him ready. — The sheriff went again the next day, and for fear of another delay, carried with him two persons to be witnesses of his demand. The Commodore asked him if he had any thing against said Fellows, besides the chief justice's warrant? He told him he had a writ from a gentleman in town, for a debt due from said Fellows. The Commodore, then said "if that is the case, he shan't come ashore; I've no intention to stop a legal prosecution, but I won't deliver the man up to private resentment." The sheriff told him, he knew of no private resentment, that his writ was for a just debt. The Commodore said he should not enter into an argument on the subject, and shew'd the sheriff the door. — Not a little surprised at this unexpected treatment, the sheriff went immediately to the chief justice, who was at the Bunch of Grapes tavern at dinner, with the G—r and C—m—rs, and calling his honour into another room, acquainted him with what had pass'd, at the Commodore's. His honour then call'd in the Governor, to whom he communicated the matter. The Governor then ask'd to what amount the debt against Fellows was, he told him about £20 sterling, he desired to see the writ, which was shewn, and after looking at the account, he ask'd his honour, if he did not imagine it was trump'd up in order to make it exceed £20 sterling. — His honour replied that Mr. Inches (whose suit it was) was a gentleman of character and reputation, and would not be guilty of a thing of that kind. It was then agreed that his honour should wait upon the Commodore; and he appointed the sheriff to meet him there, which he did, and after waiting some time (during which his honour and the Commodore, were in conferrence) the said Fellows was produced, and the writ and warrant were serv'd upon him. The Commodore giving security for Mr. Inches' debt, and Mr. Robert Hollowell deputy commissionary of the customs, and John Rowe, Esq; of this place merchant, were bail in £50 each for his personal appearance at the Superior Court for the County of Essex, to answer the criminal prosecution.

June 5

Our English divines are agreed in sentiment, relative to the morality of the Christian Sabbath, and this town from its beginning, has been remarkable for a strict observation of the Lord's day. — On the first arrival of the troops, the sober inhabitants were greatly grieved, that the military parade and music could not be dispensed with, or at least lessened on those days; they were sensible what unhappy effects, it would have on the minds of our inconsiderate youth, and the lower class of people: All application for a redress of this grievance, has been ineffectual; disorders upon the Sabbath, are increasing; our wholesome laws cannot be executed upon the soldiery: The last Lord's day, our Common was covered with great numbers of people, some of whom were diverting themselves with horse-racing, &c. in the very presence of our wardens.

June 7

On the 29th of last month there was a great consumption of powder on board the men of war in this harbour, a display of colours, &c. and the soldiers quartered upon us, appeared with oak leaves in their hats. — Upon enquiring into the cause hereof, we were told, that it was in commemoration of the preservation of King Charles the Second, who when flying from the victorious troops of the Parliament, took shelter, and remain'd conceal'd from his pursuers, in the trunk of a large oak tree. Happy has it been

for the princes, who have succeeded the family of the Stewarts, that they have always found in the hearts of their subjects a security, which we may be assured they will not be disposed to relinquish for all the alluring and flattering baits which despotism, ministers, and favourites can throw out.

June 8

An advertisement of James Murray, Esq; has appeared in the several papers, which charges the author of these Journals "with making him a traitor, a rebel, and drunkard; and calling upon him to unmask, and support his charge in public or in private, at his own option, or stand convicted of being an infamous liar, and a scoundrel, as also the publisher of a false, scandalous, malicious and seditious libel." The public may be assured, that tho' we are not intimidated with the airs of a *draw cansir*, we do not however, look upon ourselves obliged to stand forth to public view *in propria persona*, tho' so politely invited to it by no less a personage than his worship. — We have before declared to the public, that we shall be ready to support the truth of what we have related, whenever called upon, or with pleasure correct any mistakes, that may have escaped our pen: With respect to our reforming magistrate, we did assert, "that one evening his knees were seen to smite one against the other, which presently after buckled under him, whereby he received a fall, which excited the pity rather than laughter of the beholders." This is true in fact, and will be proved so by the oath of a creditable witness or witnesses, when legally called upon; if Mr. Reformer, after applying to the person who he lighted into the street, with a pipe in his mouth, should not think it needless; we did not however set him down for a *drunkard*, notwithstanding this or any equivocal circumstances; but only intimated, that it really became those, who set themselves up for *reformers*, to take good heed to their ways lest *slips* of this sort, should expose them to the *censure* and *ridicule* of all such as *oppose themselves* to reformation; as also the impropriety of employing a *lax* unbraced magistrate in the arduous work of *bracing* up government. — The advertiser, by filling up our gutted words, has charged us, with calling him a *traitor* and *rebel*, when those words not-withstanding, might be only intended to represent him as a *tory, rascal,* or almost any thing else: We are not however, at any loss to account for so much *seeming severity,* to himself: This sagacious gentleman, had not been long among us, before he perceived that men of the *most infamous characters* had been *most noticed* by a B—d, — Nay, he had even lately seen a letter of his to Lord Hillsborough, advising of his having appointed Mr. Murray, a reforming magistrate; and that he had told a counsellor who *objected his unpopularity,* that if his character had been *the reverse,* should not have nominated him to the office; might not this magistrate therefore very justly argue, that, the *more unpopular* and *odious* he could make himself appear, *the more likely* he should be *to obtain* the further preferment, he was seeking for from such an A—n— as the present.

And will not this clearly account, not only for the conduct of this intruder, in opposing himself to the *general sense of the people,* from the time of the Stamp Act to this day; but for that of *a few others,* who by a most *irritating* and *provoking* behaviour, have seemed to *invite* upon themselves, *some marks* of public resentment, upon the *merit* of which, they might ground an application for posts and pensions? — It is well that this game appears to be almost up, and that some of the most notorious of those seekers, are come to *the end of their tether.* It is to be hoped, that for the future, the true characters of men will, be more regarded by A—d—n, and that such as have gained the *goodwill* and *confidence* of their fellow citizens, by a *prudent, upright,* and *benevolent* conduct, will be thought *more proper persons* to fill up posts of *honour* and trust, than those who by a *contrary behaviour,* have justly forfeited it; *then* and not till then, may we expect *such representations* will be made by the servants of *government,* relative to the sentiments and behaviour of a *loyal people,* as will gain them the *esteem* and *favour* of their sovereign, then will our troubles *cease,* and our divisions *close,* and that much wish'd for union and harmony, between Great-Britain, and her colonies, be restored, upon which the *security* and *welfare* of *both,* doth under Providence so much depend.

June 9

The character given in sacred writ, of a true magistrate is, "that he beareth not the sword in vain;" by this we suppose it is intended, that he never fails to execute the good and wholsome laws of a community, upon all such as shall dare to violate them: But it seems our modern justice does not conceive of these words, in so confined a sense; otherwise it cannot be supposed, whatever may have been his provocation, that he would publicly intimate a readiness to draw a sword in *oppugnation* of the laws which he has been *sworn to maintain.* Whether a duel will however, be realized in this, or any other colony, we pretend not to predict; but this we are told, that a spirited inhabitant of the town, has left word with the publishers of his advertisement, that he shall be ready to gratify *the reformer,* by an appearance at the time and place, which he shall think proper to appoint for the purpose of proving to his masters, that they have pitch'd upon a very suitable officer to command in a St. George's Field engagement. — We would however, by no means, be thought to encourage any *illegal* rencounters on our behalf; whenever we are *properly* called upon, we hope we shall manifest to the world, that the pen is not the *only weapon* we can make use of, in support of constitutional government, and the rights of Americans.

June 10

All the insults and provocations, which the inhabitants of this town are daily receiving from the soldiery, cannot be inserted; such as we from time to time notice, may be sufficient to manifest to the world, the severity with which this town has been treated, for daring to distinguish themselves, in the support of the just rights of Americans, and how much a loyal and prudent people can bear, before they proceed to extremities.

June 11

A young man, an apprentice to a —— —— —— ——[1] happening to be looking

---

[1] Three or four words are blurred in the *New York Journal.*

over a fence on a small hill, near the Assembly room, in order to take a view of the company there dancing; a centinel who had been placed at the door, came behind him and gave him a blow on the head, by which he was struck to the ground, and suffered a great loss blood; the soldier's pretence for this violence, being, that he had been spat upon, by one on the hill.

June 12

A married neice of a distinguished ship builder in this town, returning home in the evening, was followed by some officers, who treated her with great rudeness, before she could recover the shelter of her uncle's house.

June 13[1]

The last night, a corporal belonging to the company of the train of artillery, who had for some time kept as a mistress the wife of a sea faring man, who sailed out of this port; came with a number of armed soldiers to the house of one Mr. Draper, of this town, having heard that the husband of the woman he had kept was there; he pretended that this woman had been beat and ill used by the husband for keeping his company, and insisted upon his being shewn to him; — the master of the house remonstrated against this riotous proceeding in vain; nay, he was struck and put in fear of his life for so doing, as was also his wife and aged mother. Having searched the house, they found the man they were looking for, whom they dragged into the street, and with their weapons beat in so cruel a manner, that had not the cry of murder brought a number of the inhabitants to his assistance, which obliged the soldiers to make off, he might have been killed in the scuffle. — This behaviour of the corporal and his party, is *the less to be wondered at*, since they had heard that the *King's-Attorney*, had entered a *nolle prosequi* on a bill found by the grand-jury against *Lieut.* M—r, for entering a house in the night in the same riotous and unlawful manner; and that the soldiers who joined him in the attempt, upon throwing themselves on the favour of the C—t, escaped the punishment which it was thought their crimes had justly merited from the hands of justice.

June 14

A worthy old gentleman, the other morning discovered a soldier in bed with a favourite grand-daughter: The aged parent, in the height of his astonishment, ordered the soldier immediately to quit the room; but he absolutely refused; saying she was his wife, and he had an undoubted right to her, and that if he went out of the house he was determined to carry her with him: Upon examining further into the matter, it was found that the soldier had found means to ingratiate himself with one of the family, and had by her aid seduced the girl with the promise of marriage; that accordingly, one evening as the girl informs, he carried her to a house in town, where as she thought, they were married by a person drest as a priest. This discovery has greatly distressed the unhappy parents, and thereby much impaired their healths. — But how must it increase our detestation of the present measures, to find that not only the *magistrates* of this metropolis are insulted *with* impugnity, but that the most *dear* and *tender* connections must be *broken* and *violated*. We would not wish to draw invidious comparisons; but surely if in the arbitrary reign of a *Stuart*, the quartering a standing army in time of peace upon the inhabitants of a town was deem'd *a grievance*, — what must it be at the present day, when English liberty is so much boasted of? But it seems *the Americans are refactory, and can claim no title to the privilege of British subjects:* This assertion with the reasoning upon it, may serve to blind the eyes of our fellow-subjects in Great-Britain, from whom the true state of things is with-held as much as possible, lest the thorough knowledge thereof should rouse that naturally humane and generous nation, to take ample vengeance on those enemies of the Constitution, who have been the authors of those scenes of *public* and *private* distress.

June 15

We hear that General Mackay, has seen fit to give out orders, forbidding horse racing, &c. in the Common on the Lord's-day, by any under his command; and that the soldiers should not be permitted to walk the streets during the time of divine service,

---

[1] Items from June 13 to June 25, inclusive, are from the *New York Journal, Supplement,* July 20, 1769, pp. 1–2.

a practice which had been very disagreeable and inconvenient to the inhabitants.

June 16

The late resolves of the Virginia Assembly are regarded with veneration; they do great honour to themselves, and give spirit to the other colonies. We see in these, the same sense of justice and value for the constitutional rights of America, the same vigour and boldness, that breath'd thro' the first resolves of that truly honourable house, and greatly contributed to form the free and generous spirit in which the colonies are now one. There is a peculiar generosity in the resolve, relating to the revival of the severe and absolute statute of Henry 8th, by the late extraordinary resolutions of Parliament, — as this was pointed not directly against themselves, but another colony. — Massachusetts ought long to remember this obligation — and as common sense dictates that each colony should feel for its neighbours under those severities to which all are exposed; there will, there must be a reciprocation of such kind of colonies, to the disappointment and confusion of those who wish to divide and enslave us.

June 17

After being deprived for almost a year, in perhaps the most troublesome and distressing time we ever saw, of the direction and support of our grand provincial Council, or General Court: At length the Governor has called one to meet in this town, in which, besides the ships of war in the harbour, there are three regiments and a train of artillery, the main guard with mounted cannon close to the door of the Court-House. — It has already been observed in this Journal, that upon the landing of the troops, the *chamber* in which the House is held, was for a considerable time changed into *barracks* for lodging the soldiery. The Governor has not appeared at all to interest himself for the removing or even *abating* in the smallest circumstance, of what cannot but be regarded as the *grossest* and most *pointed* insult ever offered to a free people and its whole legislative. — The House before they proceeded to the choice of a speaker, remonstrated upon this head to the Governor, justly esteeming it inconsistent with their rights and dignity as a free Assembly, to proceed to the elections before them, amidst the noise of drums and fifes; and while they were surrounded with armed men, sent under a pretence indeed of *aiding* the civil authority, but in reality to *enforce* ministerial measures and mandates. — The Governor refused to receive their remonstrance, or to consider them as an house till they had chosen a speaker: They protested against the grievance of the military power placed so near them, and then unanimously elected the speaker and clerk of the former house, and renewed their remonstrance to the Governor. — He replied, that he had *no authority* over the military; and every circumstance complained of remained the same. It is generally supposed, that according to charter, the election of counsellors can be made upon no other day than the *last Wednesday* in May. From *necessity* therefore, the House after a *second protest*, proceeded with the Council to the election of counsellors. — The electors were so firm in the principles of former assemblies, that the *crown officers*, about which so much has been said, were not *chosen*, while those whom the Governor had negativ'd last year were re-elected; they indeed considered it as a point of no small importance that their choice should be *free* and not *dictated* by any Governor — and that the *legislative* and *executive* departments in government, should be kept as *separate* as may be. Out of *twenty-eight* duly chosen, and presented to the Governor, he was pleased to negative *eleven*. Thus that important department of government is *weakened*, and we have a just specimen of G B's. *prudence* and *disposition* to compose the public troubles. He has in a great measure *created* these troubles, and he preserves an uniformity of character, in exerting himself to *continue* and *increase* them. — No one denies his constitutional right to negative counsellors; but still he is accountable to his royal master and the public, for the *manner* and *ends* of exercising this right. When he first began to negative, he suffered it to be known and understood as a mark of resentment towards the electors for omitting to choose the L—t G—r, *secretary*, and *judges;* and that he would continue to negative such as should be chosen in their room. This the Assembly in general has justly deemed the most *open* and *violent attack* upon the *freedom of their election*, ever made by any Governor, and to fall little short of a *claim* to nominate the persons to be chosen: They have therefore adhered from year to year with a noble firmness to their *own right*, and maintained their freedom, for which they have the thanks and applause of their country. The Governor has seen fit to be as constant to his own *rash* and *arbitrary* resolution. With the same spirit he has continued to act respecting the troops. The House have made a solemn pause, and refused for more than a fortnight to enter upon public business, while surrounded with *arms* and *cannon* pointed close to the doors of the house in which they sat; every one knows that if he has not authority to *command* their destination, his influence, had he chose to employ it, would easily have *removed* the most disagreeable and *irritating* circumstances of their situation: Tho' the House had decently remonstrated to him upon this point as the head of the civil department, this in his opinion was not sufficient; he waited to be asked to become a kind of *intercessor* for the House with the General. They deemed this below their dignity. — They *claimed* and would not *implore* of a military officer, especially thro' such a mediator, what they esteemed the *right* of the *legislative;* and because they would not descend to this humiliating circumstance —— —— —— ——[1] *civil department*, of which he himself was the head, by making it give way to the *military*, and adjourning the court to Cambridge. — The very night after this adjournment, the cannon were remov'd from before the courthouse, as tho' it had been design'd that this circumstance should not appear to be done from any regard to the Assembly. — Who can forbear to admire the wisdom and justice of Administration, in esteeming such a man the most proper to manage the King's affairs in a great and important colony, and in *rewarding* his services, that have so much contributed to bring Britain and America into their present *happy* situation.

June 18
On the 5th instant, the happy anniversary of the birth of our most gracious sovereign, was celebrated by the honourable House of Representatives of this province; they chose to meet in their own room on the evening of said day, rather than at the Council Chamber; that the presence of our Governor might not throw a gloom unbecoming the occasion. A number of his Majesty's Council, and the clergy of the province, together with many of the principal merchants and gentlemen of the town, were present by invitation, and the following toasts were drank. The *KING, QUEEN,* and ROYAL FAMILY. — North-America. — The restoration of harmony between Great-Britain and the colonies. — Prosperity and perpetuity to the British empire in all parts of the world. — The Marquis of Rockingham, and the glorious administration of 1766. — Duke of Richmond. — Lord Chatham. — Lord Cambden. — General Conway. — Lord Shelburne. — Lord Dartmouth. — The late Governor Pownal. — Col. Barre. — Mr. Burke. — Dr. Lucas. — Paschal Paoli and his brave Corsicans. — The Cantons of Switzerland. — The King of Prussia. — The King of Sardinia. —The distressed Poles. —Their high mightinesses, the States General of the Seven United Provinces. — The Farmer of Pennsylvania, and all American patriots. —The Republick of Letters. — Liberty without licentiousness to all mankind. —

June 19
On Tuesday his Excellency Governor Wentworth, with several of the Council of that province included in the Commission for the trial of piracies, felonies, &c. on the high seas arrived in town. —The next day the court was opened according to adjournment, for the trial of the persons charged with the murder of Lieut. Panton, of his Majesty's ship Rose. The plea against the jurisdiction of the court was not admitted, and the court proceeded to the examination of witnesses &c. The trial did not end until the Saturday following, when a decree was given in, *justifiable homicide*, and the prisoners set at liberty. The *noble president* of the court, *Sir Francis Bernard*, during the course of this lengthy trial gave so many

---

[1] Three or four words are blurred.

proofs of his impartiality, tenderness and ability, as a judge, as were truly *admirable.* And could not but convince the court and others, that he bid as fair to outstrip a *Jefferies,* as he has confessedly done an *Andros* in the character of a governor.[1]

June 20

By Captain Hall, lately arrived, we have it from the best authority, that about the 10th of April positive orders were issued from Lord Hillsborough's office, for requiring Governor Bernard, immediately to repair to London; and from the same authority we are told, he will never return to this government. Those few among us who are of G. B's cabal, would be inconsolable for the loss they pretend the province must sustain by the recall of a Governor, in their opinion so well disposed and adapted to allay heats, compose differences, and to promote the real interest of both countries; had they not been flattered into the belief that it was wholly owing to an apprehension) that his presence was absolutely necessary at the Court of Great-Britain for a few months at least, not only to report to Administration the true state of affairs, but to *advise* and *assist* a young American S—y in the *disposal* of offices, and a wise and popular discharge of the duties of his important station. — However, we as well as the generality of people account for the recal of this *infatuated* and *infatuating* man in a very different manner. It is known that the M—y are now plunged, and that the untoward and embarrassed situation of things with respect to the colonies and themselves, are chiefly owing to his machinations. —It appears to be chiefly upon his representations relative to the temper and conduct of this people, that the M—y have grounded their late unhappy measures respecting the colonies: They now seem to be sensible of their mistakes, and greatly suspicious of G. B. having deceived and abused *them,* as well as the *province;* we therefore think it to be as probable as it is a rational conjecture that his presence in London is required, in order to his supporting the truth of what he has written and alledged against this government; or in case of failure, to receive from his abused sovereign, the just rewards of all

his *evil devises* against as *loyal* and *constitutionally obedient* a people as can be found in any part of his wide extended dominions.

June 21

Upon the receipt of the last mail from New-York, we had the pleasure, to hear that the town would very soon be cleared of the troops now quartered among us: General Gage having received orders by the packet for the removal of the 64th and 65th Regiment, with the train of artillery to Halifax; the 29th Regiment to the Castle, and the 14th Regiment to New-York. But we have now the mortification to be told, that G. B. and the C—m—rs pretending a fear of their lives if the troops should be removed from the town notwithstanding several of them have their seats in the country which they daily visit without the least insult or molestation being given them, have applied to General Gage for the continuance of the latter regiment: It is also rumoured, that the C—m—rs in order to countenance the G—r for having advised General Mackay to stop this regiment for the present, have preferred a petition to Governor Bernard, signed by themselves and about forty of their creatures and dependents, praying that he would use his influence with the commanding officer, that the said regiment may be suffered to remain in town for the protection of their persons and properties from the rage and violence of the inhabitants — From the past conduct of G. B. and the cabal it is not unlikely that they have taken this step, as nothing seems to afford them a greater pleasure than an opportunity for doing that which has a tendency to provoke and irritate the people, if haply they may be thereby betrayed into a behaviour which shall injure their characters with the King and his ministers.

June 22

Last evening at half after 11 o'clock, the watchmen of the town hearing a disturbance in the street went out to know the cause, when they found two sergeants of the 29th Regiment quarrelling with some of the town's people; upon asking the cause of the disturbance, they were answered with, drawn bayonets, and threatened that unless they immediately retired, they should be

---

[1] The last sentence is omitted from the *Journal* as published in the *Boston Evening Post,* August 7, 1769.

sent to h—ll. — However, the watchmen were not to be intimidated with high words, and a number of the inhabitants appearing, the soldiers were obliged to decamp, under the shelter of a certain retailer of spirituous liquors, who pretended to be an officer.

June 23

A sloop arrived here from New-York, and brought 95 soldiers who belonged to one of the regiments which is to return home. These recruits are far from being sufficient to fill up the vacancies made in the several regiments quartered among us, by desertions; which notwithstanding the utmost care and vigilance of the officers, have been so numerous as fully to evince the *impolicy* of their having been quartered in this town, had no other inconveniences arisen therefrom.

June 24

It is to be hoped that the shocking fate which the Lieut. of the Rose lately met with on board a merchant ship, and the actions now commenced against several who acted under, or were concern'd with him on an attempt as illegal as it was rash and injurious, will be a sufficient caution to the commanders of our guarda-costas, and the little marine custom-house officers, which like insects have lately swarmed from the Commissioners, not to exert a power in the impressing of seamen or searching of vessels, which the laws have never given them.

June 25

On Wednesday last the 65th Regiment began to embark from Castle-Island, on board the Rippon and Rose men of war, and yesterday they sailed for Halifax. — It is the wish of this people, that the troops which still remain may soon be more usefully employed, and in places where they may be made, consistent with the honour and interest of the townsmen, more welcome than at present they can be in the town of Boston.

June 26[1]

Last Friday morning, Brigadier General Pomroy, who has commanded the King's troops here, thro' the winter, set out for New-York, in order to embark in the packet for England; and altho' it is considered by the province in general, as the greatest injustice and insult that this brave and loyal people ever experienced, the having troops quartered upon them for the purpose of quelling a rebellion that never had existence, and for keeping good order in town, that is second to none for due obedience to all constitutional laws; and however irreconcileable they ever will be to a standing army or a military government: We are yet free to acknowledge that the conduct of this officer during his residence here, has done honour to the army, and that as a gentleman he was well respected.

June 27

It comes to us from good authority, that the reason why the military parade on Lord's days has not been laid aside, or at least the music omitted in complaisance to the application made to General Pomroy, by the Selectmen, and the earnest desire of the sober inhabitants of this town, was not owing to a want of disposition in that gentleman to gratify and relieve, but to a want of power to supercede the order and regulations of a superior officer.

June 28

A gentleman from Roxford, a town in this province, writes, that, "Mr. Joseph Robinson, of this town, had a ewe that brought him four lambs this spring at a time, which are all alive and like to do well: They all suck the ewe, and look as likely to live as any lambs he had seen this year. The same ewe brought three lambs at a time last spring, and raised up two of them. As an increase of sheep will prevent our sending home for woollen goods; we may quere, — Whether G. B. will not inform L–d H——ls —gh of this instance of fecundity, and earnestly recommend another regiment of soldiers being sent, in order to have our rams castrated, or else to cause a duty to be laid upon them.

June 29

In one of the men of war which sailed for Halifax, Jonathan Sewall, Esq; Judge of Admiralty for that province, embraked: It is said the design of his voyage is to appoint

---

[1] Items from June 26 to July 5, inclusive, are from the *New York Journal, Supplement*, July 27, 1769, p. 1.

deputy judges for Halifax and Quebec; after which he is to return to Boston, the present scene of action, for all who have listed under the banners of corruption! What benefit a province can reap from a non-resident's salary of £600 per annum, when all his deputies can do the business for about the sixth part of that sum divided among them, we leave to our oeconomical Ministry to point out. Our province must however certainly esteem itself highly favoured, that this foreign judge has so long after his appointment acted among us in the several characters of Attorney-General, Advocate-General, &c. and discerning people cannot but highly applaud the wisdom of our superiors in multiplying posts and pensions in America, and making the expence of government in the new settlements and colonies, bear a goodly proportion to the civil establishment of the mother country.

June 30

The public know not which to admire at most, either the gratitude or late influence of G. B. It being confidently reported, that the sole merit of a newly created J—e of A—y, with a salary of £600 per annum, was his being an assistant to that G—r in writing a set of papers in vindication of his conduct — which not long since appeared in one of our prints, subscribed Philanthrop — When we observe in what manner the public monies have been lately turned upon the little creatures of a court, may not Americans fairly conclude that the present national *debt*, is in the opinion of the present administration a national *benefit*.

July 1

A SLOOP owned in this town, James Brown, late master, who dying on his passage from North-Carolina to Gibraltar; the mate, one James, took the command of her, and by direction of the master, altered the intended voyage to the coast of Barbary for mules, and proceeded to a Spanish port for a load of salt, from whence she was returning to Boston, but being met with by one of our little guarda costas, who found five or six quarter casks of wine, not more in quantity than was sufficient for sea stores, besides a few frails of figs and almonds, the whole being the seamen's ad-ventures: For this extraordinary breach of trade, she was seized and taken possession of by this custom-house commander, who has since libell'd the sloop wines, &c. and is now harrassing the owners with a trial in our Court of Admiralty. — Upon the first appointment of a Board of Commissioners it was asserted that the protection of the merchant was intended, but every part of their conduct convinces us nothing less is intended: — The owner of this vessel gave a full representation to the Commissioners of all circumstances and made it clearly appear, that no fraud was intended, but that the mate supposed the wines might be admitted to an entry, or he would never have suffered them to have come on board; notwithstanding this, the Commissioners informed him, that they could not interpose, but must refer him back to the Capt. a creature of their own making, as the only proper person to treat with, and may we not from hence felicitate a trading people, that the propriety of stopping, unloading, detaining and libelling vessels or cargoes, is to depend so often upon the judgment or caprice of these new created voracious and *floating* custom-house officers.

July 2

Not long since we related the behaviour of one Fellows, another of the late marine custom-house officers, towards Mr. Parsons, deputy-sheriff for the county of Essex, who was divers times fired upon by four or five people with ball and swan shot by order of Fellows, with a design to rescue a person who the sheriff had taken for a debt, which was finally effected. We also informed, that upon the sheriff's application to the Governor and Council, the King's-Attorney was directed to prosecute this marine, alias custom-house officer for his attrocious offence. — We now learn that he was brought upon trial at Ipswich court, and that the said Fellows, at first pleaded not guilty, but afterward waved his plea, and was allowed to say (or plead) that he would not contend with our sovereign lord the King, &c. a favour not usually granted in cases of importance, and to such high handed offenders. — He was then sentenced by the honourable the Superior Court to pay the sum of fifteen pounds lawful money, but before the court was ended, it is said the Chief Justice took out of his pocket a petition of the said Fellows, for an abatement, when five pounds, out of the fifteen pounds fine, was remitted him. —[1] At the same court several persons said to be in company when an infamous creature at Newberry, called an informer, was tarred and feathered, but not fired upon or in any other way put in hazard of his life, were sentenced in no less sums than 20, 30 and 40 l. respectively — We presume not to remark upon the conduct of the judges in these or other instances; shall only say that the good people of the province are greatly alarmed, and that the General Court intend making it a subject matter of their inquiry the present session.

July 3

On Tuesday morning the 27th June, a woman going to the south-market for a fish, stopt at the shop of Mr. Chase, under Liberty-Tree, appearing to be faint, they got some water, but on raising her up she died instantly. A jury of inquest was summoned, and upon examination she appeared to be one Sarah Johnson, of Bridgewater, on whom it appeared by evidence and several marks, that violence had been perpetrated the 24th inst. by soldiers unknown, which probably was the cause of her death. — Several physicians who were called in upon the occasion, declared, that upon examining the surface of the body, they observed sundry livid spots, which evidently demonstrated violence; and from the combined appearances, upon opening the body, they were of opinion that she had been recently ravished, and had resisted to the utmost; and that the over exertion of her strength, might probably terminate in a syncope or faintness, which they thought might be the immediate cause of her death.

July 4

On Monday last, one T——z P——k, an ensign of the 64th Regiment, observing a woman standing near the door of her house, made up to her, and after using a great deal of fulsome language and attempting some indecencies, she made her escape and got inside of the door, which she shut against him; he however followed her, and finding the door fastened on the inside, attempted to force it open, but not being able to do it, he went off, swearing he would return again; and on the Wednesday night following he was good as his word, the said woman being sitting at her chamber window, he accosted her, by calling her his "sweet angel, and desiring her to come down and let him in; the husband who is a person of character, being in the same room, and hearing one speak in the street, asked his wife who it was, she told him it was the same impudent fellow that had attempted a few days before to break open the door; upon which he immediately ran to the window and asked him what he wanted: — I want says he, that angel at the window; the gentleman replied, she is my wife: I don't care whose wife she is, returned he, for by G—d I'll have her in spite of all the men in the country if you are her husband, by G—d you shan't keep her long, and if you don't put your head into the window immediately, I'll be d—d if I don't blow your brains out. — The gentleman tried to keep his temper, and told him unless he retired immediately he would apply to a magistrate and have him punished for his temerity; upon which the brave officer redoubled his threats and curses, swore by G—d such a d—d ugly fellow as he, was not fit to have such a wife, and he would take her away from him at all events, for which purpose he would tarry in town till next summer, and would sacrifice him tho' death was the consequence, with abundance of other scurrilous abusive treatment; which at length provok'd the husband so much, that he took a loaded pistol which was in the room and attempted to fire it at him, but was prevented by the fright and intreaties of his wife: Mr. Ensign at last went off, and the next day the gentleman applied to a magistrate for a warrant, by virtue of which the offender was taken and obliged to give bail in £200 lawful money, to answer for his conduct at the next sessions of the peace.

July 5

On Thursday evening last, a dispute arose near the town-dock between a soldier and a

---

[1] The remaining portion of the item for July 2, is omitted from the *Journal* as published in the *Boston Evening Post*.

sailor, when the former very couragiously drew his hanger and struck the latter, who was entirely unarmed; but a good natured female standing near, put a stick into the sailor's hand, with which he so beloboured his antagonist, (notwithstanding he made several strokes at him with his hanger) that he obliged him to sheer off with considerable damage to his hull; he is since haul'd up in hospital to repair, and it is imagin'd it will be some time before he is fit for service.

July 8[1]
We have frequently had occasion to observe and point out the impolicy, not to say injustice of the late acts for raising a revenue in America; when this is discerned by those who have the lead in Administration, it may perhaps be too late to apply a remedy for a cure of those disorders which their rashness has occasioned. — The duties laid upon paper, by the late Revenue Acts, has served as a bounty to encourage our paper manufactures; those rags and materials of which paper is composed, are now carefully saved from the fire and dunghill, — the period cannot be very distant, when we shall have as little occasion to import that manufacture, as we at present have those of sithes and other implements of husbandry, which are now made use of in preference to those made in England.

A tax upon painter's colours, has set a whole continent to explore their hills and mountains in consequence of which we have discovered, and now actually make use of a red and yellow ocre, superior in quality to what was imported from England. — Oil is extracted from our flax-seed, not only for our own consumption, but for exports; white lead so necessary for the painters, which it was imagined could not be obtained, has been made in Boston, equal in goodness to the British; and if the fairest prospect should not deceive, a mine of lead, not far from water carriage, owned by a gentleman of property will be quickly worked to such advantage as to afford a full supply of that article for all the painters in America. Manufacturers of pipes, delph glass, linen and woolen wares are set and setting up in this town, and while the ministers of the British court are postponing a repeal of the Revenue Acts and a redress of grievances, until as they say it can be done consistent with the *dignity* of Government, and so as not to weaken the supreme authority of Parliament; Americans are laying a most solid foundation for their future grandeur and felicity, by greatly increasing their growth of hemp and flax, and multiplying their flocks of sheep; spinning schools are opened and filled with learners in Boston and other parts of the province; and the following articles of intelligence, out of many others, may serve to show the progress of industry, and what methods are taken to countenance and encourage so laudable and beneficial an employment. —

July 9
We are informed from Dorchester, that about sixty of the fair sex in that town, assembled at the house of the Rev. Mr. Jonathan Bowman, with wheels, and the greater part of them with flax, and spent the day there in the much to be recommended and encouraged business of spinning. The order in which they were ranged on the green, before the house, at which they met; the decent behaviour, pleasantry, and industry, visible among them in the work of the day, gave sincere and singular pleasure to the numerous surrounding spectators of this and other towns. About sunset the wheels ceased going, and the reels and combs made use of by others, were laid aside: And the many skeins all well spun; at the aforesaid house, together with those sent in on that day, are enough, as is judged to make eighty yards of cloth, more than three quarters wide. — Provision for the repast or entertainment of the ladies, was freely sent in and gratefully accepted; as was the work of their hands.

July 10
We are also informed from Beverly, that last Tuesday, very early in the morning, sixty young ladies of various ages, belonging to that town, assembled at the house of the Rev. Mr. Champney, with their spinning wheels, flax, and cotton wool, and entered

---

[1] Items from July 8 to July 17, inclusive, are from the *New York Journal, Supplement*, August 24, 1769, p. 1. Apparently there were no items in the *Journal* for July 6 and 7. The *Boston Evening Post*, August 21, 1769, closes its item of the *Journal* for July 5 with the statement "No further of the *Journal* is yet come to hand."

upon the business and design of their meeting together, — with pleasure and spirit, with skill and dexterity, and so spent the day with great application. The music of their wheels ceased only for their refreshment; — No uneasiness appeared among them for the whole day. — They spun one hundred twenty knot skeins, which they generously gave to him and family, as also considerable cotton and flax, for want of time to spin them.

July 11

We hear that eighty-three industrious young females, met at the house of the Rev. Mr. Robbins, in Milton, where they spent the day in the delightful employment of spinning, and at sunset, what was spun and presented, amounted to four hundred and sixty skeins, excluding tow; about half of them spun their yarn at the rate of 140 knots to the pound, which was done incomparably well; and sixty weight of the flax, was, of Mr. Robbins's own raising.

July 12

They write from Braintree, that a number of young ladies met at the house of the Rev. Mr. Weld, in that place, and according to the laudable practice in many other parts, spent the day in spinning; and generously gave both their labour and yarn; — and what is especially remarkable, a young miss of 9 years old wound off her two double skeins, excellently well spun, — a good omen for the times. — An example of industry well worthy the ambition of others.

July 13

We are informed from Ipswick, that the young ladies of a parish called Chebacco, to the number of seventy-seven, assembled at the house of the Rev. Mr. John Cleavland, with their spinning wheels; and though the weather that day was extremely hot, and divers of the young ladies were but about thirteen years of age, yet by six o'clock in the afternoon, they spun of linen yarn four hundred and forty knots, and carded and spun of cotton seven hundred and thirty knots, and of tow six hundred, in all 1770 knots, which make 177 ten knot skeins, all good yard, and generously gave their work, and some brought cotton and flax with

them, more than they spun themselves, as a present; and several of the people were kind and generous upon this occasion. And it may be worthy of noting, that one spun of good linen yarn, 52 knots, and another of cotton 60 knots, it being carded for her. — After the music of the wheels was over, Mr. Cleaveland entertained them with a sermon, on Prov. xiv. 1. Every wise woman buildeth her house; but the foolish plucketh it down with her hands:—which he concluded by observing, how the women might recover to this country the full and free enjoyment of all our rights, properties and privileges, (which is more than the men have been able to do) and so have the honour, of building, not only their own, but the houses of many thousands, and perhaps prevent the ruin of the whole British empire, viz. by living upon, as far as possible, only the produce of this country; and to be sure to lay aside the use of all foreign teas, also, by wearing, as far as possible, only clothing of this country's manufacturing.

July 14

We hear from Wenham, that early in the morning, there came a number of young women, to the house of the Rev. Joseph Swain, with flax, wool, and wheels, in order to spend the day in spinning, which they did till 6 o'clock P. M. with cheerfulness, discretion and industry. Their diligence and industry, in the business of the day, will appear by comparing the number of spinners, and the quantity of yarn spun. The spinners were in number 38; the quantity of yarn was 75 run; all which they generously gave to him and family, besides a considerable quantity of flax and wool, which was left unspun.

July 15

We hear that a number of young ladies belonging to Mr. Haven's parish in Dedham, lately made Mrs. Haven a visit, and presented her with 102 skeins of good yarn, mostly linen: each skein containing 20 knots, which they had before spun at their several homes, and of their own materials. Their professed design was to encourage industry and our own manufactures, and to testify their affectionate regard to their minister, and to his family; which many of the fair sex in several towns, have lately been doing.

They preferred this method of doing it, to that of carrying their wheels and flax to their minister's house to spin there; as they hereby avoid much trouble and parade, and had an opportunity for a more pleasant visit, and free conversation, and to animate one another to a course of persevering industry and frugality, which is necessary to save our country from impending ruin. The disposition which they discovered was applauded and encouraged, and their gratuity thankfully received.

On the 12th of July, the good women of the second precinct in Brookfield, — true daughters of liberty & industry, stimulated by their fair sisters, met at the house of the Rev. Mr. Forbes, to the number of fifty-five, with thirty four wheels; and from 5 o'clock in the morning, to 7 in the evening, picked, carded, and spun, of cotton wool and tow, 762 knots, and a few threads; and of flax, hatcheled and spun 936 knots and 35 threads, all which they generously gave to Mr. Forbes. The young lady that excelled at the linen wheel, spun 70 knots: And among the matrons there was one, who did the morning work of a large family, made her cheese, &c. and then rode more than two miles, and carried her own wheel, and sat down to spin at nine in the morning; and by seven in the evening, span 53 knots, and went home to milking. As the cool of the evening came on, about five o'clock, they all descended from the chambers and rooms of the house, into the front yard, on the green; where, with their buzzing wheels, innocent chat, neat and decent apparel, (chiefly homespun) friendly activity, and the very perfection of female harmony, made a most agreeable appearance. The next day, and for several succeeding days; others as well affected to their minister and the cause of liberty and industry, but could not leave their families to join their sisters on the said day, sent in their forty knots each, spun out of their own materials: — A very striking example to generosity and public oeconomy.¹

July 16
Newport. July 10. We can assure the public, that spinning is so much encouraged among us, that a lady in town, who is in very affluent circumstances, and who is between 70 and 80 years of age, has within about three weeks become a very good spinner, though she never spun a thread in her life before. — Thus has the love of liberty and dread of tyranny, kindled in the breast of old and young, — a glorious flame, which will eminently distinguish the fair sex of the present time, through far distant ages.

July 17
We are informed that two vessels have lately arrived at Falmouth from Scotland, the design of the owners was to purchase their cargo of lumber, with British manufactures, as had been usually done but the inhabitants of that town, having came into the agreement relative to non-importation of foreign merchandize; The loading of those vessels could not be procured with any thing but the *money*. — *The colonies can supply themselves with almost every necessary for wearing apparel, the large sums which Britain has annually drawn from us, should be placed to the account of our luxury and extravagance, rather than to our wants; were we but wise and frugal, silver and gold would soon flow in upon us, as pay for our fish, oil, lumber, and other commodities, required at European markets.*

July 18²
We shall continue to hold up the actions of our military gentry, not merely for the information of Americans, but that the people of Britain may perceive the wisdom of Administration, in appointing such a set of men as aids de camps to the civil magistrates, in the execution of the laws and conservation of the peace.

July 19
A respectable tradesman of this town, returning home one evening through Boarded

---

¹ The items from July 9 to July 16, inclusive are omitted from the *Journal* in the *Boston Evening Post*, September 4, 1769, p. 1. The following is inserted in italics: "(Here follows a long account of several spinning matches of the female sex, particularly at the house of the Rev. Mr. Bowman of Dorchester; — at the Rev. Mr. Champney's of Beverley; — at the Rev. Mr. Robins's in Milton; — at the Rev. Mr. Weld's in Braintree; — at the Rev. Mr. Cleaveland's in Ipswich; — at the Rev. Mr. Swain's in Wenham; — at the Rev. Mr. Haven's in Dedham; — at the Rev. Mr. Forbes's in Brookfield; — and at Newport, Rhode Island; but as these have already been published in the news paper here, we think it needless to reprint them again)."

² Items from July 18 to July 24, inclusive, are from the *Boston Evening Post*, September 25, 1769, p. 1.

alley, was without the least provocation, knocked down by a grenadier of the 29th Regiment; he soon came to himself, and having recovered his cane, was quietly walking off; but soon perceived was followed by the same soldier, who he called upon to stand back, but this not being regarded he made so good a use of his cane, as to protect himself from any further abuse for that time; however, it seems this fellow, who had that night got a terrible drubbing from other persons whom he had insulted, took it in his head to lay the whole of what he had received upon the beforementioned tradesman, and having met him about a fortnight afterwards, near the Common, tho' before sunset, he dared to assault & wound him with his bayonet, in a most cruel manner, a number of soldiers looking on, and had it not been for the timely assistance of some of the inhabitants passing by at that time, he would probably have been murdered: This person was confined to his house a considerable time, by means of the wounds received. The soldier had a bill found against him by the grand jury, but this being suspected before it was given in, the criminal deserted, or rather was concealed for a time, and then, as is supposed, conveyed away, as others had been before him, out of the reach of the law, which must have fallen heavy upon him.

July 20

A young man was standing in the street some evenings past, as Capt. M—h was passing, a stick which this officer said he flung at a dog, struck the young fellow, and occasioned some altercations, the Captain soon drew his sword, and made a stroke at the other, by which he was wounded; the people soon gathered, and might have treated the officer with as little ceremony, had not he immediately sought and found a shelter in a gentleman's house, not far from the scene of action.

July 21

As a captain of a vessel was standing by his street door, he heard the cries of two ladies, whom some soldiers were treating with great rudeness; he did not fail to expostulate & then threaten, for which he was knocked down and much hurt by the soldiers.

July 22

An officer of the navy came into a taylor's shop in the day time, accompanied by several soldiers, when pretending he had been affronted, he drew his hanger, and beat in a cruel manner, a young fellow who was setting on his board, notwithstanding all the intreaties of his father, who was present, a number of people rushing into the shop, obliged this hero and his party to decamp and march off with precipitation.

July 23

Last evening as two women of unblemished reputation, one married, the other single, were returning home about nine o'clock, from a visit, they were stopped in the street, near the brick meeting-house, by an officer, who insisted upon waiting upon them home, upon being told they were near home, and had no occasion for company, he began to use very foul language, and finally, in a very courageous, and soldierly manner, took his leave, with about a dozen smart strokes of a rattan, upon the shoulders of the unmarried and defenceless lady.

July 24

Some Sabbaths past, as the guards, placed near the Town-House, were relieving, there was a considerable concourse of people, chiefly boys and Negroes to partake of the entertainment given by their band of music; the wardens having by their laudable exertions dispersed the rabble, soon perceived that Mr. John Bernard, our Governor's second son, had made one among them, and still kept his standing; upon which they very civilly accosted him desiring that he would walk off, lest his being suffered to remain, should give occasion for their being taxed with partiality in the execution of their trust; Mr. Bernard then seemed to be walking away, when Capt. M—s—h, who commanded the guard, called to him, desiring that he would come into the square, where he should be protected from the wardens; the young man accepted of so pressing and polite an invitation; but the wardens called to him as he was going into the square, praying him to desist, as they would otherwise be put to the disagreeable necessity of returning his name to a magistrate, the Monday following; upon this the officer of the guard, in a sneering manner, called upon the musicians to play up the Yankee Doodle tune, which compleated the conquest of the military, and afforded them a temporary triumph. The wardens made good their promise, and discharged their duty, by entering a complaint with a magistrate, against Mr. Bernard, for breach of Sabbath, when he was convicted, and punished agreeable to law.

July 25[1]

A country butcher who frequents the market, having been in discourse with one Riley, a grenadier of the 14th Regiment, who he said had before abused him, thought proper to offer such verbal resentment as led the soldier to give him a blow, which felled the butcher to the ground, and left other proofs of his violence. The assaulter was had before Mr. Justice Quincy, convicted and fined, and upon refusing to make payment, was ordered to goal; but rescued out of the hands of the constable, by a number of armed soldiers, in the sight of the justice, when they carried their rescued comrade, in triumph, thro' the main street to his barracks, flourishing their naked cutlasses, giving out that they had good support in what they were doing, and that they defied all opposition. — The inhabitants were greatly offended at this audacity of the military, and the call was very general, that the posse commitatus might be raised in order to recover the prisoner out of their hands; this was not a little alarming, even to the General himself, he apprehended, from the resentment of the people, and tho' he was to have embarked in the Rippon man of war in a few days, he immediately laid aside the thoughts of it. — It being soon given out, that the soldier thus rescued had deserted, or was taken out of the way in order to prevent a discovery in the course of tryal of those who had encouraged so illegal and dangerous an attempt: The friends of peace and order advised the constable and one of his assistants, who was also wounded, to proceed immediately to Cambridge, in order to make representation to the General Assembly, who were then just upon rising, of the behaviour of the military, which they accordingly did; when the House of Representatives, after giving them a hearing, appointed a committee to examine into this matter, and transmit the state thereof to their agent in London.

Affidavits were accordingly taken, but not in the Bernardinian manner, *exparte;* some of them are here inserted, that the world may have the most authentick proof in what manner the civil magistrate has been assisted by those modern conservators of the peace.

EDMUND QUINCY, of Boston, in the county of Suffolk, Esq; and one of his Majesty's justices of the peace for the said county, deposeth, that on the 13th day of July current, at Boston, aforesaid, Jonathan Winship of Cambridge, in the county of Middlesex, victualler, came into the office of the deponent, and complained in his Majesty's name, that he had been assaulted and beat, the same day, by John Riley, a grenadier of his Majesty's 14th Regiment of Foot, in said Boston; the complainant at the same time, producing full evidence of the assault and battery; that on the same day, by force of a warrant, issued by the deponent, the said John Riley, was by Peter Barbour, one of the constables of the town of Boston, brought to answer to the said complaint, and pleading guilty, was by the deponent fined in the sum of five shillings to his Majesty, and ordered to pay costs of prosecution, and to *stand committed until sentence be performed;* that pleading his inability to pay his fine and costs, was indulged till next day; a serjeant of the company, one John Phillips, becoming responsible for the return of the offender into custody, in default of payment; — that the said serjeant did the next day, at the hour appointed, return the said offender to the office of the deponent, the abovementioned constable being there ready to receive him; that the said offender being asked whether he was ready to pay his fine and costs, returned for answer, *"he would not pay it,"* whereupon the deponent said to the offender, that he must then commit him: Soon after which, while the deponent was writing a Mittimas, the said offender attempted to wrest himself out of the hands of

---

[1] Items from July 25 to July 30, inclusive, are from the *Boston Evening Post*, October 2, 1769, pp. 1–2.

the said officer, then having hold of him in the said office, and in the attempt, very suddenly forced himself, with the officer into the street; after which the deponent going to the door of his office, and seeing the hostile approach of (as he apprehended) about 20 grenadiers and other soldiers, many if not most of them armed with cutlasses, swords and other instruments of death, and the same handling in a menacing manner, went to the door of his said office, and commanded the said soldiers to disperse themselves, but as a non-compliance with the order was soon visible, the deponent immediately said to Mr. Ross, (a lieutenant of the company of grenadiers of the beforementioned 14th Regiment) who just before entered the office that he desired he would order those men to their barracks, and after a most urgent repetition of the request, the deponent received for answer, from the said Mr. Ross, that he did not know what to do with them, or words of similar import; but after hearing that the constable was wounded, the said Lieutenant Ross went, and (as the deponent was soon after informed) ordered those soldiers who still remained before the office, to disperse and go to their barracks. — The deponent further saith, that the prisoner, John Riley, through countenance and aid of the said grenadiers, and other of his Majesty's soldiers, was rescued from the hands of Justice, and has ever since been so concealed, that as the deponent verily believes the officer has not been able to retake him.

EDMUND QUINCY.

Suffolk, ss. ⊳ *Boston, July* 24 1769. Edmund Quincy, Esq; before named, appeared before us, two of his Majesty's justices of the peace for the said county of Suffolk, and made oath to the truth of the before written affidavit. Taken in consequence of an order of the Honorable House of Representatives of this Province, to perpetuate the Remembrance of the thing.

Before me, RD. DANA, Justice of the Peace, and of the Quorum.

BEL. NOYES, Jus. of the Peace.

I Peter Barbour, one of the constables of the town of Boston, testify and say, That on the 13th day of July inst. a warrant was committed to me the deponent, by Ed.

Quincy, Esq; one of his Majesty's justices of the peace for the county of Suffolk, against one John Riley, a grenadier in the 14th Regiment, for assaulting and beating one Jonathan Winship a butcher, usually attending the public market; by virtue of said warrant I took into my custody the said John Riley, and carried before the aforesaid justice, who, upon a full hearing of the case, ordered the said John Riley, to pay a fine of five shillings, lawful money, and costs, and to stand committed until the said sentence should be performed; but the said John pleading his inability to pay the fine and costs, was indulged, till the next day; — a serjeant of the same company, John Phillips, by name, becoming responsible for the return of the said Riley into custody the next day, in default of payment; and on the next day the said John Riley, was by the said Serjeant Phillips, bro't before the said justice, where the said Riley refused to pay his fine and costs; whereupon the said justice said he should be committed to prison; and whilst the said Justice was making out a mittimus to commit the said Riley to goal, one Lieutenant Ross of the said regiment, came into the said justice's house; and upon the said Riley's saying he would neither pay the fine nor go to goal, the said Lieut. Ross turned himself to the said John Riley, and bid him go; upon which said Riley attempted to retire out of the house, and I endeavored to stop him, and seized him by the collar, and held him until the said Lieut. Ross rushed in upon me and broke my hold, whereby the said Riley escaped, and got out of the doors, notwithstanding all I the deponent, with my assistance could do to prevent it: I immediately followed the prisoner to the door, and as soon as the said Riley had got out of the door, he drew his cutlass and struck me upon my head, which blow brought me down upon my knees. I then said to the prisoner, for God's sake don't strike me again, but the said Riley immediately struck me another blow, upon the head with his cutlass, which bro't me to the ground, which was the last thing I knew for a considerable time; and further I the deponent say not.

PETER BARBOUR.

Sworn to as the First.

I Jeremiah Belknap, of lawful age, testify and say, that on the 14th day of this inst. July, as I was passing thro' dock square, I saw a number of soldiers, (the names to the deponent unknown) armed with broad swords, some of which soldiers I then heard say, damn him, we will wait for him; when after being absent about a quarter of an hour, and returning the same way to my house, the deponent saw a number of soldiers standing before the door of Edmund Quincy, Esq; one of the justices of the peace for the county of Suffolk, where one John Riley, as I soon after understood, was then convened for breach of the peace; which soldiers the deponent apprehends and verily believes to be the same he had heard say in dock-square, aforesaid, damn him, they would wait for him, and as the deponent passed by the said soldiers he heard them say that the said John Riley should not be carried to goal; upon which the deponent turned to some of the inhabitants, who stood near, and told them there was like to be a riot and desired them to hinder it, by supporting the civil officers in the execution of their office, and then went to the justice's window, where he was called upon by the constable to assist him, the deponent then went into the justice's house, and told the said justice that there was like to be a riot at his door, for those soldiers that were standing there had swore (in his hearing) by God, that the said Riley should not go to goal; upon which the said justice turned to Lieut. Ross, an officer in the same company, to which the said Riley belongs, and desired him to take care of his men, in order to prevent a riot; the said Ross answered he could not, and immediately gave way, upon which the said Riley made towards the door; then Peter Barbour, the constable aforesaid, declared the said Riley should not go, and laid hold of him, in order to prevent his escape: The deponent then endeavouring, by order of the said constable to assist, and prevent the said Riley from escaping was, with the constable forced out of the justice's door, where the same soldiers, as he believes, with drawn swords, rushed upon us, & struck at those who were endeavouring to aid and assist the said constable in the execution of his office, by one of which strokes the deponent was much wounded by being cut in his hand; and the deponent further says that the soldiers around the justice's door were about 20, with arms, viz cutlasses, &c.

JEREMIAH BELKNAP.

Sworn to in the same manner as the first.

July 28

I John Loring of Boston, Physician, of lawful age, testify and declare, that being on the 14th day of July, current, near his dwelling house in Cornhill, about 3 o'clock P. M. observing a number of the grenadiers of the 14th Regiment, following and insulting a country butcher as he was riding on his cart, which stopping a few rods from said house, the deponent went near the cart and heard the butcher talking to the soldiers, desiring them to let him go about his business, when Col. Dalrymple came by and asked what was the matter. The butcher got off his cart, and with his hat in his hand told him he was insulted by the soldiers, who hindered him from going about his business; and that one of the regiment yesterday had knocked him down, the Colonel said to him, "you are a damned scoundrel, you was saucy, they served you right, and I don't care if they knock you down again," and directly walked away; the soldiers took off their hats, and exultingly said, there's a noble gentlemen, do you hear what the noble gentleman says, the deponent then went into Mr. Justice Quincy's office, and told him he was apprehensive of a riot, and desired him to go out and disperse them, he went out and spoke to them but to no effect; soon after, Lieut. Ross of the grenadier company of the 14th Regiment, being sent for by one of the soldiers, came to the said office, the deponent standing near the said office, among the soldiers, and hearing them very abusive, and swearing that Riley the prisoner should not be carried to goal, went into the office and told Lieut. Ross what the soldiers said & threatened; his answer was, I can't help it, other persons particularly Mr. Justice Quincy spoke to him to the same effect, and he gave like answers; in a few minutes after, the prisoner being by the door of said office, near said Ross, and attempting an escape, was seized by the constable Barbour, who commanded assistance;

a number of swords were immediately drawn by the soldiers in the street, and Mr. Jeremiah Belknap coming into the office, with the blood running from his hand, the deponent again spoke to the said Ross, and asked him how he could stand by and see such outrageous behaviour, and he answered, what would you have me do, I can't help it; the deponent then left them, some body telling him the constable was wounded, the deponent found said constable with a cut on the forehead and the blood following very freely from the wound, and going to his own house for proper dressings, saw said Ross in the street, and told him the constable was for aught he, the deponent knew, dangerously wounded, and the said Lieut. Ross answered him, "I am sorry, but can't help it," and further saith not.

J. LORING.

Sworn to in the same manner as the first.

July 29

I Edward Jackson, of Boston, of lawful age, testify and say, that on the 14th instant, July, between 2 & 3 o'clock P. M. I saw about 12 soldiers together, on dock square, and hearing of Mr. Winship's being knocked down the day before by a soldier, I went to said Winship, and told him I believe they were consulting some mischief against him, and advised him to go home immediately; upon which he got into his cart, and as he was riding along, these soldiers hollowed after him & followed him, upon which he stopped against Justice Quincy's, and the soldier who had assaulted him the day before, challenged him to fight; upon which Mr. Winship said he never struck any body in his life, and never desired to fight with any body; while he was speaking, Col. Dalrymple passed by, I advised Mr. Winship to speak to the Colonel and acquaint him with the treatment he received from his men, he accordingly went up to Col. Dalrymple in a respectful manner, and acquainted him he had been abused; the Colonel replied with a raised voice, that he was an impudent rascal, and that he had not been abused half enough, & if he did not lick him he would, upon which one of the soldiers replied, that the Colonel was a

gentleman, and that they would not take it as they had done; another soldier said, they, meaning the inhabitants, would not be easy till they lost a leg or an arm.

EDWARD JACKSON.

Sworn to in the same manner as the first.

July 30

I Stephen Greenleaf, of lawful age, testify and declare, than on the 14th instant, as I was standing by Mr. Gardner's shop, between the hours of 2 and 3 o'clock, I saw a number of people coming up the street fronting dock-square, and went to see what the matter was, and saw one Riley, who had been taken up the day before for knocking down a butcher, named Jonathan Winship, going to Mr. Justice Quincy's, a number of other soldiers accompanying of him, the said Winship was also with them, and one of the soldiers was challenging him to fight, the said Winship replied, that he never struck a man in his life, and never intended to, and the said Winship seeing Col. Dalrymple passing by went up to him, in a respectful manner, and acquainted how he had been abused by one of his men the day before, upon which Col. Dalrymple inquired of some of the soldiers, what was the occasion of his abusing the man, the soldier made some reply, which the deponent could not hear, upon which the Colonel said to said Winship, that he was a damned rascal, that he had not been beaten half enough, and speaking to the soldier, he said knock him down again if he (meaning Winship) abused him; if he did not he would, upon which he passed off, and soon turning about said, *understand me;* soon after this, I saw the prisoner, viz. John Riley, coming out of Mr. Justice Quincy's, with a drawn sword, and uttering these expressions, take me, *take me now if you dare,* upon which a number of other soldiers drew their swords, and said also, *take him, take him now if you dare;* upon which the prisoner went off in a triumphant manner, flourishing his sword: — About half an hour after this, as I was passing by Mr. Payson's shop, the retailer, in which were a number of soldiers, among whom was John Riley, aforesaid, who seeing Mr. Barbour the constable passing by, drew his sword, and said, there is the sword that did the jobb, damn his eyes, I wish I had cut his head wholly off: And the deponent further declares, that he apprehends that there was to the number of 20 soldiers, at Mr. Justice Quincy's door, all armed, when the said Riley went off.

STEPHEN GREENLEAF.

August 1[1]

IN the letters of Governor Bernard, to the Secretary of State, not long since published, and some more lately arrived, we have a true picture of the man drawn by his own hand. — Never did a minister of state receive, even from the lowest servant of the crown, such a budget of little malicious stories, of inflammatory details, and gross misrepresentations. Never did the Governor of a great and respectable province, sink so far beneath his character, as this letter writer has done, and so totally forget what he ow'd to candour, to truth, to his own station, to the people whom he govern'd, and from whom he had been enriched, to the honour and service of his sovereign, and the interest of the nation, at a very critical season. The man is now held up to public view in his true colours, to whom the misunderstanding between Britain and her colonies, is more owing than perhaps to any other person, tho' he has not been without base coadjutors and mercenary tools. Not content with relating plain important facts, and leaving Administration to judge of them, which is all that a man of common candour and humanity would have done, considering the severe inclinations of the Ministry, and the delicate situation of the town and province, he has heap'd up and disguised little incidents to irritate and inflame: He has reported as facts, what never existed: He has given a malevolent turn to what is true; and not only suggested the most violent, distressing, and unconstitutional measures; but has laboured to shew, by a series of misrepresentations, that such measures are absolutely necessary. He has aim'd the most false and malignant aspersions, not only at particular characters, but the most respectable bodies of men; at the Council, the Selectmen, the Overseers,

and the Justices of the town of Boston. In the course of business with these bodies, he has meanly tamper'd with particular members, as appears from his letters, endeavouring to draw out something that might be dropt in a debate, by individuals to one another, in a private manner, in order to furnish matter of representation to the Ministry; and when he could not find fault with the determination itself, — He has insinuated that it might proceed from the basest motives. In these, and innumerable other instances, he has acted the part of an infamous pimp to a Secretary of State, who instead of encouraging, ought to have known himself dishonoured and affronted, by having such accounts addressed to him, even if they had been true. His representations of the town of Boston, and the disposition of its inhabitants, and particularly his assertions of a design form'd to seize the Castle, are beyond example, false and abusive;— But his rancor is not confined to this town; it extends to the whole province, to its charter privileges, and the rights of America, which he has employed every base method in his power to destroy; he has plainly signified in his letters, his inclination, that not only the judges, but all the justices thro' the colonies, should hold their commissions during pleasure; which must at once destroy the grand security, which the British Constitution gives, for the free and impartial administration of justice. — With respect to the charter of this province, he expressly says, that the destruction of it is an event devoutly to be wished. — And yet such meanness was this man capable of adding to his malignity, that just before authentic copies of his letters were received, he repeatedly declared to the honourable speaker of the House, and other gentlemen of character, that he was a sincere friend to the province, and its charter privileges; that he had never wrote against either, and if he were at liberty to shew his letters, their candour and moderation must be acknowledged by all. — His whole conduct has been of a piece with his letters, and both demonstrate how totally unqualified, he was, to sustain any department of government with

---

[1] The following item is from the *New York Journal, Supplement,* November 30, 1769, pp. 1–2. The heading is "continued from No. 1393, Sept. 14." This item is not printed in the *Boston Evening Post* whose last item is July 30 and does not have "To be continued."

honour, and to promote the true service of the crown. — We have already remarked upon his behaviour in the General Court, as far as the adjournment to Cambridge. — This adjournment had the effect which might naturally be expected from it. — Instead of abating, it raised the tone of the Assembly. — The contempt with which he had treated their just remonstrances, and the inclination he had so plainly discovered, to keep up every mark of superiority and insult in the military, over the legislative of the province, served to convince them more of the necessity of supporting their constitutional rights: and furnished matter of irritation to men already warm'd with a high sense of liberty. — In all their replies they could not avoid holding up the opinion they had formed of him, as a determined enemy, to the rights of this, and indeed of every colony: And his speeches, his letter, and his conduct, demonstrate to all the world the justice of this opinion. Full of this idea, and knowing that he was soon to embark for England, and that he had already been paid as Governor, till August, they suspended the grant usually made at the beginning of the year, upon which no doubt his heart was much set, and which it is tho't he was weak enough to expect: — They passed a new set of spirited resolves; they refused to make any provision for the military, introduc'd into the town of Boston, not only without the call, but contrary to the sentiments and declarations of the civil magistrate, and quartered there, in the teeth of an act of Parliament, and proceeded to vote articles of complaint against the Governor, and a petition for his removal from the government: — In all these proceedings of the House, there was great unanimity, and they were supported by the almost universal sentiments of their constituents. — At length, the Governor, after a speech, in his usual strain, prorogued the Court to January, — whether in this he meant to affront the Lieutenant G—r, in whom he shewed so intire a confidence, by preventing, as far as he was able, his meeting the Assembly, whatever occasion might offer, within six months; or whether this step was concerted between them, we pretend not to determine: It is however certain, that such long prorogations at so critical a

time, as they tend to prevent a true idea of the state of things from being seasonably placed before the British government and nation, can never promote the true service of his Majesty, or the tranquility of his good subjects.

Governor Bernard, a year before his departure for England, had received hints from the Ministry, that his presence in London would not be disagreeable; but foolishly disregarding this soft language, he was now obliged to obey positive orders. — He gave up with a heavy heart, the hopes he had entertained of enjoying a good share in the American revenue, besides his salary and perquisites as Governor, under the security of a military power. — Upon his departure every demonstration of joy was to be seen in his government, in which all America partook. — Whatever may be his first reception at home, impartial history will hang him up as a warning to his successors, who have any sense of character, and perhaps his future fortune may be such as to teach even the most selfish of them not to tread in his steps.

The Commissioners not long since published an advertisement, relative to the stripping and feathering of one Jessee Tavilla, a tidesman in the town of Providence, Rhode-Island, promising a reward of £50 sterling, for the discovery of any one concerned in this illegal distribution of punishment. — *Well may such princely rewards be offered by a set of men, who* are under less controul in the disposal of the revenue, arising from the new duties, than is the K—g himself, respecting the national monies! —

The House of Assembly of New-Castle on Delaware, in consequence of a letter from the Speaker of the late House of Burgesses of Virginia, inclosing their resolves, relative to the advice given to his Majesty, by the Houses of Parliament, for the seizing and carrying off any person to England from America that may be obnoxious to the King's governor or minister, have thought fit to adopt those resolves, in expressions as well as sentiment; if this is done in the other governments, when permitted to meet in Assembly, it will be the best evidence of *unanimity* that can be given. —

The sloop Liberty, lately owned by Mr. Hancock, and by way of insult to the merchant, fitted out by the C—m—rs, at a most enormous expence to the crown, as a guarda costa, having for some time past greatly distressed the fair trader, has at length come to an untimely end, in the harbour of New-Port Rhode-Island, where a number of persons exasperated at the imprudent behaviour of the captain and some of his people, went on board her as she lay at anchor, cut the cable, let her drift ashore, and then set her on fire. — It is unhappy both for the mother country and colonies, that the power of stopping, seizing vessels, &c. in our several harbours, has been committed to the little injudicious officers of petty guarda costas, and that when any have behaved in an illegal and abusive manner, they have been screened from due justice, and continued in his Majesty's service, as has been lately related of one *Fellows*, an officer in one of those vessels, who rescued a prisoner in Cape Ann, out of the hands of the sheriff, and with his people fired several times upon the sheriff and his assistants, with powder and ball, to the greatly endangering their lives.

The spirited behaviour of the merchants and traders of Philadelphia and New-York, respecting those who have imported goods into those provinces, contrary to the spirit of their agreements, relative to an non-importation of foreign goods, plainly shews, that they are in earnest, and must serve, if any thing will, to awaken the British merchants and manufacturers, to a sense of their own interest. — The following are selected from many instances of the same nature.

A vessel arrived at Philadelphia from Yarmouth, with a load of malt, shipped in May last; the merchants assembled, and voted it contrary to the spirit of their agreement, and an attempt to counter act the same, which ought to be discouraged; — the brewers attended in a body, with an agreement drawn and signed, wherein they engage that they will not purchase any part of it, nor brew of the same for any person whatsoever; this agreement was read and received with applause, — after which it was unanimously voted, That in order effectually to discourage such attempts for the future, no person ought to purchase any part of this cargo. — And that such as

should purchase or assist in the sale of any part thereof, or be any ways concerned in the unloading, storing or removing it, shall be considered as a person who has not a just sense of liberty, and as an enemy to his country. —

In consequence of the foregoing resolutions, it is said the said vessel with her malt, sailed for Cork, a few days after.

At New-York, as we are informed, one Simeon Cooley having been discovered in acting counter to the agreement of the merchants and traders of that city, was called upon to account for the same; he at first refused, and apply'd to a major of the Regulars for a protection of the soldiery, which was inconsiderately granted, but soon recalled by a superior officer, to prevent a flame which was enkindling; he then retired to the fort, but soon thought it expedient to come forth and make an *amende honourable* in the presence of several thousands of the inhabitants, for his contempt, and opposition to the North-America agreement, relative to non-importation of foreign goods; he begged pardon of all his fellow citizens, promised never to offend again in like manner, and engaged to send to the public store an equivalent to the goods he had sold, together with all those he had in possession, that were imported contrary to the agreement, there to remain till the Revenue Acts were repealed, and so to conduct for the future as not to render himself obnoxious to the contempt and just resentment of an injured people.

On the 25th of last month, his Majesty's 64th Regiment embarked for Nova Scotia, as the 65th Regiment, which had been quartered on Castle Island had done some time before. — The loss of men which the regiment, placed in this town have sustained by dissertion, may alone afford full conviction, that Boston is a very unsuitable place for quartering of soldiers; it is a gross abuse upon the inhabitants to have it given out, that those desertions were owing to their practices; a liking to the country, and a prospect of carrying on their several manufactures to mutual benefit, may account for the numerous desertions, from the several regiments, without recurring to any other causes. —

Many letters have been lately received from our friends on the other side the water, acquainting us with the methods taken by the present Ministry, to quiet the minds of the people of England, which were greatly disturbed by their conduct, in rejecting the colony petitions, and postponing the consideration of American affairs, until another session of Parliament, one of those methods was to have it given out as from them, that the acts of Parliament relative to a revenue would be certainly repealed, and every conciliating measure adopted with respect to their future treatment of the colonies, and that letters had been transmitted to the several governors, to acquaint them with this determination of Ministry. — For the information and satisfaction of our brethren at home, we shall give the sense of Lord Hillsborough's letter to the Governor of Rh. Island, respecting this matter, and this almost in his own words. His Lordship begins his letter by advising that he had inclos'd his Majesty's speech at the rising of Parliament, and particularly refers to what is therein said, with regard to the measures which have been pursued in America. — And the satisfaction his Majesty expresses in having the approbation of his Parliament thereon. — The resolution of their firm support, and that the concurrence of every branch of the legislature cannot fail of the most salutary effects. — He infers from hence, it will be understood the whole legislature are of opinion with his Majesty's servants, that no measures ought to be taken, which can any ways derogate from the legislative authority of Britain over the colonies; but at the same time assures, that though men of factious and seditious views had insinuated, that other taxes would be laid on; yet the Administration at no time had a design to propose any further taxes, for the purpose of raising a revenue; — that at present it was their intention to propose, at the next session of Parliament, to take off the duties upon glass, paper, and colours, on consideration of their being laid contrary to the true principles of commerce. — His lordship further observes, that these have been, and still are, the principles of the present servants of his Majesty, with respect to America, and concludes with observing his Majesty's reliance upon the prudence

and fidelity of the several Governors and Assemblies, in explaining these measures, that they may tend to remove the prejudices excited by means of misrepresentation, from the enemies to the prosperity of Britain and America, and to re-establish mutual confidence and affection, on which the safety and glory of the British empire depend."

Americans are too enlightened and knowing a people, to suffer their understanding to be imposed upon, by the arts and unfair practices of a British Minister, who appears as much lost to a sense of his own dignity, as he is to the true national interest, and too spirited to receive the grossest insult with indifference. The effect of L—d H—sb—gh's letter, relative to a repeal, has been similar to those occasioned by his former circular letter; — it has been treated with due contempt, and instead of shaking the agreement of the merchants, respecting a non-importation of foreign goods, it has greatly strengthened the same: The merchants of this province and indeed of a whole continent, have again solemnly engaged not to start from one of their resolutions, until the revenue acts are repealed, and the objects of their agreement fully realized. —

The inhabitants of this town have for a long while been acquainted with the true character and behaviour of C. P. Esq; late a surveyor and searcher for the port of B—n, now swelled into a Commissioner of the Customs. It is therefore no surprise to us, to be told, that in a discourse with a respectable merchant of this town, before copies of Governor Bernard and the Commissioners letters were received, he should utter what follows, "Pray Mr. S—, what can be the meaning that I am so much despised and hated in town — I was not made a Com—r by my own seeking, — I had no desire that there ever should be a Board established here — I had £400 a year before, and I have but £500 now, — I never wished for any troops or ships, — I never wrote for any, — I think it very wrong that any ever came, and I hope they'll soon be gone; — I always said that the Revenue Acts were bad in every respect, and I hope and believe they'll all soon be repealed, and things put upon their old footing, and I wish the town would not think me its enemy." — Our friends in England may however, by perus-

ing his letters, lately published, and acquainting themselves with his late intrigues
with Ministry, be fully satisfied what sort
of men are agreeable to the present Administration, and how well Mr. P——n has
merited the *five hundred pounds per annum,*
granted him out of the spoils of the American
commerce —[1]

---

[1] There is no notation at the close of this item that it was to be continued as had been customary throughout
the *Journal.* No further sections of it have been found, hence it is assumed that it was discontinued at this point.

INDEX

Admiralty, Court of: suit against Hancock and others for smuggling wine starts, 19; trial of Hancock postponed, 28; new judges appointed, and salaries raised to £ 600 per year, 28; again postpones the trial of Hancock, 31, 34; merchants oppressed with charges of minor infractions of revenue laws, 40–41; first witnesses heard against Hancock, 42; further considers Hancock's case, 44–45; unusual procedure in Hancock's trial, questions of constitutional rights raised, 46–47; commissions for new judges arrive in Boston, 53; trial of Hancock continued, unfair tactics used, 56–57; coasting vessel condemned for minor offense, 65; trial of Hancock continued, witnesses heard in his defense, 66; trial of Hancock, arguments heard, 67; important questions of legal procedure raised, 68; ruling of court on procedure in Hancock's trial, discussion of same, 72; trial of Hancock dropped, 83–84; extension of jurisdiction of, a serious grievance, 98–99. See *Customs, Commissioners of; Guarda Costa; Hancock;* and *Soldiers.*

American Union: reasons for unified sentiment in support of Massachusetts, 65.

Amherst, General Jeffery: mentioned, 8; displaced as commander-in-chief in America, 13.

Annis, Joseph, soldier: indicted for assaulting Justice Hemmingway, 91.

Arms: right of Americans to have, defended, 60–61.

Army, officers of: engage in fight with town watch, 54; agree not to disturb future concerts, 65–66; break the Sabbath, 57. See, *Boston, Soldiers, Troops.*

Arnes, Richard, private 14th Regiment: shot publicly for desertion, 17.

Ashley, John, soldier: indicted for assaulting Justice Hemmingway, 91.

Assistance, writs of: collector of customs at New London, Connecticut, made a second application for, refused, 92; granted by superior court to custom house officers at Charlestown, 92; discussion of nature, illegality and undesirability of, 92–93; officers of custom applied to courts in several colonies for and were refused, 93.

Assembly, of Massachusetts: election of new members to, 97; character of new men elected to, 103; comments on conditions facing the new session, 109–110.

Attorney General: of Massachusetts, refuses to prosecute soldiers for assault on Gray, 47; checks prosecution of soldiers for assault on inhabitants of Boston, 57–58. Of England: rules coasting vessels should not be required to enter and clear, 49.

Auchmuty, Robert: made Judge of Admiralty with salary from American revenue, 23; confirmed as Judge of Admiralty, 28; also made a local justice of peace in Boston, 58; commission as Judge of Admiralty read in open court, 83.

Augustine: report of arrival there of troops from Pensacola, 37.

Avery, John, justice of peace: refuses to quarter troops, 11.

Bahama Islands: arrival of Governor Shirley at, 30.

Balston, Nathaniel, justice of peace: refuses to quarter troops, 11.

Barbour, Peter: affidavit of rescue of Riley from Justice Quincy's court, 120.

Barrè, Isaac: sent petition of citizens of Boston, 87–88.

Beaver, warship: at Boston, 1, 23.

Bedford, Duke of: seconds Hillsborough's resolutions in House of Lords, 82.

Belknap, Jeremiah: affidavit concerning forcible rescue of Riley from officers of law, 121.

Berdt, Denys de, agent of Massachusetts Assembly: difficulty in presenting petitions, 19; appointed agent for Delaware, 22; letter concerning Hillsborough's opposition to trials of soldiers, 92.

Bermuda: troops from reported sent to Boston, 22.

Bernard, Francis, Governor of Massachusetts: referred to, 1, 20; portrait of mutilated, 3; misrepresents billeting of troops in papers, 3; maintains land of town was the King's and could be used by troops, 4; accused of having secured troops by misrepresentations, 4; ordered sheriff to carry copy of riot act to be read so troops could be used, 7; suggests Council refer question of billeting to judges, 11; lays letter from Hillsborough before Council, 12; appoints James Murray justice for Suffolk County, 12; demands Council do all work with him present, 12; presents letter of Hillsborough recommending changes in Boston magistrates, 18; proposes a proclamation concerning the justices of the town, refused by Council, 21; denies Council can petition King, 24; advises that all money from the revenue be spent in America, 24; orders a day of thanksgiving, 25; effigy of burned in New York, 26–27; efficiency of contrasted with that of previous governors, 30–31; home guarded by soldiers, 31; appoints James Murray and William Coffin justices in Boston, 32; asks Council to defend Sheriff Greenleaf against suit for trespass, 37–38; further attempts to protect Sheriff Greenleaf, 41–42; makes serious incident of a prank of some boys, 50; controversy with, over rescinding Circular Letter, 53; designs upon the charter of Massachusetts, 55–56; spying on people of Boston, 56; appoints more partisans as local justices, 58; shows anonymous letter accusing Boston leaders with plotting a revolt, 60; address to, of Selectmen.